Note
by
Note

◆ FriesenPress

Suite 300 - 990 Fort St
Victoria, BC, V8V 3K2
Canada

www.friesenpress.com

ISBN
978-1-5255-5420-9 (Hardcover)
978-1-5255-5421-6 (Paperback)
978-1-5255-5422-3 (eBook)

1. BIOGRAPHY & AUTOBIOGRAPHY, PERSONAL MEMOIRS

Distributed to the trade by The Ingram Book Company

Note *by* Note

A Tale of Trauma, Recovery and Musical Discovery

Kristi Magraw

To my clients, thank you for trusting me.
To my sisters, friends, musical mentors,
and my partner, Tijmen Tieleman;
your love and caring made this book possible.

Contents

Introduction:
Motifs of My Life

Dreams have always been important to me, both those that arrive in the night and those that lead my days. I have kept some form of dream journal since I studied Jung in my late teens. My study of music (piano and guitar lessons) and interest in songwriting also began early in life. Eventually these two interests joined, and many of my songs have been inspired by a dream image. On my CD, the song "If I Can Sing, You Can Do Anything" came from a dream about a horse running on the water. This song poetically expresses an idea I aim to model to my clients, students, and friends: "Perseverance in facing trauma and the adversity it generates can pay off in physical healing, connection, creativity, and fulfillment."

I was born with a hearing disability: My left ear was undeveloped in both the inner and outer tissues and structures. This condition is now called Microtia, but in the 1950s, when I was growing up, it had no specific label, and all physical disabilities were considered shameful and best hidden away. I acquired a further disability when I was nine years old, during an operation that was supposed to "fix" my ear but instead caused the muscles in the left side of my face to become semi-paralyzed. This was the consequence of a partially severed facial nerve—a medical accident that was the surgeon's mistake.

The shock of going from having a hidden disability (my small ear) to an obvious one (my crooked smile) was a major trauma that reverberated into my future as post-traumatic stress syndrome (PTSD), which was not diagnosed until many years later. I lived a functional life in many ways, because I developed a "survivor pattern," as many people with PTSD do. I define a survivor pattern as a narrowed life that is built on top of an iceberg of fear and despair caused by trauma. I looked mostly normal on the outside, but the PTSD pattern required me to block emotions, avoid potential triggers by not taking risks, and develop various coping mechanisms, including a work addiction.

My experience has characteristics in common with other trauma survivors but also with people who have pain (emotional or physical) due to "normal" and environmental stress. In the course of my healing journey, I came to believe that none of us needs to remain stuck in our discomfort. Everybody has the gift to heal themselves (though often we require many and varied kinds of help, of course).

Crucially, I was missing joy and meaningful connections to others and to music, as you will read about in the chapters of this book. However, my saving grace was in searching for answers to solve the mysteries of my existence and in developing my skills to help other people solve theirs. Following a path of perseverance has enabled me to develop my own synthesis of modalities: The Magraw Method. It has inspired me to write songs and instrumentals and has seen me through losing my singing voice three times. In the pages ahead, I tell my story to inspire others to tell their stories. I share the layers of trials I underwent while learning to use my body as a guide. I explain different types of pain signals I encountered, and the many different healers and modalities I found to help me recover and lead a life of creativity and calmness. This is the work I've been doing for myself, and in one-on-one sessions with clients, and now I invite you, my readers, to join me in this calm, creative space.

I wrote this book to understand my story and use it as an illustration of the power of body work and music as healing modalities. I wanted to have a coherent narrative for my life, instead of a fragmented, doors-shutting, bottom-falling-out set of memories. This kind of narrative therapy is recommended by people such as Daniel Seigel, MD, in his book *Mindsight: The New Science of Personal Transformation*.[1] I wanted to know the darkness I denied, so that I would be able to stay present with it when it was triggered. I also wanted to inspire and educate others, to connect with people—both healthcare professionals and survivors of hospital trauma—about the mind-body connection and PTSD.

As Tara Westover put it, "I had come to believe that the ability to evaluate many ideas, many histories, many points of view, was at the heart of what it means to self-create."[2] I titled this book *Note by Note* to express the degree of patience and belief in myself necessary to pursue my dream of singing and playing the guitar. I have had to face my disabilities realistically but with energy to push the envelope and find outlets that bring satisfaction for my musical nature.

As a coherent narrative of my life unfolded during my writing process, I grew in my understanding of the overlapping effect of having had both a hidden disability and hidden PTSD and living with family secrets. All these experiences had a disconnecting effect that led to isolation. Reading Pauline Dakin's excellent 2017 memoir *Run Hide Repeat* helped me appreciate how a childhood can be defined by a web of secrets.[3] My childhood was also defined by various forms of secrecy and omissions, especially on the part of my mother. As it is for many people, understanding and forgiving the disappointments in my relationship with my mother became an essential task within my wider healing journey. Pauline's story helped me accept my own. Reading about her struggles for forgiveness validated my many years of therapy dealing with similar issues. The insights gained have given me new resolve to explain the hidden power of secrets. I ask my readers to keep in mind that these are my memories, and that I respect the fact that others sometimes have different memories.

I began my career learning to heal the body as a massage therapist and Shiatsu practitioner. I then moved into psychotherapy training, doing thirteen years in psychodrama and eventually becoming a licensed psychotherapist. During my training and subsequent career, I worked as a body-oriented psychotherapist, putting in the long hours of observation necessary to understand the mind-body connection. Having retired from psychotherapy, I now teach and coach, passing on what I have learned from helping myself and others recover from trauma and body pain.

This is why I am writing: to encourage people who are carrying the weight of trauma and/or secrets of their own, of their parents or even of more distant generations, in order to find their way out. This "way" is different for each person, and often long and winding, but we can learn from each other. I was biased against doctors and medical approaches in my early years as a massage therapist, because of my medical trauma, the hippie environments that I gravitated to, my parents' views, and the paradigms of the time. But on my circuitous path, I gradually realized that I did not believe in extreme points of view but rather in bridging them—especially between standard medical and alternative practices. I did not want to be "right." I wanted to question everything. I wanted to be collaborative and effective. I now want to communicate to other trauma survivors, and people in general, the philosophy and practices I have accumulated on my journey, such as it is okay to believe in antibiotics for infections and homeopathy for the immune system. It is okay to use neurofeedback for some "mind problems" and antidepressants for others. The placebo effect is present to some degree in all methods and sometimes very helpful because of the strength of our mind to affect our body. Help comes in many forms; what is essential is to learn to ask for and receive it.

I use music as my vehicle for change—it provides energy, direction and structure--much as the epigraphs gleaned from my songs and poems do at the beginning of each chapter. And there are many means available to help us reach the journey's end: physical health and freedom from pain, contentment with self and others, wellbeing and fulfillment of dreams (both those that come from the unconscious as "messages" and those from aspirations realized).

There was a point in the process of writing this book that I could feel myself being swept backward, whirling down the tunnels of traumatic memory. I knew I needed something to ground me in the "better present." In the process of talking to family, reading my archive of journals, and reflecting on my journey, I found that my spiritual part—my inner voice of wisdom—had pulled me out of the depths of depression many times. I can see how the hand of my Innate Intelligence, as I call it, was at work the whole time. I felt its guidance in various ways. Most often it came to me in what I call "message dreams." To relate some of that guidance here, I've included a series of letters to myself as if written by my Innate Intelligence. These appear at the end of each chapter. I composed them as a strategy to understand and reassure myself as I continued to write this book. As a grounding device, it worked immediately—I could sleep again—and as an inspirational tool, it helped me see the shape of my circuitous healing journey. As a narrative device, I intend them to illustrate both the dissonance and harmony in my life, especially during periods when I didn't understand the shape of the larger symphony.

Writing a letter to your younger self is a technique employed by many modalities to encourage connection between different parts of the self. You can write letters from your present self to your younger selves, or from the healthy part of yourself to the less healthy parts. Just hand the pen or the keyboard to your inner voice of wisdom. Give yourself comfort, acknowledgement, and advice. If you're so inclined, give it a try right now.

There are many other techniques I have developed for readers who wish to explore their mind-body, connect to their emotions in an embodied way, and understand their own trauma and what healing could look like for them. For an even more practical and instructional reading experience, I've included several of these techniques in the sections called "Techniques for Keeping the Body in Mind." These easy techniques require no special knowledge or equipment. Try them for yourself, either on your own, with a support group, or with a trusted therapist or another healing practitioner. All the techniques invite you to make friends with your body, your pain, and the general state of "what is" in the present moment, including emotions. In other words, they can teach you to stay connected.

They are also premised on a couple of essential principles: the body and mind are one, and healing trauma is best done with interventions and support from multiple points of view—allopathic and alternative, scientific and artistic. Our bodies are sources of pleasure and pain. They take us into action and let us know whether that action brings satisfaction or dissatisfaction. Our bodies are mirrors of our emotions and tools of our truth. Most important, we are in relationship with our body—married to it until we die. The phrase "keeping the body in mind" means just that. Recognizing the mind-body relationship can make life variously more interesting, easier, less painful, and more sensuous. When my mind (what I call the "I") is in relationship with my body, the pitfalls of living become less mysterious and the lessons more accessible.

For example, my shoulder suddenly starts hurting, and I use my mind to question and guess at the sources of that pain—maybe using a metaphor to tease out the emotional cause; maybe using deduction to rule in or out a mechanical cause and medical approach; maybe using insight or mindfulness to let the real "matter" rise to the surface of my mind. Or, I realize that I am feeling blue and go to an exercise class to help myself feel optimistic again. With many options and techniques to bridge the mind-body gap, my body becomes my friend instead of my enemy.

Keeping the body in mind is an art, learned over time through experimentation and practice. Anyone can do it and each person's way of doing will be their own. There is no "one size fits all".

My life has been enriched by starting a conversation with my body at a young age. This is how I learned that emotions speak through body sensations and how I could disperse body pain by facing my emotions. This conversation gradually brought me back from a dissociated state, plagued by flashbacks and chronic sore muscles to a contented body and peaceful mind.

The key is to face oneself, befriend oneself, and take action for oneself within a community—both inner and outer—because my mind-body is also in relationship with other people's mind-body.

Western society imagines we can divide the body and mind. As I read about in *Descartes Error* by Antonio Damasio,[4] this began with Descartes and continues to be the habit of some practitioners. Often, psychologists don't pay attention to the body, and doctors sometimes don't pay attention to the mind (even though this is slowly changing). Emotions often have a bad name all around, and when they are dysregulated (experienced in a disconnected way), they really are not so useful. I suggest working with experts and practitioners who understand that we are more than just a mind, more than just a brain full of chemicals and synapses, and more than just a body. Choose practitioners who are willing to see different points of view and often refer clients to others who work outside their field. Choose someone who can think around corners in an inquisitive and humble manner.

One of the most powerful discoveries I made while writing this book was that my Uncle Dick, whom I respected but did not know very well as a child because he lived far away, was a widely respected doctor and published author himself. He worked, from the 1940s to the 1990s, as a clinician (both an internist and psychiatrist), an educator, and a medical-school executive leader. Throughout his career, he devoted himself to interdisciplinary collaboration and developing a method called "Asking the Right Question," which urged medical specialists to be more patient-focused and holistic in the way they delivered their medical care. His example is incredibly inspiring, and I only found out the extent of it in 2017, when I read his book, *Ferment in Medicine*. Throughout my career, I had been following in his footsteps and I didn't know it:

> If the doctor really understands the patient's complaint, he should be able to answer the following questions: (1) Exactly what does the patient mean by the words he uses? Is he for example speaking allegorically? "I have no strength in me" may mean something quite different than "I feel weak." (2) Exactly what about his symptoms bothers the patient? How does it hurt or interfere with his life? (3) Why does he come at just this time? (4) What does he think he has? … The doctor must be aware of how the patient may interfere with communication, but even more important, he must recognize his own habits of work and thought that may hinder (his) understanding…. We speak of a "chief complaint," which implies we want only one specific brief complaint, as though fearful that by opening up we will let loose a Pandora's box of symptoms. By the phrase "taking a history" we imply we extract the information we want rather than encouraging a spontaneous story from the patient…. The doctor's orientation and training obligate him to identify the diseases present; consequently, he tends to treat first his own anxiety by deciding what disease entity the patient has rather than focusing on what bothers the patient.[5]

He was definitely ahead of his time, as I was. Only in the last decade or so has the area of "trauma-informed, patient-focused" therapy been developing and hitting the mainstream consciousness, thanks to works by Dr. Bessel Van der Kolk, Dr. Gabor Mate, Peter Levine, John Kabat Zinn, Ruth Lanius, and Judith Herman.

In 2016, I received a powerful affirmation from Uncle Dick. He wrote in a birthday letter to the family:

I come now to the real reason for writing this letter. I hope you will indulge my advanced years to the extent of accepting a letter to you on the occasion of my 97th birthday. I don't expect to be around much longer, so I'm taking this milestone as an excuse for making a couple of statements of awards, which I have gratuitously and grandiosely "trumped up" to express my gratitude and heartfelt approval of some of the members of our extended family. I am labeling these awards (with apologies for my insolence) the "Magraw Family Hero" awards.

The first and perhaps foremost award goes to Kristi Magraw, (Jack and Lizanne's second daughter). She, through courage and perseverance, has a remarkable lifetime achievement behind her wherein she triumphed over an early disability, which could have blighted her life.

I don't know about being a "hero," but I do recognize that I've shown courage and persevered in the face of difficulties. My main method of keeping on track with my body was always my love of music, and my secondary method was bodywork. In the chapters to follow, you will see how I eventually healed my trauma by exploring a variety of practices with an open mind, by filtering the results of those practices, by listening to my own mind-body, and by learning the important lesson of how to ask for and receive help.

At last I can talk openly about my sensory differences and disabilities, thus making possible self-advocacy. No longer caught in dissociation, I can reliably find out what my body needs. And, finally in a romantic relationship in which I am not keeping secrets and neither is he, I realize what I missed: an easiness and relaxation that leads to deeper connection. This is what I would have wished for my mother. This is what I wish for my readers.

Chapter 1
Island Home:
My Touchstone

She said, "I come to this beach in the late afternoon
To look through the decades of views,
All different because I was changing
But the shape of the islands remains the same."
"Odd," I said, "I lay under the poplar trees in the late afternoon,
Looking up at the green against blue,
Remembering the decades of this view;
I was changing but the trees stay the same."
She said, "It must be telling us something about life.
How strange that things can change yet stay the same."
I said, "Yes—a beautiful paradox."

My family was living on Eagle Island when I was born, the second of five girls. We lived in an old creaky house surrounded by huge, Lombardy poplar trees behind and a large bonsai-shaped blood plum tree in front (we called them blood plums because of their red flesh). There was ivy growing under and up the trees, and a quince tree sheltering the driftwood for the fireplace that we had gathered from the beach. To the south of the outhouse was a Juniper, and an apple and pear orchard just beyond that. Today, most of the poplars and some of the old fruit trees remain.

My mother had to travel in a small plane to the mainland to give birth to me. My father remained on the island to care for my older sister, Alison. Alone in a hospital in Everett, Washington, my mother held me in her arms for the first time and had the shock of seeing a little lump of flesh and cartilage where my left ear should have been.

At that time, there was not a recognized scientific name for the disability I was born with, but it's now known as "Microtia," a congenital deformity that occurs in approximately one in 10,000 births. Having never faced her own scoliosis (curved spine), it must have made her feel fearful for me and ashamed of her own body for bearing me deformed (which was a common term for disability in 1952). However, she was reassured by the doctor and enjoyed our initial connection. She sent me a letter when I was in my twenties that recalled those early days:

> *"Reaching over to pick up the small bundle which was you from a plastic bassinette and feel your warmth next to me on the bed— having the doctor come to tell me about your ear—to try to assure me that you were a fine healthy baby. And you were. I felt very close to you in those first few days because I wasn't as afraid as I had been when Alison was born and because I was able to have you with me all the time after the first few hours. I remember coming back to the island with you while the plum tree was still in bloom, which seemed an added blessing because I thought it would have faded while we were off island. That warm feeling of closeness is what I treasure."*

My sisters, Alison the oldest, Linnea the next one after me, then Melanie and Martha, were an important part of my growing up and that bond has continued to the present, with two major interruptions: my operation and the disruption that caused, and later, my move to Toronto. We played together, explored the woods together, and worked all our chores together. One year, it was just us and one other girl in school. Another year, when Mama was upgrading her teaching certificate, we helped our father run the household. I felt proud of us as individuals and as a unit, and I still do now. We had different talents: Alison was neat and orderly, liked to write and made good plans; I supplied the energy and initiative; Linnea was good at crafts, gardening, and staying calm; Melanie was lively, creative, and good at building relationships; and Martha was curious, cheerful, friendly, and an excellent problem solver (this is the short list). We all learned to garden, cook, and bake. Linnea and Melanie learned to sew (our mother was an excellent seamstress), and all of us learned to do the planning necessary for living on an island. Our close connection and these differing skills have made it possible for us to prepare large meals together, do work bees, put on weddings and unique birthday parties, develop a plan for the land, and support each other in difficult times over the years.

My life in the family and community was full and mostly happy. A birthday party was a big deal on the island. Every child was invited, along with their mothers and any fathers that were on island. My mother would use her Norwegian baking skills to make delicious angel-food cake and we would play games while the adults drank tea in the brilliant green of our backyard, if it was spring, or crowded around the dining table when it was raining. They would swap stories and gossip until the children complained of hunger and then load into the dilapidated trucks and cars that coughed their way along the bumpy dirt roads home.

In the community and in my family, there was little awareness of the immediate impact of hearing in only one ear or how this would affect my life to come. I learned early to ignore the little lump of flesh and cartilage where my left ear should have been. My friend Merry, who lived across the field, remembers caressing and curiously examining my ear—I think she was the only one who wasn't afraid of it.

Music was a big part of my childhood. There were dances in the post office (a large old log building) transformed with flowers and colourfully dressed people. My mother, because she was a seamstress, always had one of the prettiest dresses, and she would curl the ends of her hair with big curlers and wear bright red lipstick. My mom and dad were both excellent ballroom dancers and danced late into the night, while we children were piled in a dark corner, under coats, to sleep. Occasionally my dad would sweep me up in his arms and whirl around the dance floor. One of my favorite dance tunes was "Hernando's Hideaway." Even then I was attracted to Spanish and Latin sounds.

Nature (and its glory) was up close and personal. I began writing poetry at an early age to express in metaphor my feelings about the beaches, the wind, the wildflowers, the birds, and the stars that filled the sky at night. I was proud of the Eagle Island way of life: the strenuous nature of it and the unique community of old timers, bohemians, and back-to-the-land idealists. It wasn't by any means a perfect childhood, but the energy of the land and the water comforted and eased my pain. The physical hardships helped me develop muscles and resourcefulness. Much as I complained about garden work, I loved our big rambling garden and the delicious vegetables that sprung from it. My parents were truly happy in the garden.

There were potlucks with singing around a beach fire—folk songs and protest songs—with the waves lapping and the stars falling in streaks across the sky. In the winter, there was the school Christmas play (with humour, music and songs), and then afterward, a group sing-along from the fireside songbook, with Marietta playing the piano. At Christmas, we sang carols, riding around the island in a wagon of hay pulled by a tractor, stopping at every house for cookies and hot drinks. I loved the melodies and complex harmonies of Christmas carols. My favorites were, "It Came Upon a Midnight Clear," "Oh Holy Night," and "The Coventry Carol."

One of the most fun musical things I did was climbing trees with Merry. I would run across the field to her house, and we would go on adventures. For example, climbing every kind of tree: white firs (not really white), Douglas firs (lots of pitch), madrona (with their smooth red limbs), and apple trees (that poked you with random branches). Once perched, each on our own branch of the largest madrona tree, we would sing songs we knew from the fireside songbook and whatever else we could remember. Songs like "Oh My Darling Clementine," "What Shall we do with the Drunken Sailor?" "Sally Go Round the Roses," "Home on the Range," and many more. We competed to remember the most lines or sing the longest. Later, we would stand around the fireplace in Merry's log-cabin home, warming ourselves on the metal fireplace hood while we sang along to rock and roll songs on the radio.

When I was six, I studied piano with Frances, the only piano teacher on the island at that time. I never really clicked with her, but I enjoyed learning the piano. Several years later, when I began studying with Marietta, whom I admired and liked, I was inspired to write small piano songs. We had an old piano in our house with thick curlicue legs and several keys missing. My sisters and I would practice on it, and we used it as a place to keep song books and general knickknacks. It was underused.

I loved music. A story my grandmother told in her journal from one of her visits showed how emotional I was about music. There was to be a music evening at Frances's place and my grandmother and grandfather were going, taking Alison with them. I was not allowed to go and threw a crying fit as they were leaving. She wondered how long it took me to get over it. I imagine that I was upset about missing the music.

When I was eight, there were more children than usual in school: fifteen kids between the ages of six and thirteen. We developed a complex game that involved much running, hiding, and finally capturing the flag, following the strategy devised by the "big kids." That year we, put on a play called *The Christmas Cuckoo.* I was the cuckoo and had fun popping out of the fireplace to make my speech. I liked the attention that I received from performing. We also sang a beautiful carol, "The Boars head Carol"—another musical highpoint for me. At the spring play, Alison and I sang "My Old Kentucky Home." It was a year of fun and carefree creativity.

I ran around with my sisters on the beach and the dirt roads, enjoying the vivid smells of each season: the spicy flowering current and delicate plum blossoms in spring, the salty smell of low tide and heated pine needles in summer, the dry smell of maple leaves in the fall, and the wet smell of mud and sheep in the winter. We climbed fir trees, getting our hands covered with sticky pitch, celebrated the birth of lambs (but hated chasing sheep), and had the occasional, very exciting sightings of bald eagles or otters. We went barefoot from May to October, challenging each other to be the toughest by walking on the exposed barnacles at low tide. We had no television, so we developed games and read books— lots of books. For example, *Swallows and Amazons*, a series about a group of English children who explored and mapped their small lake world. We decided to do the same thing. Alison had very neat handwriting, so we elected her to be our scribe and chose different areas of the woods and fields to explore and map: swamps, old falling-down cabins, odd-looking trees, and the deep drainage ditch on the old Allen property down the beach, which we called "the Gully." It was totally fun to explore, and in the quiet of the woods, my one-eared hearing problem was not obvious.

In the fifties and sixties, there was a high value placed on community. The Eagle Island community reflected this and had a very busy social calendar, especially during the summer months, when an influx of people came to the island to camp and improve their summer cabins. We knew we had to hide our secret places from the "summer folk," and we hoped they were secret from our parents as well. I became attached to our secret places and would think up reasons to go out and play there (this was probably connected to my love of quiet). One was a cedar grove: a stand of big cedar trees set in the middle of a blackberry patch. There was only one way to get there, and we were sure that we had discovered it. The trees in the grove were majestic and mysterious. Underneath was a carpeting of dead cedar needles—no thorns! We would perform invented ceremonies and have picnics under the low-hanging bows, sure that the people who owned the land would not find us.

The other secret place was also protected by thorns. Close to the beach, it was a small meadow set in the middle of a Nootka Rose (wild rose) patch. It had a small apple tree and some interesting rocks. It was only a ten-minute walk from our house, and I would sometimes go there when I was upset.

No one talked about my ear when I was young. My parents didn't touch it, except when washing my hair and, even then, not overtly. By this time, my sisters and I all had long hair. Getting it washed was a time-consuming process, performed only by our mother. We helped each other untangle, brush, and braid our hair so it wouldn't tangle again. The braid hid my left ear.

I don't remember ever having been taunted because of my one-eared disability. Perhaps it was because my ears were hidden. However, this disability caused odd behavioral habits to develop, like not saying hello when I entered a room. My mother called me "thoughtless." She was referring to my manners, but I surmise that my behavior was less related to attitude and more to my not being able to hear audio cues and sometimes becoming overwhelmed by sound. At the time, I thought nothing of it and didn't consider that I might be perceiving the world around me any differently than my family and friends. I was probably more concerned with getting outside to play in one of my secret places or wondering when the food would be served.

I enjoyed the island work bees, which were focused around tasks such as roofing, building a house, or doing school clean up, more than

I did potlucks, which had large numbers of people and lots of noise. I was a good little worker, highly motivated by the praise and attention it brought me. There was always much work to be done: weeding the large garden, picking vegetables and fruits to can, gathering wood from the beach for the fireplace and the forest for the woodstove, gathering hay for the sheep, and the laborious process of washing clothes (there were few automatic washers on the island).

Our little red tractor ran the washing machine (as well as cut the hay and hauled the wood). Then all of us girls had to take turns feeding the wringer and hanging the flattened clothes on the extensive clotheslines that a family of seven needed. We often argued over these tasks. Washing dishes was a daily chore. My mother was a good and somewhat elaborate cook, and I remember I often felt annoyed about washing the eggbeater (but I enjoyed the food).

Many boat trips came with living on an island. We would take picnic expeditions to other small islands and commute to the close, big islands for supplies. Because we were all crowded together in a small, slow motorboat, I received more physical attention than normal (always good for me), and the motor prevented conversations, so I didn't have to strain to sort out sense from cross talk. I would hum along to the sound of the outboard motor, relaxing my ears. Back then, I didn't know why, I just enjoyed boats.

Our mail arrived by boat three times a week. The post office was a fancy log cabin with a large porch—perfect for all the socializing that happened there. As kids, we looked forward to running down to the dock to greet the boat, hoping there were letters, books, or clothes for us.

Tibb's beach was the gathering place for island events in the spring and summer. There was road access and a sandy beach with a view across bright blue water to the islands of Canada. In a flat, grassy area with small windblown fir trees, just right for setting up food-laden picnic tables, the community gathered. Ray and Mary Tibb, an older couple, were warm and welcoming.

It was at Tibb's beach that we celebrated the Fourth of July one year with a big potluck feast, including the rarities of watermelon and ice cream. Because there was little refrigeration available at that time, we had to use dry ice to keep the ice cream frozen. And eat it quickly! My sisters and I hung close to our mother; we were "the shy Magraw girls." I wasn't actually shy, but in a potluck, the chaotic noise levels were high. People who had not seen each other recently would yell, laugh, and call out greetings. The little kids running around would cry and shout, not to mention the brisk wind off North Bay making waves crash, and various truck motors with no mufflers, making a noise environment where I could get "lost," and not know who was calling out to me. This created an uncertain social experience for me, and I am sure I looked shy.

Then the Huntleys would arrive in an old beat-up truck, typical for islanders. I would feel my mother tense up and move away when their son Aaron, who had Cerebral Palsy, was unloaded with his special wheelchair, and she would flinch when their other son Rory, who had Down's syndrome, was running around being extra friendly. I don't recall seeing their second son, Shawn, who did not have a disability. Perhaps he was avoiding attention, as he told me later that he often did, because the enormous pressure to be "the success" was stressful. His true needs must have been lost in the shuffle of drama and pity surrounding the "disaster of disability" that, in those days, was a common attitude toward people with a visible disability. From this atmosphere, I got the idea that people who looked different were too scary and unpleasant to deal with. It made me afraid too—afraid of being like them. Looking from today's standpoint, it may be hard to understand how isolated people with disabilities and families with a disabled child were.

My father would fly off island to work as a salesman. He had taken on this career when it became obvious that working in the government would not be possible due to his prison record for being a conscientious objector in the Second World War (it was the McCarthy era). His gregarious and persuasive nature made him well suited to sales work, and it gave him the freedom to live part time on Eagle Island and also do what he could to improve socio-economic conditions, such as volunteer to build housing on the reservation of the Lummi tribe, engage in a variety of peace efforts, and take draft dodgers to Canada. My father wanted to help make the world a better place.

To makes ends meet, my mother had to work as a teacher, which she did at the Eagle Island school. For a few years, I saw a lot of my mother at home and at school. This was okay, unless she was in an anxious mood; if that was the case, I just did as I was told and escaped into a book.

I am sure my father's absences affected all of us, as did the stretched-thin quality of his life, but when he was on the island, he would immerse himself in island life, fixing fences, shearing sheep, gathering wood, and planting the garden. He was well tuned in to the importance of fun and adventure too, piling us into the canoe to have picnics at Mark's cove or driving our rattling old car up the mountain for a wildflower walk. The smell of the warm pine needles and the vivid blue, white, and lavender flowers would fill me with contentment, and I would forget that he had ever been gone.

Every night he was home, my father read aloud to us girls in front of the fire in the stone fireplace he had built. This was one of the most relaxing, calming activities for me: to be in physical contact and have a story to listen to. I became deeply attached to my father and to books.

My parents listened to jazz on the radio, as well as news from Canadian stations, which were easy to tune in. My father liked the Glenn Miller big band music and Dixieland jazz. He would carry us on his shoulders while dancing around the living room. My mother also enjoyed music and played the piano a bit, although more often than playing piano, she worked in the kitchen and reminded us to do our chores. In retrospect, I can't help but think this was a missed opportunity for her. What I did get from my mother throughout my childhood was a love of words. Encouraged by her, Alison and I would make up stories from lists of words. We would write poetry and short stories, and I remember they made her happy. In town, she edited all my high-school essays. We played scrabble frequently. Words became our meeting place.

I had dreams of being a conductor of an orchestra or choir. I knew what a conductor was, because my father listened to choral music on the radio (the Mormon Tabernacle choir was his favorite), and he explained to me what a conductor's job was. The idea of directing musicians to make music sounded exciting. When I was very small, my father sang in the island barbershop group, and he would sing us lullabies on the way home from community events: "Merrily We Roll along," "Swing Low Sweet Chariot," "Good Night Irene." It was soothing and wonderful to hear the rumble of his voice as he carried me home in his arms.

I knew there was a dark side to both my parents' lives. We were not close with my mother's family, and we learned not to ask questions about it. We visited Minnesota (where all the grandparents lived) infrequently, and I have more vivid memories of my father's parents coming to visit the island with gifts and helpfulness. My father never talked in detail about his time in prison during the war, when he had walked out from a camp for conscientious objectors and gone to work in the ghettos of Detroit during the food riots. Now and then, he would mention it briefly, and I had the feeling that he was proud of his defiance of the system. But his silence about his prison time was puzzling, because he was a "talker" about many other subjects of a political nature.

My mother's darkness was harder to define but affected me more. One of my early difficult memories is of a dark and stormy night when my mother abruptly left the house. After a while, my father went to look for her, leaving us children alone. He found her crying in the barn. He carried her back to the house and put her to bed, telling us that she would be better in the morning. I wondered what had made her cry. I believe this is where I began to take on the job of being my mother's caretaker.

The one-room schoolhouse that I attended was like a second home. The large maple tree just outside the door was covered in soft moss, and its giant arms supported our bodies as we invented games and swung on the rope swing. Around the side was a new swing set with bars and a shiny pole. Inside were old wooden desks, nicked and carved but smooth with repeated use. There was a clock on one wall, George Washington's portrait on the other, and big windows to let in the winter light. The teacher would read aloud at lunch as we munched on delicious sandwiches and many varieties of apples. We did not have visitors to the school very often, and they always seemed exciting, even if the visitor was a school nurse. As I rode my old bike to school one fateful day, when a nurse was to visit from the mainland, I wondered what kind of person she would be. Little did I know that she would initiate a process that led to the main trauma in my life.

Innate Intelligence Letter

Dear little Kristi,

You have a spark in you. You have music. You have a beautiful place to grow up in. I know things are confusing for you sometimes and nobody touches your cute little ear. There is nothing about your body to be ashamed of.

It's okay to say what you are feeling. It's okay to ask questions. It's okay to have big dreams. Reach out for what you want and spend time where you feel comfortable and with the people who make space for you. You have the right to leave the noisy places and loud people.

Even though your family can be confusing, they love you, even if sometimes they don't know how to care for you in the ways that you need.

Stay open to the joy of nature and listen for the music in your heart

Love,

Innate Intelligence

Chapter 2
Silence: My Ear Operation and the Trauma of Isolation

No One Knew
The wind is tossing the trees about—they spring back mostly
Except when a gust catches a weakened branch
And it falls to the ground, broken
In the hospital bed waiting for the operation
I wondered, Who will I be when I have two ears?
The drugs kept me silent
My misplaced nerves were caught in the wind of medical inexperience
My smile was broken
Afraid to feel the bandage around my head
The pain of skin peeled off
Afraid of knowing the loss
Of Nerves, muscles, and self cut into unfamiliar shapes
I knew my life would never be the same
I had no idea how to accept the mistake I felt I was—
Bad for causing my mother anxiety
With my identity in pieces
I could not shield myself from her fears
We were nauseous, nightmarish, and guilty together
No one knew

The nurse was very direct and spoke openly about my "deformed" ear. I remember the room going still as I went into emotional shock. I could feel my mother's tension build as the nurse addressed her in front of all the other students and their parents, who were assembled for this scheduled group medical consultation. The nurse talked calmly about the possibility of school environments being difficult for me in the future because of having one ear. Oblivious to the loaded atmosphere in the room, she mentioned a special government program that might subsidize an operation for my ear. The nurse's implied criticism of my mother in front of her community must have been awful for her.

Shortly thereafter, on July 1961 in Bellingham, Washington, at St Joseph's Hospital, my life changed. I was only nine years old. Here is my story about being broken and surviving it. Dear reader may I remind you that my memories are mine and other's may differ.

This is what I remember: My parents inquired further after the nurse's visit that winter and found out that the State would provide funding for an operation to construct an eardrum and an earlobe, both of which were missing in my ear anatomy. They applied for and received funding, but the government reserved the right to choose the doctor and the hospital.

I remember tension around filling out the forms and then a long wait. Suddenly a doctor was available, and even though my father was away on a business trip and my mother had just returned from a trip to Minnesota to see her ill mother, she thought that this was our only chance and didn't want to turn it down. She decided to go ahead (even though my father was still on the road), hurriedly arranging childcare for my sisters, feeding me breakfast, and rushing to the three-seater Cessna airplane that took us to Bellingham.

We arrived at the Catholic hospital that had many nuns walking around in full habits—another odd thing in a day of strangeness. There were more forms to fill out, including a release, and the doctor newly informing us that there was a chance that a nerve would be cut. My mother signed. Finally, I was put in a bed and given drugs to make me relax. My mother was reading *Treasure Island* aloud to me in a very tense voice. It was not relaxing.

I knew that they were going to do something to my ear to make it better and that would help me hear more easily in school. I still felt strange that now there was something wrong with me, when before there had not been. Trying to explain how anesthesia worked, the nurse said, "You won't remember anything," and in my child's mind I thought that she meant I wouldn't remember my entire life. I was very frightened but already losing consciousness. I tried to say something about this fear, but the words wouldn't come out.

During the operation, I woke up feeling a searing pain on my stomach, where they were taking off skin for a graft on my ear. I tried to say something, but I couldn't. I remember the anxious voices of the doctor and nurse talking about my ear, and then I went blank again until I woke up hours later (the whole operation had taken seven hours) in recovery, throwing up violently, because my mother didn't know that I was not supposed to eat on the day of the operation. My father was at my bedside, and I felt the relief of recognizing him. (I exist as myself after all!) In that moment, I became even more attached to my father. I also developed a phobia of vomiting.

Slowly, as I awakened, I realized that some very wrong things had happened to my body. I couldn't feel the left side of my face, and my ear and my stomach hurt. I had a big bandage around my head, covering my ear. I don't remember looking in the mirror for the first time, but gradually I became aware that my face was different: I had lost half my smile.

The surgery was intended to be both functional and cosmetic: to improve my hearing and to create an ear that matched the other one. However, there was no improvement in my sense of hearing. I had an earlobe where before there was a figure eight of flesh, but no ear rim. (I guess they never anticipated that I might have to wear glasses someday!) The surgery could hardly be called successful. One of the worst parts for the nine-year-old me was the damage to my self-esteem, because of the surgeon's error in partially severing the facial nerve, which made the left side of my face collapse into a semi-paralyzed state. Overnight, I had changed from a person with a hidden disability (Microtia) to a person with a visible disability (facial paralysis and synkinesis).

I was in the hospital for several weeks, and my parents must have come and gone several times but I have no memories of my mother being there and just a few of my father. The only other visitors I had were my piano teacher Marietta from the island, and Chuck, Mildred, and Merry Ludwig, who had moved to Bellingham, where the hospital was located. Even though I knew these people, I didn't feel like myself, and the social contact felt awkward.

I was aware that I was missing a very special boat trip. Apparently, the island kids were going out on a big tugboat. I would look longingly out over the blue water that I could see from the hospital balcony. All my upset feelings about my changed appearance were channeled into literally missing the boat.

One day, I attended a concert put on at the hospital for the children who were recovering from operations. Sitting there with a bandage on my head and half a smile, I thought sadly that I would never be able to be onstage looking like I did. I would always be in the audience. I loved music, but my relationship to it had radically changed; my music dreams had been stolen by the stigma of facial disfigurement. I had learned that people with disabilities stayed in the background. I began to shut down my eagerness for new experiences and enthusiasm for the music of life. I began to shut down my connections with the people around me. Here is what my parents put in that year's Christmas letter to friends.

> Kristi's quiet voice has a more penetrating way of coming through the jumble of rush hour jams to point out the essential course of action—an ability she has developed to see her through several operations to improve her hearing…. Before there was time to gather up the loose ends of an eventful five days (Lizanne's visit to ill mother), Lizanne was back in Bellingham with Kristi for an exploratory operation on her ear arranged through the state department for the conservation of hearing. We were not prepared for the anxious and physically exhausting days which followed as Kristi endured two seven-hour operations in three days; but what seemed to be a grueling experience for Kristi and us was also difficult time for the doctor who skillfully constructed an inner ear where there had been none, and painstakingly repaired a damaged facial nerve.

What I really needed was validation of the reality of what had happened and identification of the doctor at fault (not my body). I needed recognition and comfort.

My friend Merry Ludwig was going to school in Bellingham, and during one of my stays with the Ludwigs, I ran ahead of the adults up a long set of steps. After this, I don't remember the visit. She told me many years later that when I smiled at her that day as I burst in the door, she could see that my face was all crooked, and she felt shocked. She said that I had asked her, "I really look different, don't I?" Seeing my self-consciousness, Merry realized in that moment that I needed her friendship. She instinctively took me outside to the juniper tree in their front yard to play, as we had played so many times on the Eagle Island beaches. On the ground beneath the juniper, we found a tiny elephant pendant—a treasure from another time and place. The adult Merry (now called Meredith) said she still had the pendant and gave it to me, and most importantly, helped me remember that magical moment. I have always trusted Meredith. She was one of the few people I spoke to about my face before I shut everything down in a fog of distrust.

Back on the island, no one talked about what had happened. They just looked at me with fear and pity. On mail day, that previously exciting social occasion, I would catch people regarding me with sad expressions on their faces. I still had my bandages on. I stopped going to mail day until my bandages were off. Within my family it was the same: No one talked. This was the beginning of a distance growing between me and my sisters that took years to overcome. None of my sisters remember my parents ever discussing what happened to me.

Once, at the beach, when we were sitting together on a log, my dad tried to talk with me, but all I would mention was missing the boat trip, and he didn't know how to ask the difficult questions. One of these questions needed to be, "Why don't you sing anymore?" After the shock of losing my smile had come an even deeper loss: I opened my mouth to sing at a beach fire and no singing came out. The big mystery began: Why could I talk but not sing? Later, on my own, I tried to sing again and my voice would shake uncontrollably—a physically uncomfortable feeling and very odd sounding. Singing was my chosen way of expression and solace, and now I desperately needed it but didn't have it. The loss was unbearable, so I tried not to think about it. Confused about this strange symptom and deeply distrustful, I stopped singing and told no one. The loss of both my voice and smile seemed impossible to face. This was not the end of strange symptoms. Confusion, compensation, and hiding became my way of coping until I gradually received the right help, from people who had the information I lacked and effective techniques to solve the mystery. There would be three more operations the following summer for reconstructing the outer ear. My memories of them are blurry and confused. The surgeon who had made the mistake of cutting my facial nerve did not talk directly about what had happened. He never apologized to me for the mistake he had made. The follow-up appointments were tense and what stuck in my head were his words, "Well, at least you can now wear earrings."

I don't know what my parents were going through at the time. They never talked about it to me in any depth or detail. My sisters. Like Shawn, the Huntleys' second son, must have felt lost in the shuffle. For some years—because the family's resources were spent surviving the "disaster" that I had become (a person with a visible disability)—there was not enough left to meet the true needs of my siblings. Alison later told me that she felt her social anxiety as a child had never been addressed. I did not know what my sisters were going through. In my distress, I paid them little mind. Later, when I was twenty and living in Toronto, I had some growing awareness of the gaps that had opened between us after these traumatic times. I wrote to Melanie, hoping my other family members would read it,

> "I really miss you and Martha, Alison, and Linnea. I never appreciated you enough, especially Linnea. I feel sad about that. I'm sure you're reading this letter and so I'd like to tell you, 'I love you, Linnea, and wish I knew you better and hope the opportunity will arise when we meet again.'"

In fact, it took many years for me to open up and establish a "knowing" relationship.

After my mother died, I found out that my uncles, my father's brothers, Chuck and Dick, felt terrible about my operation. They felt especially guilty because they were both medical doctors and yet neither had been able to convince my parents to get a second opinion or let me come to the Eastern states to have the procedure done. My cousin told me that the day my uncle Chuck found out that my facial nerve had been cut during surgery, he "yelled so loud we were afraid. We knew he was very upset about it." My parents had already refused their advice and wouldn't make use of their medical wisdom. The neighbors on Eagle Island said that they could see that my mother was depressed for several years after. Here is a quote from the 1962 Christmas letter.

> *"Kristi and Lizanne made three trips to St Joseph's hospital in Bellingham, where Kristi had several stages of reconstruction on her outer ear. Kristi is placid, yet spritely; spends much time reading."*

Through the years, I had various confirmations of the "what could have happened." These later confirmations of the reality I had experienced in contrast to the other possibilities, given better resources, were key in the healing of the PTSD that resulted from that botched medical procedure. For example, when I was forty, an ear, nose, and throat specialist (ENT) in Toronto told me that the doctor had no business doing an operation of that delicacy at that time. In 1961, he would not have had the necessary education. I thought, *if we had been connected to my uncles, they would have gotten a second opinion and maybe the medical accident would have been averted—or at least they would have been connected enough to see that I needed more follow up.* Even though this didn't happen, the possible alternative reality brought me relief. It loosened the hold that my "fate" had on me.

After my mother died in 2000, and I felt free to ask questions, a close neighbor on Eagle Island said, "Well, it was a big tragedy but no one talked about it. Do you think it would have made a difference if people in the community had talked?"

I said, "Yes." He nodded in acknowledgement.

In the same way as I had learned to ignore my little lump of an ear—to the extent that I didn't even know that it was actually a figure eight—I learned to ignore my scars from skin grafts and my crooked smile. Because of being numb to it, I just wasn't very aware of where my left side was in general, and I hurt it many times. I had a bad cut on my left foot, an infected piece of wood in my left knee, a bad cut on my left thumb, and a pitchfork stab on my left little finger. In photos from the years after my operation, I hid my face as much as I could and the left side looks absent or asleep. I practiced not smiling, because when I did smile, kids from off island would make comments like, "You have a funny smile" or "What happened to your ear?" or the worst, "She has a crooked smile, ha ha." I didn't know what to say, so I said nothing and just disappeared within myself. I am not smiling in any photos after my operation.

The Eagle Island kids, taking a cue from their parents, never mentioned my ear or my smile. I learned to avoid social contact with unknown kids. I had nightmares about forest fires. I think the fires represented my fears that something terrible was about to happen and nobody could stop it. I had chronic indigestion, and I remember my stomach hurting frequently. I refused comfort from my mother. The trauma had broken the attachment cord.

Attachment

When we are born, we are naturally attached to our parents for survival and growth. Some popular books on this subject have been published in recent years, drawing on the foundational research by John Bowlby in the 1930s and evolving through his collaboration with Mary Ainsworth to produce Attachment and Loss, volume 1, about parent-child relationships.[1] Insecure attachment styles have become a common way of understanding behavioral challenges in children and even dysfunction in the romantic relationships of adults. This attachment, if it is not disturbed, goes through different stages but endures from birth through adolescence. It allows the child to process their emotions safely and feel protected as they go out into the world. It teaches the child interactive skills they will use all their lives and take into other intimate relationships. When it is disturbed or broken, the child has an insecure attachment pattern, which creates feelings of alienation, disconnection, and loneliness. My metaphor for this feeling is a lost seed being blown through life—never finding her resting place. See more in chapter 7.

My father's busy house wares sales job continued to take him off the island for work. Sometimes he would take longer trips back to Chicago for conventions. I would feel very lonely when he left, because he was my main attachment figure (I felt safe and grounded when he was near), and I could relax when he was home.

My saving grace was books, music, and the people who created them. One year, I read 114 carefully counted, thick, hardcover books that I had borrowed from the Bellingham library. My friend Belle, who went to school with me that year after the operation, remembers that I always had my hair covering my face and my nose in a book. One of the most fun experiences of this dark time were the stories she told us (cleverly illustrated on the large blackboard), after school when the light was fading and we were supposed to be doing our janitorial jobs. It was fun and exciting to be breaking "the rules." Another continuing comfort was my dad reading aloud to us girls when he was home. I was attached to the characters in the books. I wrote letters to my favorite authors (Farley Mowat was one of them) and, magically, it seemed to me, received answers. I carefully saved those letters.

One time, a violinist came to the island—a friend of my father's—and I fell in love with her music and her. I embroidered a little handkerchief with the words "I Love You." It was awkward giving it to her, because my mother didn't like her, but I did it anyway. I wrote a letter to Julian Bream, a classical guitarist, and received an answer from him. I felt validated and inspired, as if the artists were taking care of me.

I turned to knitting as well. I would set myself goals: two hundred stitches, three sweaters, etc. I didn't really love it like I did music, but I wanted to feel competent at something. Another comforting activity was listening to the radio. The signals drifting down from Canada would come in loud and clear; CBC Radio was much clearer than the US stations. Eating lunch and listening to the familiar voices of the Rawhide noontime show or the news was a reassuring ritual. Though I didn't know this back then, it was also extra relaxing for me because all the sound was coming from one source (the radio) and my ears didn't have to screen out the background noise. I became attached to radio and would often use it to soothe myself.

The unacknowledged cost of losing my singing voice was both social and of my musical soul. I couldn't sing with my friends, at caroling time or at the endless parade of birthday parties, which I used to love but grew to hate. I didn't understand what had happened. I kept trying and failing to sing happy birthday. I couldn't make up my little songs or sing high up a tree. No one seemed to care if I sang, so I tried not to care either. Except the truth was that I did care. My little singing heart was broken. My dream of being a conductor evaporated, and I could not envision what my musical "place" would be. This was the first but not the last time I fell into a depression from lack of musical expression.

My father once took Alison and me to see the blues singer Lightnin' Hopkins in Seattle. The concert took place in an old theater named Washington Hall. The theater was ornately decorated with chandeliers and carvings in gold and red. Everything was big and noisy, and I felt small and confused. My dad guided us into our plush seats, and the lights were dimmed. Suddenly I could focus and enjoy myself. I was happy to have another place to enjoy music. Alison remembers this as a particularly magical moment that instilled in her a love of the blues, as it did for me.

Music was a seed growing deep inside me, and soon it would be transplanted into a guitar; a family friend had given us girls her unused one. I took possession of it and began to learn chords. In 1962, when I was ten years old, my family went to the Seattle World's Fair just before my second series of operations, which were intended to further "fix" my ear. When I reviewed my father's letters from that summer, I saw how much uncertainty my ear operations caused in our family. My dad writes,

> "We are trying to get ready for Kristi's operation. It will involve most of July, I guess. I plan to stay on the island all the time that month…. Our plans are not at all set with the possibilities of Kristi having to have a couple more operations, although we don't know about that either…. It hardly seems just a week until Kristi has to go to the hospital."

Most of the fair was too loud and chaotic for me, but when we entered the darkened tent of the flamenco performers, magic happened. I loved the passionate singing (the rending open of the heart), the angry stomping of the dancers' feet and, most of all, the percussive sound of the guitars. I decided I wanted to learn to play flamenco. I had my operations. It was all a blur of purposefully forgetting.

What I do remember is that, for some months after the operation, still a ten-year-old, I would travel to Bellingham by plane to receive physiotherapy for the paralyzed muscles in the left side of my face. My parents couldn't come to all the appointments, so often I went by myself.

I would sit captive, waiting for my turn with the physiotherapist, watching her torture other oddly shaped or injured children. I didn't want to be a part of that group, and I really didn't want the searing pain of the shock treatment. The physiotherapist—a large, rough, taciturn woman—would apply electric shock to various facial points, and it would hurt like hell. Afterward, I would walk to the library, get as many books as I could, then walk to the hotel where the taxi waited to take me to the small airplane that flew back to the island.

One time, I got lost trying to find the library. (I wasn't a forgetful child and I didn't usually have trouble finding my way, but in those days, nothing made much sense to me.) Finally, a stranger asked me if I was lost. Crying, I admitted, "Yes," and he helped me get back to the hotel where the airport van would pick me up. I am sure my dissociation, or "numbness," played a role in my forgetfulness.

Dissociation

Dissociation is a defensive response that happens when events are too painful or overwhelming to bear. It is the equivalent of an animal "playing dead" to escape death at the hands of a predator. The dorsal vagal system kicks in and numbs our senses, removes blood from our periphery, shuts down our frontal lobe functions, and blocks our memories. Animals shake their bodies to recover and return to their normal state. Often, human beings remain numb and shut down, not able to connect with their bodies or other people. This is one of the symptoms of post-traumatic stress disorder (PTSD). An extreme version of dissociation is dissociative Identity disorder (DID) where the psyche spits into "parts" in order to contain the distress. This often happens to survivors of sexual abuse. For more, see chapter 5.

After some months of these electrical-shock treatments, they gave us a home unit. My mother tried it on my face once, but after that I totally refused to let her use it on me. I felt anger and shame. We didn't talk about it, and I didn't go back to Bellingham for follow up. I don't remember any doctor or physiotherapy appointments after this incident in the winter of 1962–63. (They may have still happened, but I blocked all memory of them.)

Fortunately, that year a woman from Berkeley was living on the island. She was a good flamenco guitarist. Alison and I began to take lessons. She only stayed a year, but it was a good introduction to music I loved. My dad wrote in a letter to his folks in 1963, just before a family reunion,

> *"Everyone is getting quite excited about the trip. Lizanne is busy making matching seersucker outfits and the girls are busy practicing on the guitar. Kristi does very well with it.... I plan to go back tomorrow afternoon to the island. Will meet Kristi at the doctor's office in Bellingham and then take the plane out. We are hoping it will be possible to postpone any operations this summer—there is too much going on.... In the school closing program, Alison sang with Kristi playing the guitar. They both are doing well with it. We got new strings and they both practice every day."*

This is when the guitar became my comfort and constant companion. I am grateful for the music lessons that I received and my father's obvious support. I had lessons sporadically over the next five years, and this was wonderful. I am not really sure what my mother's position was, because my memories of what happened at the family reunion in 1963, when I was eleven years old, erased whatever support for my music she may have given me previously.

We traveled to Minnesota for this first-ever reunion of my father's side of the family. It was during the height of my "lost seed" years. I was not securely attached to my mother but was hyper-sensitive to her emotions. She spent much of her time before we left sewing the six matching seersucker suits and acting tense. I don't remember much about the reunion itself except the awful humidity and thunderstorms, the nervousness of my mother, and most importantly, the talent night. By this time, my singing voice would sporadically be there and then not be there, and I had optimistically planned to sing a Connie Frances song, "The Wayward Wind." I really loved this song, expressing as it did my feeling of being adrift. I had wanted to bring my guitar for the performance, but that idea had been rejected by my parents as being too difficult. During the performance, I had to stop partway through—maybe because my voice gave out in the noisy environment, maybe because I wasn't playing my own guitar. Everyone, especially my mother, wanted to hurry past my failure to perform/sing. I could feel her shame, and afterward, not once did anyone talk to me about what had happened. I was ashamed and confused, and experienced intense feelings that something was wrong with me. Why couldn't I just sing!? In a dissociated state, I blocked out much of the rest of the festivities and felt isolated from my parents. I told myself I would never perform again.

Here is my parents' version of that reunion written up in the Christmas letter and thoroughly erasing mine:

> *"It's the best vacation we've ever had." Our girls were talking about the enjoyable three-week trip we took to Minn. This was a memorable experience for everyone, meeting and getting acquainted with nieces and nephews and cousins—seventeen in all. Lively guitar, banjo, uke and mandolin jam sessions and a couple of bugles too, kept us jumping when we weren't out on brisk jaunts in Dick's sailing canoe, cruising on a pontoon boat or competing in a volleyball free for all. We did appreciate the warm water, which proved a boon in encouraging the girls to improve their swimming.*

I never learned to swim.

My creativity found another outlet two years later when my seventh-grade classmates and I decided to make a newspaper. We called it *The Where and When*. It was a social and creative effort that encouraged me to wake up my inner writer, and I discovered that I was quite good at capturing the little stories of island life. I got feedback that my words counted. This was important for a girl who had lost her voice in the medical-accident trauma.

It was during this time that I discovered that songs and certain singers could speak for me and comfort me. Odetta was my first "singing mother." When she sang "Sometimes I Feel Like a Motherless Child," the sound of her voice would comfort my sadness. I loved the song "Wayfaring Stranger" because it captured my feelings of unrelieved hardship. I would try (unsuccessfully) to sing it.

When I heard Buffy Sainte-Marie, I recognized the sound of struggle in her voice as being like mine, and I identified with her fighting spirit in "Universal Soldier." These musical moments nurtured the hope that maybe someday I would be musical again and kept me from drifting away from the world like a lost seed.

My parents were members of The Society of Friends, a left-leaning Quaker group, and when I was twelve and thirteen, I began to go to Yearly Meeting. Those experiences strengthened both my spiritual and musical self. In the quiet of the meeting for worship, I found a social connection that was suited to my one-eared existence. I found the discussion groups had enough audio space in them so I could speak up about my ideas. In many environments, when my ear was busy trying to sort out one person's words from another, it was difficult for me to enter a conversation. Sounds were frequently just a big jumble. At Yearly Meeting, I found adults I could talk to and kids my own age to folk dance with. I especially liked the Jewish folk dances like the Hora. I felt I belonged with this group.

My last school year on Eagle Island (eighth grade, five years after my operation) before my family moved off so I could attend junior high, I regained my place in my peer community with the help of a game. Alison had gone off that year for high school, staying with family friends. I hung around with my sisters, Linnea and Melanie, and the Burn kids, Cameron and Lisa. In this gang, I was the oldest, so I became the leader of explorations and games. I felt at home and not judged, so I finally relaxed.

We had an old wagon—heavily built but usable. I decided we could play gypsies, which was what we called the Romani people in those days. I don't think we'd ever met a Romani person, but they figured in many of our favorite songs and books. We made a cover for the wagon with old bedspreads, scrounged up a few old plates and mugs (the older the better), and gave ourselves what we figured were "gypsy names." It took all five of us to haul the wagon around to various locations (Bitte's Drive, Ralph's road, Tibb's beach, and the lower field). We then set up our fire pit following careful instructions from our parents. We would cook our small meal, sing songs like Joan Baez's "Dona Dona"—with only sporadic participation from me—and generally have a good time. Somehow, I had found a piece of my singing voice, though it was still quite unreliable.

Sometimes we would sleep overnight there, all crammed into the bed of the wagon.

I managed to sing "Dona Dona" for the school play that year, and I don't think it's an accident that the image of the wagon comes in the first verse and that sorrow is acknowledged with a hopeful tone. I can still remember the lyrics to this day without looking them up on YouTube. They stick in my mind because that was a time when I felt connected with my little group of friends, so those memories are deep and accessible to me. Experiences like these solidified my identity and lessened the chronic fear of rejection. Though I had many ups and downs to go on the road of reconnecting with music, people, and myself, for the space of a year, I had a place.

Innate Intelligence Letter

Dear Kristi,

You are suffering. It is not your fault. It is true that your parents are making a mistake—so is the doctor. Do not doubt your perceptions. Do your best to stay connected with yourself. Use the trees and water to comfort you and reach out as best you can. Merry is a good friend—you can talk to her freely.

You will recover but very slowly. I will send you inspiration through books and music. I am glad you write letters to your favorite authors and do embroidery for your favorite musician. Your gratefulness is a sign of healing.

Touch your little ear—do not hate it. Just like it is not your fault that you were born different, it is not your ear's fault that the doctor didn't fix it. Eventually you will be able to talk about what happened, and in the meantime, you can talk to me.

Love,

Innate Intelligence

Chapter 3
Not Facing My Face:
A Teenager in the City

Back on the coast in '69
I was a teenage landmine
Cool chick on the outside hid a crying heart
Never knew that I was lost in the dark
Was acting old as Methuselah
Dressing like Mother Teresa
I'd never been to a drive-in movie
Never knew someone like you would choose me

Chorus
But now I'm workin' on a big smile
A joker in disguise, I'm changin' my style
Yes, I'm counting on a big smile
And baby, you're part of this rare event
Come on, let's get crazy and bent
Now I'm ready for a big smile

I was a groupie of the high-school band
I'd bring along the bread and the jam
They'd be playing and laughing all night long
Never knew that I could learn those songs

When I was fourteen years old, our family moved to Seattle. We left our island home for my father's work, my mother's entry into teaching in Seattle and access to city schools, so my three younger sisters could go to school with more kids their age, I could go to junior high, and Alison could go to high school. (The Eagle Island school only taught kids up to grade eight.) This was a big change for our family, and I missed the island terribly.

I was a facially disfigured young person who could not bear to face her face and could yodel but not sing. I wasn't even close to acknowledging that I had a hearing disability as if it was the fault of my ear that all these other bad things had happened. I avoided looking at myself in the mirror or consciously dealing with my disability in any way. I was determined to be "normal" but deep down knew I wasn't. From photos, I can see I still looked like someone who has Bell's Palsy; my left eye didn't close fully, my smile was incomplete, and when I tried to smile, other muscles on the left side of my face would tighten, causing my eye to squint. This condition, called Synkinesis, is caused by the misfiring of nerves, usually after some kind of trauma. Involuntary muscular movements accompany voluntary movements. I could hide my ear with my hair but my face and smile were another matter. I grew my hair even longer and let it fall romantically over my face. I made it a practice to look mysterious, thus hiding the difference of my appearance as best I could.

The shock of entering a large junior high school was hard to adjust to, especially after having become the leader of the school kids in my final year on Eagle Island. I had to learn how to negotiate a new social scene and all that noise: echoing halls and gyms, loud voices, transistor radios, locker doors banging, and teenage crosstalk. This cacophony added to my social confusion. I didn't know how to make my way. I would walk bleakly down the school halls, pretending I was physically invisible to defend against the idea that I actually was socially invisible.

An emotionally difficult incident happened at a party with some of the "in crowd" girls. One of them said, "Do you ever pluck your eyebrows?" I had never heard of doing this and reluctantly allowed her to show me how. Looking in the mirror was traumatic. I did not see the point in doing anything to make myself pretty, because I felt I was hopelessly ugly. This incident led to a decision to stay away from the girls and hang out with the boys. I didn't wear makeup or earrings until I was in my forties.

In keeping with unspoken family rules, I kept all this angst and confusion hidden from everyone. In the annual Christmas letter that my family sent out, I revealed little with the paragraph I contributed:

> *"The past year has been a growing year for me. I finally adjusted toward the end of last semester and found my own group of friends."*

Meanwhile, my sentiments in my diary spoke of isolation and loneliness. Not knowing what was wrong with me, I attempted to describe what dissociation felt like when I wrote:

> *"I am in a separate world, insulated against all hurt. Voices constantly hit my mysterious shield and are absorbed soundlessly. I feel like there is cotton all around and can't decide whether it's a pleasant or horrible sensation. Now I am in a glass tube but it must be plastic because it bends and writhes. I feel like a worm in a can of water that has no bottom ... sides are useless without a bottom to keep me from sinking into infinity and without a bottom I have to race from side to side to keep alive."*

I knew I was different from others but not to what extent. I knew certain environments were uncomfortable for me but not why. I wanted to prove that I was okay, so this led to pretense and dissociation. If a kind, persistent person had asked me how I felt and why, I probably would have been able to tell them, but no one did.

Later that year, I recovered my optimism and wrote:

> *"I am at the Weirs's (family friends who were part of the Friends Yearly Meeting crowd) looking at the trees silhouetted against the sky.... The sun has set and it is lavender-grey. A star just came out, everything is piercingly and endlessly peaceful. I am listening to some weird but cool guitar and flute music [Laurindo Almeida and Jean-Pierre Rampal] that just fits the way this moment is and the way I feel.... My wish upon that star is that I will always be able to completely enjoy things like I do now—forever."*

My inner moods were very up and down, and I learned to keep a mask on them all. For example, I was in a choir class and enjoyed it but was always worried about my voice. The mystery of its sporadic appearances kept me unbalanced. Eventually I felt too discouraged and quit, because I had no one to talk to about it. The words of my teenage self revealed a pattern that would keep on repeating far into the future:

> *I haven't seen about getting into the talent show—don't really know if I want to or what—all mixed up. Did and said about a thousand stupid things today but have buried them somewhere (I wonder where) so I don't lose my self-respect. I think one main function of a memory is to forget things like that.*

In the latter part of ninth grade, I returned to my interest in writing and became the editor of the Meany junior high school newspaper. In the editorial meetings, I met Kyle, an artist who also identified with the outcasts of the school. He had two friends, Harlan and Kit. We began to hang out together and eventually Kyle became my boyfriend. We were all into hippie things, like Jimi Hendrix, Jefferson Airplane, smoking pot, tie-dye, wild art, and radical politics. I took my first acid trip in the basement rec room of Kyle's parents' house. I did many fun things with the boys.

We would sneak out of our respective homes at night. Luckily, I had a ground floor bedroom, so I could open the window ahead of time, putting a roll of clothes in my bed and hoping my sister Linnea, whom I shared a room with, wouldn't wake (she later told me that she did wake, worrying about me getting caught). I would slide out of the window. We would go down to the stadium and scale the fences to get in. Construction was going on, and Kit, our most adventurous member, had discovered a way to get into the infrastructure for water drainage and electrical wiring that ran underneath the stadium and nearby hospital. We called them underground steam tunnels, and they were indeed steamy and echoing. We knew it was illegal, but the boys enjoyed the thrill of breaking the law and I enjoyed the camaraderie. Trying not to feel trapped in the hot, dimly lit tunnels, I would run after them—sometimes emerging in the hospital (that was scary) and sometimes at the bottom of a construction opening. We would climb up a long ladder, escaping to breathe the fresh night air. It was probably quite dangerous, but I felt I belonged with them.

I was musically "waking up" again, thanks to the help of a wonderful flamenco teacher. The lessons were the high point of my week. I learned to roll my fingers in a rasgueado, do trills, and to distinguish the different song forms of flamenco music. None of it was easy, but I kept trying. I happily studied with him for a year. Then he had to leave town. I was heartbroken, and somehow my parents didn't seem to notice my upset or to follow up with any other lessons. Perhaps they were distracted by their own struggles. After a summer on the island, we came back and I entered high school. Kyle went to a different high school and broke up with me. Our little group came apart.

Occasionally, Alison and I would hang out with the ex-Eagle Island kids who also lived in town so that they could go to high school. We would smoke pot and listen to R&B music. I did not feel I belonged with this group—maybe I didn't share enough of myself. The music we listened to kept me from getting bored. My favourites were: Dionne Warwick's "Say a Little Prayer for Me" (I needed lots of them) and "(Sittin' On) the dock in the Bay" by Otis Redding, which would make me feel homesick for Eagle Island. During the Seattle years, my younger sisters Linnea, Melanie, and Martha had their own friends and would go folk dancing with our father. I didn't hang out with them at all (how sad).

The sixties were in full swing in 1968, and our school was a center of activism. My dad, being a strong activist, was right in the middle of it, organizing the other parents to help make changes in outdated policies. But for me, the large inner-city school was noisy and intimidating, and I had no one to talk to about how overwhelming it felt.

I still didn't know how to negotiate normal high-school activities, such as games in gym class. My coordination was terrible, partly because my left side was semi- blocked from sensation, and I couldn't locate it in space. I would be out on the field and suddenly a ball would arrive. I would try to catch it, but it would slip out of my fingers, or I would be a several feet away from it. The other girls would get angry with me. I would just get confused. In softball games, I would not be chosen for a team. I drifted off into a dissociated state: numbing, agitation, and preoccupation with others' problems and possible future disasters were the subjects of my mind. It's the very nature of dissociation that one feels alone; nothing gets in or out. It is difficult to express emotions and to receive love and attention.

At times, the world seemed less colorful, and my body was hard to drag around. In contrast, when I came back to the present, mostly when I was on Eagle Island, I felt energized and settled at the same time. Food tasted good and many things seemed possible. An up-and-down existence such as this was very confusing, much like my on-again off-again singing voice.

I don't remember going to any school dances, but I did try going to a modern-dance class. This was a disaster. The teacher was mean and would yell at me about my left leg dragging. I couldn't feel what she was talking about and was quite freaked out. I quit the class, confused again. I joined the jazz music class, and though the teacher (a well-known jazz saxophonist) was sympathetic, the class was all boys and very noisy. I didn't understand why it was so hard for me to play with others. I practiced my parts at home, but when I came to class, my fingers would be clumsy and stiff on the fingerboard, which had suddenly become a strange landscape. I felt isolated and confused, not knowing what was wrong with me.

At the end of my sophomore year, I met my next boyfriend. Raoul was Filipino/American and lived with his grandmother in a tiny house in a rundown area of town close to the high school. He played the electric guitar and drove a small golf-cart type vehicle. It may sound odd, but I found it romantic riding around with the wind in my hair. We would go to rock concerts at Eagles auditorium and smoke pot. I remember liking the jazz-oriented artists, such as Charles Lloyd, better than Janis Joplin, but I pretended to like them all. My true favorite was Judy Collins, who sang the Leonard Cohen song "Suzanne." Even then I could recognize a good melancholy lyric.

Raoul was creative but not very attentive. Before I went on the pill (which I talked my parents into letting me have at age 16), I had a sexual experience with him when we were making out and thought I was going to get pregnant. I shut down so thoroughly from the fear of getting pregnant that it took me years to wake up my sexual sensation again. But worse than losing my budding sexuality was selling my guitar so that he could buy an amp. No one questioned this action. Even though it was the "liberated" sixties, his musical adventures seemed more important than mine. He had a friend who played the violin. They performed as a musical duo, called themselves "Seagull" and found a financial backer: a Mexican hairdresser named Gabe. We would go to Gabe's hippie pad, Raoul and Joe would practice, and I would listen to Nina Simone singing the Randy Newman song, "I Think It's Going to Rain Today." The song and her voice perfectly captured my inner despair. I was becoming even more convinced that I was not a musician and that my musical aspirations didn't matter.

Before I completely gave up, I did try to work with my voice a bit more by taking singing lessons but made almost no progress with it and quit after the teacher (a large, elderly man) tried to molest me. At first, I trusted the teacher and didn't think to question his motives, even though he probably gave me reasons to be suspicious. I was only paying attention to my desire to reconnect with my singing voice, and my emotions were wrapped up in the rejection I felt from the members of "Seagull." I had something to prove, and I walked right into a dangerous situation. It wouldn't be the last time.

A man followed me on the street, and I scared him away by growling, then I was almost raped by a guy who had picked me up hitch-hiking through Seattle at night. He took me to a dark ravine, and somehow, I convinced him it was not a good idea. I think I acted crazy. It's possible that the invasive experience of the operation set me up for sexually invasive experiences. Certainly, I was numbed out to the degree that I would make bad choices (like hitch-hiking in a large city).

We took a family trip east and saw my Uncle Chuck's family for the first time in many years. My sisters remember that trip quite well, but I don't. Uncle Chuck was a doctor in Boston, and he had many connections. He knew about the trauma of my operation, although I didn't know he knew. He had arranged an appointment for me with a Boston specialist. Because we hadn't been talking about my medical accident or the appointment, I was shocked when it was announced that we were to go to an ENT so he could look at my ear.

I remember only two things from that trip. One was standing in the doctor's office with my mother, father, uncle, and the doctor. He was looking at my ear and said that nothing else could be done for the facial nerve, and I was lucky I had an earlobe and could wear earrings. I had heard that before. That another doctor had made a flip remark about wearing earrings, a comment grossly at odds with the degree of loss I experienced, and the fact that no adult spoke up for me, led me to feel hugely betrayed. I could hardly wait to get out of that office.

The second thing I remember is staring at the pattern on the rug in my uncle's house for a long, long time. I think I used it to help me dissociate. Perhaps my preferred method of shutting myself away and forgetting—putting my nose in a book—was too impolite under the circumstances. I already avoided wearing earrings and makeup, but after this, even looking in a mirror became an unbearable activity. I resorted to filling my time with work. This was the height of a phase during which my accumulated trauma reactions and dissociations caused me a deep sense of loss of self and of my body sensation. I later learned that this state is called *depersonalization*.

Music and the magic of the islands began to bring me back to life. I broke up with Raoul and went through a transformation, taking LSD more frequently and dating a guy named Steve, whose family had a place on another island in the cluster of islands of which Eagle Island was a part. He was good with boats, and I admired that. We would go to his island and hang out. One time, a group of us took an LSD trip by a lake high up in the middle of the island. I got separated from the rest of the group and wandered around the steep cliffs, enjoying the smell of fir trees and dry grass, and hallucinating in green and lavender patterns. Impulsively, I decided I would try yodeling, which I had not done since I was thirteen years old. I opened my mouth and let out a sound that echoed nicely against the rocks. After a few minutes of yodeling, I began to sing. I don't remember exactly what I sang, but from that moment I believed that my singing voice could come back. It was a life-changing moment to have something return that I thought had gone forever.

When I was eighteen years old, I lived on my own in Seattle, working at a co-op grocery store. My parents and younger sisters had moved back to the island, but my dad came to town frequently for work. It was the early 1970s, and the radical sentiments of the sixties were still a big influence. There were peace marches, music festivals, and pot smoking, not to mention tie-dye t-shirts and bedspreads with paisley designs. At the co-op, I liked making cheap healthy food available to people. My dad had co-founded it, and he was very enthusiastic about health food— ahead of his time. He also introduced me to Re-evaluation counseling, a peer group that put emphasis on listening to and expressing emotions. The first group he took me to was intriguing but also scary, because he expressed emotions about feeling "left out," which were a complete surprise to me. I had him on a pedestal, and it was hard to integrate this side of his personality. Although I never went to a group with him again, I got enthusiastically into Re-evaluation counseling (RC). It was my first foray into alternative therapy and very valuable.

At this time, I was still experiencing quite a bit of dissociation, especially around things associated with my ears and face. This longstanding habit had four main factors: the tissue damage from the operation and resulting PTSD; my mother's pattern of extreme privacy and secrecy; the attitudes in the 1960s regarding disability and facial difference; and a traumatic experience with one of my first healers, a naturopath named Dr. Stiber.

Dr. Stiber had been recommended by one of my father's radical friends. Supposedly he had special methods for working with facial trauma. Stiber told me he could do a special "balloon technique" on me, which involved inserting a balloon into my sinus cavity and then pumping air into it to expand and enliven the surrounding tissues. This was the first attention my face had received since the unbearably painful electric-shock stimulation when I was nine.

The treatments went on for about a year, during which time I moved back to the island for some months. Although my dad paid for the sessions, he did not ask me much about them. During one of the sessions, Dr. Stiber made an unusual and surprising comment: He told me my uterus was tipped, and he could re-align it, and that would help my face. I believed him, and even though I was uncomfortable, I let him stick his fingers inside my vagina and manipulate my muscles. It still seemed professional, and it was the hippie days when anything was okay. Also, I was used to being compliant.

Then, in another session, he was looking in my left ear and exclaimed with horror, "Your ear is full of hardened wax. No one has cleaned this for years!" I felt shame, for myself and my parents. How could my ear have been so neglected? He proposed that he clean it out, and I said, "Yes, please."

He said he would have to do it after hours, in his hotel room (he traveled up from Portland, Oregon) because it would take so long to pick it out. He said he wouldn't charge me for it. So that process began. It took several sessions of extracting the wax. The night it was finally cleared, he was very pleased with himself. I was getting ready to leave, and he called me into the room where the bed was. He was sitting on the bed, clothes off, with an erection. He said, "Can you help me?" I had a conflicting array of feelings; I was grateful for how he had cleaned my ear and wanted to show that; I was disgusted with him; I felt shame that I had gotten myself into this situation. I think I dissociated, because I don't remember how I got out of that room. I don't believe I carried through with anything, but I am sure he said that I was not to tell anyone. And I didn't.

This man's treatment of me sealed the silence that my mother and father had begun. Feelings of shame generate hiding and secrecy. When I had this bad experience at the hands of a professional who was supposed to be helping me, my shame compounded. I mentioned it once obliquely in a letter to my mother, but she didn't ask any questions so I didn't talk any further. That was my strategy: I would throw out a clue, and if the other person didn't pick up on it and ask questions, I would remain silent. Of course, my clues were fairly hidden too. It is no wonder that I didn't get the attention I wanted. I could connect and feel good when I was alone, reading, enjoying nature, and sometimes using drugs, but when I was with others, especially doctors and musical "experts," I would get into uncomfortable situations where my boundaries would be transgressed because I was not "all there."

That year, a few other significant things happened: I acquired a new guitar and began to write songs with it—songs with melodies that skipped over the holes in my range where my voice couldn't sustain a singing note. My favorite was "Bicycle Rhythm." I stayed on the island that winter before going to Toronto. The island musicians, Matt, Bill, and Cal, encouraged my song writing and that was great. But I still couldn't sing the Dylan song "Easy Chair," which was one of my favorites. I was confused as to why I couldn't sing other people's songs but happy that I could write my own. I still have a record of the lyrics to a lot of my first songs saved in my journals from those years.

I attended my first therapy group other than peer counseling. This group was based on bio-energetic theory and involved emotional release, which was familiar to me from the RC groups I had gone to in Seattle. We did lots of crying and yelling. I can remember having an anger release about my face that revealed the neglect I had experienced. I remember a sense of strong resistance to dealing with the concept of my mother as less than perfect.

Bio-Energetics

Bio-energetics is a form of therapy developed by Alexander Lowen in the 1940s and early 50s. A mind-body therapy, it's based on the idea that we store emotions in our bodies. He developed a series of positions that put stress on large muscle groups that help the participants access the emotions held there.

A Jungian study group was organized by our neighbor, and my mother was a part of it. Neither of us revealed much, but it was interesting to learn about Jungian typology and especially dreams. I began to write down my dreams then and never stopped.

I was reading many books about spirituality. The Buddhist ideas expressed by Chögyam Trungpa, a Tibetan monk, in his book *Meditation in Action,* evoked earlier feelings of inner peace that I had when I went to Friends Yearly Meeting. I attended a meditation group and was beginning to develop a spiritual base of my own.

Before I left Seattle, I was living in a very small coach house in an alleyway. My kitchen was like a boat's galley, my bedroom held just my bed (a futon on the floor), and my living room wasn't much bigger, though for some reason there was a piano in it (mostly unused). There was also a large mirror propped against the wall. I was experimenting with taking LSD alone—an urge coming from a spiritual intuition perhaps. As the drug took effect, I was sitting in my tiny house listening to Jimi Hendrix and flautist Charles Lloyd and feeling my body change.

Then, uncharacteristically, I decided to look in the mirror. I was nervous at first about what I would see. I had big resistance from years of not looking. But I stuck with it, and soon I was hallucinating patterns on my face, and then suddenly, I saw the symmetry behind the asymmetry. I felt amazed and more accepting of my face. I think I may have cried. This signalled the beginning of facing my face.

Innate Intelligence Letter

Dear Kristi,

You bounced back once and you can do it as many times as you need to. The social stuff is really hard when you have a facial difference. But you have an instinct for people who are good for you. You will also get lost with people who are not so good for you. But all the time you are learning. Follow the writing path. You have learned good skills from your mother.

Play your guitar, even if you don't have a teacher, and buy many guitars—whenever you need a steady companion! It was a mistake to sacrifice yourself for a damaged and angry young man who didn't realize the cost of his requests. You are reaching for healing and that is good, but don't get fooled, there are many charlatans out in the world.

It is a fact that Dr. Stiber molested you and misused his power. You have a right to protest. Just because you are not "pretty" doesn't mean you have to put up with abuse. Those are not good situations and will just compound your feelings of shame.

I am here in your brain, in the music, and in the wind.

Love,

Innate Intelligence

Chapter 4
Adventure Calls:
I Strive to Become a
Sherlock Holmes of the Body

Waking up and reaching in will reveal the mystery
So I'll dance with me on the edge of the earth
To the music of birth in search of mirth
To heal the wounds and tell a new story

In 1973, I was living on Eagle Island but dreaming about the wider world. I was spending much of my time with a couple called the Adams. She was a physiotherapist, and he was a classical guitarist. I studied massage and anatomy with her and guitar with him. It was a perfect combination, and their excellent teaching and mentorship provided me a good grounding in music and bodywork. Later, during summer vacations back from Toronto, I taught them Tai Chi.

In 1972, I had acquired my Washington State massage license, but I wanted to learn more—more about the body, about how to relieve stress and to unlock comforting experiences for myself and others. I sensed that the body would be a good mystery to solve. I was fascinated by how the unconscious could show itself in the body. I had read the books on my parents' bookshelf about improving one's life by examining it, by authors as varied as Abraham Maslow, Rollo May, and Carl Jung. They contained examples of concepts I only half understood but yearned for. This reading was the beginning of my ability to distill what was useful for my life from a book. I entered a path that would solve mysteries and create my method.

My own body was hungry for touch and frequently in pain. I had no idea how to put together the clues I was noticing to reach a conclusion, but I did recognize them as clues. It was no surprise that my favourite board game at the time was Clue. (Who killed Mrs. Plum with what weapon in which room?)

By the fall, I felt a strong need for new experiences. I left the Island to go on an adventure. In Seattle the year before, I had been part of a New Age meditation group. My housemates, Ned and Rob, both Canadians, were members too. They moved to Toronto and said, "It is great here. We have a leader and we think the whole group should come. It's the place to be." Toronto was very hip and creatively active in those days, with the Riverboat and the Edge coffee houses, Nancy White, Ellen McIlwaine and Bruce Cockburn, along with every New Age group in the book, so it very much was the place to be. It also turned out to be the place I would call home for forty-five years.

I boarded the cross-country train to Toronto in November 1973, with a pack, my dog Karuna (in the baggage car), all my suppressed disability "baggage," and high hopes. It was my first long trip by myself. I felt accomplished and grown up, managing to get to my dog from where he shivered in the baggage car to take him out for walks in the cold Canadian towns we passed through. I wondered what this new country would be like.

I arrived in Toronto to stay with friends of Rob who were all part of a spiritual group called the "White Table." A chiropractor, Daniel, was the leader, medium, and father figure of the group—tall and distinguished looking. He was married to a ballet dancer, Darcy, who danced with the National Ballet Company. Rob, who had a limp left over from childhood polio and who I had lived with in a Seattle commune, was the convener. A lawyer, Dalton, and his wife, Iris, made up the occupants of two newly renovated Cabbagetown semis. This is from my first letter home:

> *"I am sitting in the living room looking out the door to the sundeck. There are huge maple trees all around it with a few yellow leaves and strong black trunks. It is quiet here for a city and*

the neighborhood has beautiful old homes that remind me of my picture of England; close together, tall and skinny with small front yards and picket fences."

The sophisticated setting was intimidating to me, having so recently come from the country setting of Eagle Island. At the same time, it was something I yearned for. But my clothes weren't stylish, my cooking had too many spices, and I had a long-haired dog. I did my best to be a good guest; I cooked, cleaned, and kept my dog out of the way, feeling all the while that I was somehow inferior.

I worked as a foot reflexologist and also did work around the house, cleaning and contributing songs and chants to the meditations of the White Table group in exchange for accommodation and meals. At some point, I found out that to continue practicing massage legally I had to go to school in Ontario and get a license, but when I went to check out the school, I realized that it was a sham operation set up to deliver "workers" to massage parlors (places to buy sex). I felt shocked. Was this really what society thought about my chosen career? Around the same time, another masseur showed up on the scene, and he was really close friends with Daniel, the leader of the group. I was worried that I would not be treated fairly by society in general or by the people I was living with.

It was difficult for me to have left home, where I had a role in community and a landscape I loved, and to have ended up in a less-than-secure situation with customs and ways of eating that were new. I tried to comfort myself with my songwriting. Here is one lyric I remember:

"Will you be with me as I find my way through the pain of a leave taking?
Will you be with me as I find my way into the pain of an opening?"

I was yearning for creative fulfillment, not understanding everything that was going on for me. I could sense something was blocking me, and referred to it as "the elephant" in a poem that I sent in a letter to my mother"

Untitled

Like irises out of compost heaps
This emotion called happiness leaps
Out of my depression
It began inside when I got to the bottom of the
rubbish pile
My eyes began to peer out from under the covers
over me
Smiles of people who I never knew before
A look of recognition making sparkles inside
The quietness of nature spreading its soft presence
through my earthquake pain
Healing flows up like rising sap
Sticky with the fresh smell of new life, new ways
Clearly defined I swing out of the rut
Precisely pointed and growing again
Carefully reaching out because I dare not come too
close to life too soon
Or the invisible elephant will crush me (by accident
of course)
Since I haven't learned to see it yet
So I hold the inner petals folded gently around
my heart
'Til one exquisite day I reach a shining bell tower in a
crystal white spire
And stepping stones to a shimmering star
High on top of my world
I cannot bear to be alone anymore
I feel so filled with rainbows I must share some with
the wind
which rushes everywhere in everyone
It will carry the message of my delicate structure to
a Japanese garden or a clear mountain stream
Impossible to stay poised on my pinnacle for more
than a moment
I will remember to return there and learn.

And though the pencil goes up and down graphing the
hills and valleys of my life
I can get higher all the time and join the wind
that dances
On plateaus of shared happiness.

It's a wonder that my mother didn't question me about depression or what the elephant might represent. I know now that she never faced her disability (scoliosis) or her many bouts of depression but just learned to hide them with clothing and outward persona. This understanding leads me toward forgiveness. Looking back, I also feel compassion for the silently "giving up" young adult that was me, who had learned she was really "on her own" and had to prioritize survival above creativity.

I'd been feeling blocked and depressed for a while. Another letter I wrote, this one just before I left the island, is also revealing of my creative frustrations:

> We got on an unbelievable high at Bill and Alison's playing music. We were all singing quite well and there was some talk about getting down and practicing more and arranging for the tentative goal of having a group of songs of recording quality. We want to do more of our own music because there is often more feeling power behind it than other people's songs. I want to write a song but I have some fear that keeps a large part of what is creative in me held down, buried under this burden of self-consciousness.
>
> This self-conscious part says to the creative part, "You can't do anything until you do it perfect or you will not be accepted by me." But bringing the unconscious "feeling inspiration" into conscious form takes practice, trial and error, and learning from both successes and mistakes. Oh, that is what it is! I am so afraid of making mistakes! I want to get rid of all this junk in me keeping me from doing what I want, this over-concern about what other people will think. I want to do it and learn from what happens—not running from it but feeling it with my whole self. I am learning that there is no way I can push my creative self. My ego pushes, afraid that "me" is not good enough—I have to prove myself.... What I can

do is share what I really think and feel and then the creative will come out from under the expectations I have pressed upon it.

Many people, especially creative types, will recognize this overly critical self-talk. Now I know that the criticism had a distinct message that I was not hearing. Unconsciously, I viewed myself as a "mistake" because I had a disability. This deeply hidden identity was blocking my progress. I was afraid of the "unbearable pain" of facing my shame at not "being able." A family friend told me many years later, "After your operation, you had a driven quality, as if you had to prove yourself."

I continued to flex my creative muscles in Toronto, a city full of experimental people. The new experiences kept on coming. I write as much in a letter to a friend:

Another "self-shaking" experience I am having is the massage trade-off sessions I am doing with John Cox. When he works on me, it often turns into a therapy session. I go deeper than I ever have into my emotional state and return with a new strength that comes with (emotional) dying and re-birth. I have surprised myself considerably, and when I see how an unacknowledged or suppressed emotional attitude can control me more than an admitted, accepted one, I want to discover more—painful as it might be. I find that, if I am aware of an emotion, I can choose whether or not to actively express it … also, my accepted emotions pass away much more quickly. It is rather disconcerting to run across attitudes that I used to have in high school. It's also difficult when I think someone is not going to like me for feeling a certain way. Then I have to remember that, even though I try to conceal it, they can probably see it anyway. He encourages me to deal more directly with my anger. Day to day, I am so unaware that what I am feeling is anger. But my body lets me know. I have these points in my shoulders that knot up and hurt until I admit that I feel angry about something.

I was learning about how anger felt in my body, as well as starting to notice what brought me to a relaxed state: "I finished learning the Tai Chi set and now the real work begins—achieving a dynamic flow—stillness in movement. It's really good for my body and mind—bringing a focused attention to the rotation of the spine. I can really feel the Chi energy."

Many of my learning experiences happened outside formal classes, in casual social situations that happen when you hang around with people who are deeply involved in art, self-expression, healing, and spirituality. In my scene in the seventies in Toronto, these people surrounded me daily. At one of our communal house parties on a warm, fragrant spring evening, I had an interesting "face experience." A couple named Mitch and Anna arrived at a party in a small row house in Cabbage town. Anna had an asymmetrical face, mirroring mine. I wrote home about how excited I was to meet someone with a face similar to mine. After talking with her for just a few hours, I felt as though I knew her, because of our common experiences. We were so tuned into each other, I felt like she was my sister. However, the friendship did not last. I have no memory of why—just a feeling of shame. I had many friendships end during those early years without knowing why.

My younger sister Melanie and I were in a creative collaboration that began before I left for Toronto. We would write simple chants together. In a letter home I write:

> "I am so glad you did the recording. I really miss the music and singing with you. There are not many musicians here at the Center. I am chief chanter. We chant frequently and everyone really likes the Eagle Island chants. It is a new dimension to be lead singer and sing without accompaniment and do any harmony that is being done. I think my voice is improving. Could you send me the chords for some of our songs?"

I asked her for "I Gotta Stop Lying," "Don't Worry Mama," "The World and All Its Sorrows," and "Spiral Rainbow," all of which I co-wrote with Melanie. I must have been in one of my 'better voice' moments and chanting, being more like speaking, was easier for me. I don't have a record of the lyrics, but the song titles suggest that I was already identifying some of the psychological themes that kept emerging: pretending I was okay to please those around me and being generally secretive, being enmeshed with my mother and her anxiety, taking on the burdens of the world as well as my family, and finding a spiritual path that would help pull me up again.

These lyrics for a blues song—one of my first "song babies"—express a mix of despair and hopefulness that became a hallmark for my lyrics through the years:

"I got the can't-see blues tonight
They are the blindest blues I ever had
Everywhere all I see is an ocean of uncertainty
And I ain't got no money and hardly any friends
I'm a long ways from home
I can't see what I'm supposed to do
I can't find the place I fit into
Everything I thought was a solid rock has dissolved beneath my feet
I can't see who I am
I can't see who you are
I don't know what this all means to me
But there is one thing that I do know
I'm not an ugly duckling no more
Inside my heart is a precious jewel
I can see it in you too
When I can feel that I'm really worthwhile
I begin to live with a deeper smile"

Even though I knew nothing about the craft of songwriting, I could write a song to help myself out of a hard place.

Eventually, the underground dynamics of the White Table group tore it apart. Everyone except me and Rob moved out. The leader, Daniel, lived in the other semi with his wife, Darcy. By now, I was studying Tai Chi and teaching it. I was doing Re-evaluation counseling and teaching it too. Some good people and support could be found in the counseling community, but I tended not to open up about what was really going on for me. Like my mother, I was prickly on the outside to protect my fragile sense of self. I was doing some reflexology and massage for people, as I had learned to do on the island, but I practiced "discreetly," because I did not have an Ontario massage license yet. I was struggling to establish myself in the big city.

Finally, Daniel asked me if I would like a ticket back to Seattle. This was a shock to me, because I looked up to him and took this comment as a vote of non-confidence. I proudly refused and moved into an unsuitable rooming house with my dog and continued to work at the Center where Daniel had his chiropractic offices. I taught Tai Chi and yoga and treated people in the women's change room. I scraped by with very little money while developing my style of massage that included Touch for Health—a shiatsu- and kinesiology-based system. My work also included the beginnings of my verbal style, which would grow into the Magraw Method: active listening and encouragement of the client's imagination in "talking/listening" to their bodies.

During that time, I would have spells of deep despair, probably emerging from my unacknowledged PTSD that I described in a letter to my sister Melanie:

> "The last couple of days have been hell. When I look at it logically, there have not been such terrible things that you [referring to myself in the second person] should feel crazy, but I have been feeling really crazy and freaked out. Several subtle things came together in such a way to make me feel worthless and rejected. I have to travel two buses and a subway between where I live and the Center where I work and I can't afford it —the other people in the house don't like my dog—Jon Cox the man I was doing exchanges with said I was speedy, graceless, and insensitive in my touch. My illusions came crashing down and it was very painful to be exposed. Then Rob (who I thought had my back) said he thought I should find a home away from the Center. I came apart at the seams. I was just about to give up and come home to the island. A part of me misinterpreted all the events

of the past week and has been saying to the rest of me, 'See, I knew you couldn't make it. I knew you were no good. I knew no one liked you.' It was scary to be so exposed to that part. Then I went into the White Table meditation room, cried for a while, rested, and gradually a calm came over me and I saw how I had been exaggerating and negatively projecting on myself. I said, 'If nothing else, I am still a channel for universal love.' By evening, I was ready to change course and take the next sensible steps. I am not leaving TO but instead am finding a better place to live. I am not giving up on massage. I am going to let people come to me for friendship instead of chasing after them. What a bugger of a pattern this self-rejection and self-pity is. I want to grow out of it soon, find my inner jokester, and learn to laugh. I feel like all I've been doing is crying. However, I am improving as a yoga teacher; I am a talented massage student; I am reading up on energy flows (like acupuncture), beginning to feel energetic auras, and my upper vocal range is coming together slowly but surely."

I feel empathy for the young woman, so isolated and unsupported, and wonder that no one questioned her about feeling "crazy." Perhaps she hid it too well.

As I was caught up in making a sparse living and helping to build the White Table group, music kept asking to have its place in my life. I had moved to Toronto without a guitar, but four months after I arrived, I bought a $60 Brazilian guitar and was playing folksongs. In a letter home, I say that it was hard to play and sing at the same time, and that my rhythm was all screwed up, but a drummer had given me some help. This guitar inspired and comforted me enough to begin singing a little more. Then I had two open-stage experiences. At the Process coffeehouse, I sang through a microphone for the first time and really liked it and felt good about my performance. This memory was lost, however, in a different coffeehouse, where there was also a mike but so much background noise that I couldn't sing or play well, and I totally blew it. I was so confused by the latter event that I stopped playing my guitar and singing for several months.

After this bad on-stage experience at the open stage, I gave up performing in public for another two years, though my musical self was always trying to find a way to share. I would sing for family and in spiritual and therapy groups, and for friends and lovers—quieter situations that were easier. I sang with my sister Melanie when I was on the island. Emotionally, I compensated for my musical disappointments by attaching to certain singers and players. I was passionate about Bruce Cockburn, Pink Floyd, and Pentangle.

One day, at the coffeehouse that had been the scene of my open-stage failure, I met Arthur, a.k.a. "Shandor," who would go on to woo me and ultimately persuade me to marry him. We were married for a disastrous nine months. "Disastrous" is not overstating it; it began with a proposal I accepted under duress. "I will kill myself if you don't marry me," he said. What I didn't know then was that he suffered from Dissociative Identity Disorder (DID), previously called multiple personality.

He said he was a medium. I was very confused about what "channeling a spirit" was and was not. Interacting with him and his alters (what the sub-personalities are called) was startling and felt like a seductive responsibility. One part would persuade me that I could save the other part. My experiences in the White Table group didn't help with this confusion. Part of the group's activities involved channelling spirits. I wrote to a friend during that time:

> Last night we agreed to limit the group to a specific number of people until we had a regular medium reaching a high spirit. Several people in the group have been going into trance states regularly and receiving various entities. We don't know what sort the one that comes through me is. All I know is I feel really good and cheerful while it's happening, then filled with energy when it leaves. It's a very peculiar feeling to have something moving my arms and hands and making me laugh.

Mediumship was big stuff, but I was there mostly for the singing opportunities, because singing in a group made me feel grounded and connected.

Being in a relationship with Shandor, a man with DID, was scary for the still young woman that I was, afraid of being "crazy" herself. We would go on "normal" dates sometimes, like long walks or breakfast at the coffeehouse. We'd talk about beginning an archery program at the school where he studied, but none of the future plans ever came to pass, and we never really talked about what was important. There was so much secrecy, denial, and dissociation on my part as well as his. Operating in survival and rescue mode, I went ahead with the wedding.

The ceremony was on Eagle Island. It involved more pretending than I had ever done before. While I had a beautiful outdoor ceremony, I felt shame and isolation in my heart.

In that year's Christmas letter, my parents write:

> "The highlight of the year was Kristi's wedding. Kristi, who has lived in Toronto since 1973, came home in July with Shandor Boudreau to be married. The ceremony in the manner of Friends (Quakers) was held in our orchard followed by a splendid feast in the backyard, music and dancing in the barn. Having [my father] Jack's parents here for the occasion was an added joy. All four generations of the family were on hand."

They were very much invested in keeping up appearances.

In a 2016 conversation with my sister Melanie regarding my first marriage, she asked, "Yes what was all that about? None of us could figure out what you were doing!" The truth of it was that Shandor (in his distress and mental illness) unconsciously took advantage of my vulnerable state and my helping nature. I was struggling to keep things normal in a very strange and scary situation: his DID, my confusion about mediumship, and my wanting out of the marriage. I spoke to my family about the normal activities Shandor and I engaged in, like walking my dog in Toronto's autumn beauty, but we were actually struggling just to survive. I was acting out my desire to be noticed and rescued. "Yes, there really is something the matter" were the words I wanted to say but couldn't. I have blocked many memories from that time.

At the beginning of 1975, I wrote this sugar-coated, convoluted cry for help to my mother, still not able to admit how bad things were:

> "Dear Mama, Your letters give me warm rushes of energy. Breathing deep Eagle Island scenes, I am renewed. Sometimes I

feel so dumb and quite ashamed of myself for being as blind as I was, yet it all makes sense in terms of growth, in terms of these testing times. I see it all around—people going through their heaviest of heavies. It's sink or swim time. We are being given incredible opportunities for becoming strong in ourselves and our spirits. Also people around the Center are beginning to help deal with the negativity that frequently spouts from Shandor. I do alright but sometimes I get so tired and angry with myself for ever having a hand in creating a situation that is like a constantly grinding pain. I hope I can turn it into a pearl of wisdom and beauty."

In the spring of 1975, the pretense of having a marriage that was working was no longer viable. Shandor and I finally broke up, and I filed for divorce. My mother didn't put that in the Christmas letter that year.

There were no songs while I was surviving the humiliations of my "faux marriage" or afterward while I continued to survive and eke out a living as a body worker in Toronto. How did music find its way back? After my divorce, I found Tibetan Buddhism in the form of a meditation group that met in a community center in the east end of the city. I was so excited when I found out they chanted! I had previously been attracted to the Tibetan Buddhist philosophy, but the chanting sealed the deal. I wanted to be a part of this group and most of the people involved seemed quite grounded.

This was important after a year of dealing with an unstable husband. I felt disappointed in the White Table group and became more discriminating about what kind of groups I would be a part of. White Table had morphed into a group called SOIL (Society of Integrated Living) and bought a farm in the country. By this time, I was getting wary of "high-flying new-age rhetoric" and by nature I was a practical person. As Matthias, my new boyfriend put it, "You were refreshingly direct and grounded compared with the star-children culture of the SOIL community." Matthias was Dutch and a musician. He was a very good man and interested in spiritual things. I remember thinking I wasn't a good enough person to be with him. I think I was still reeling from my faux marriage. In a recent conversation he said, "You played your cards close to your chest. You didn't talk about your marriage, and I didn't know that music was that important to you. At the same time, I experienced you as being quite direct and open. More than I had experienced before. I learned to look at myself more closely."

———————————

I was feeling shame about my marriage, but my desire for healing led to my next adventure. Up to this point, my only training in bodywork had been in peer counseling, bio-energetics, massage, and self-taught shiatsu. Despite that lack of formal training, many people would have emotional releases and insights on my table: "I don't entirely understand what is happening, but 'it' keeps happening and I am having difficulties keeping my workload down. Also, I have been discovering some not-so-pure motivations behind my choice of the healing profession and have become frightened. I think maybe I shouldn't do it anymore." During that time, I knew that fear wasn't a good motivation for action, but I wasn't sure what a good motivation was. I was a confused mess. So, I went abroad to take a break and hopefully to get some perspective.

I landed in London with an impossibly huge knapsack and an equally huge desire to find direction for my life and work. My destination was Findhorn, an alternative community in Northern Scotland that specialized in new-age pursuits and growing very large vegetables. Along the way, I took the time to meet and learn what I could from many artistic and spiritual people. I had never traveled outside the United States, so it was strange and mostly stressful (I was nervous about missing buses and getting lost). I had the most fun in places like Scotland, which reminded me of Eagle Island.

I was yearning for a higher level of discernment after the confusion about what was true spiritual channeling and what was mental disturbance. I wanted to know what to do to handle my clients and students in an appropriate way. I wanted to make sure I was not going down a wrong path.

I traveled around the UK, meeting people and having spiritual experiences. One of these was being inhabited by Bach's Brandenburg concertos. I felt the music in my body! Another was sitting in a field in the midlands of England, with a mirror, making friends with my face again. I cried when I saw the beauty beyond my judgements. I felt the comfort of the sun on my skin and the wind in my hair. It was a poignant moment that had benefits for a long time.

In a letter to Matthias, I described another experience, my continued experiment with Bach:

> I am sitting listening to Bach on the headphones. It is so beautiful. In his book Island, Huxley says Bach is the closest music to silence. I am using the headphones to try to re-train my left ear to hear. What I do is turn it up loud enough so I can hear something in my left ear, then turn the right one off and on. After a while, my left ear gets all warm. I have been going to a Bates teacher (an eye re-training method), which has renewed my inspiration in enlivening my left eye and ear and corresponding part of the brain that I have been told is the creative receptor and focus. The first day I faced this difficulty, I freaked out. At first, I was confused, but eventually I understood it as fear. My left eye is frightened of my ear! It wants to be like the right eye—perfect—but it isn't. This desire creates strain. The Bates method is an incredible spiritual tool.

I didn't have someone tracking me, so this intuitive experience—like so many others of that time—was left by the wayside. However, I was getting the idea that tuning in to my body held some of the answers.

The Bates Method

The Bates method of eye relaxation was developed by William Horatio Bates (1860-1931). It is an alternative method to improve eyesight without wearing glasses and largely consists of relaxation techniques. Research has now shown that its claims for improving eyesight do not hold up. I used it for relaxation purposes, not to improve my sight. It was good for me in that it raised my awareness of sensation in my left eye and ear, where I was numb.

After a few weeks of exploring, I made it to the fresh breezes and beautiful expanse of rocky Scotland. I liked the plant-oriented spirituality of Findhorn. The community reminded me of Eagle Island, and I realized how much I missed my home. In Findhorn, I met a new-age healer named Ludi. I told her my story of confusion regarding working with clients and asked her what I should do. She looked at me very directly and said, "Get training and learn how to deal with it."

I felt two things in that moment. One was embarrassment at how obvious that solution seemed; and the other was resistance, a blind "I can't" feeling.

On the surface that resistance could be read as reluctance to undertake formal training, which was expensive; I had been barely making a living for the past two years. But deeper down, that resistance was based in my traumatic experiences of hospitals and doctors (classified in my mind as mainstream systems, and therefore, bad) and my learned bias toward alternative approaches. Doing anything that might remind survivors of their traumas (for war vets, it can be airplane sounds, and for me, it is paperwork and institutional environments) is often avoided before we even become aware of the fact that we are afraid. I didn't know the depth of my disillusionment with the medical system. I mistakenly felt that training would involve getting captured by "the system."

I thanked Ludi and arrived at the conclusion that I would not stop helping people, but I would do my work from a different motivation and then see what happened. But my courage and her encouragement had made an impact. When I returned to Toronto, I went to school. First to a newly opened massage school to get my license and then to Shiatsu school for a Shiatsu certification. When I saw how these two efforts had moved me ahead, I was grateful for Ludi's plain speaking.

My rented house in the late 70's was big and old, on a street lined with large maple trees close to the University of Toronto. There was a park nearby, where I walked my dog Karuna while composing songs in my head. Being in charge of the house I sublet rooms to an artistic Australian woman, a Japanese woman who did martial arts, and a songwriter. Yams and rice were my dietary staples. I decorated it hippie style with paisley bedspreads and crystals.

I had a massage practice in a tree-surrounded room on the first floor, and a sound-proofed room in the basement for clients who did emotional release. I also resumed Tai Chi classes at the Hagerman street club in Toronto, run by the enigmatic Mr. Moy. I felt enthusiastic about bodywork and the mysteries of the unconscious. I worked long hours, but I was still broke. School fees had put me in debt. However, because of being more educated, I was feeling optimistic. Then my lower back went into spasm. The gnawing ache made it difficult to do massage and walk my dog. I felt frustrated with the pain and myself. I had to work! I had not had this pain before and my usual methods of self-massage, exercise, and emotional release were not working to move it. I had to find a new kind of help. I had heard about a method of postural realignment called the Alexander Technique, and a deep inner knowing combined with desperation to resolve the pain told me it could be good for me. I decided to try it out.

Verna Johnson, the Alexander teacher, had her office in a large old house in the Annex area of Toronto. I lay on her table with two soft-cover books under my head as she explained the principles of the technique. Then she laid her hands gently on my body and slowly began to re-align my spine. I began to relax in a familiar and good way. After this, I practiced sitting, standing, and walking in the new, more aligned way as she gently cued my body away from its old habits. I could feel immediately that I was in the right place to solve my current problem.

The Alexander Technique

The Alexander Technique was invented by Frederick Matthias Alexander, an Australian actor, who lived from 1869 to 1955. He had recurring problems with laryngitis while performing and managed to help himself by observing his habitual postural tendencies and gradually eliminating them. Subsequently he taught actors and singers to improve their voice production by changing their posture. He discovered that gently re-aligning the head, neck, and back relationship produced improved vocal production. Actors use the Alexander technique to this day for improving their performances. It works. Alexander developed the Alexander Technique specifically to recalibrate the kinaesthetic sense, and to bring it in line with our conscious intention. Nowadays many practitioners in the area of postural training have adopted his principles.

I recovered from my back pain quickly and gained an understanding of my posture. I had a habit of pushing my upper body forward, and as result, had an exaggerated lumbar (lower back) curve. I used my right side more than my left, which created a twist in my torso. I did not know how to let my body align in a way that it would be supported in an Alexander sense: the legs resting on the feet, the pelvis over the legs, the spine resting on the pelvis, my back muscles lengthened and widened, my neck aligned over my shoulders, and my head lifted up. Instead I had been straining and twisting to hear and to compensate for physical scar tissue and numb areas of my body.

As I continued lessons with Verna, I became aware of the underlying emotional issues connected with my posture. I had my first conscious encounter with the emotion of fear. I certainly had experienced nervousness before, but this was different, deeper. As I changed my posture to allow my upper body to receive the support of my lower body, I experienced this sensation of fear in my chest. Then, just as I was falling asleep, I would jerk awake in a panic. I gradually became aware that this fear of falling asleep was related to the sensation of going under anesthesia. This insight led me to do my first round of emotional release work on the trauma of my operation. From Alexander lessons, I learned the power of posture to conceal and defend against traumatic memory. Feeling safer as a result of this insight, I opened my awareness to my internal sensations and the joy of feeling a body that was more aligned.

Things were coming together for me. From a place of both pain and optimism, I had sensed a new kind of help was needed, available, and I had been brave enough to show up and try it. This was my first full experience of the Help Curve. The Help Curve is a metaphor I developed later in life but was intuitively pursuing at this time. These were the steps that my intuition led me through:

» I had awareness of the possibility of help:
The Alexander Technique.

» I had newly acquired openness to the technique: I had faced the fact that my other pain-relief techniques were not working.

» I asked for specific help: a way for my body to learn a new posture.

» I received the help: I trusted the teacher and became pain free.

» I felt grateful: The postural education had opened me to my bad habits of straining.

» I did round one of forgiving myself and doctors and integrated the help: I transferred the new postural understanding to all my other activities. I could have periods of deep rest.

As my healing progressed, I began to be able to savour my progress along the Help Curve, over and over again. I learned that a better quality of giving emerged in my work when I poured from my own full cup. I learned that, if I stayed current with my needs for help, my body hurt less. I learned that resting was part of the process.

The Help Curve

Human beings have a hard time asking for help, even though our brains are wired for social engagement. Why is this, when we are social creatures and need help in order to stay connected and healthy? My best answer so far is that the defenses built from attachment and other traumas harden around us. They are created to protect us from hurt but often end up closing us off to help. The basic building blocks of asking for help are being able to discern an unmet need, having the courage to let go of outmoded defenses, and asking until you find the resource that will meet it.

I constructed the metaphor of the "Help Curve" to facilitate the flow of getting help. Metaphors are useful in both approaching a difficult topic and for holding and remembering the information that emerges from the body and the unconscious.

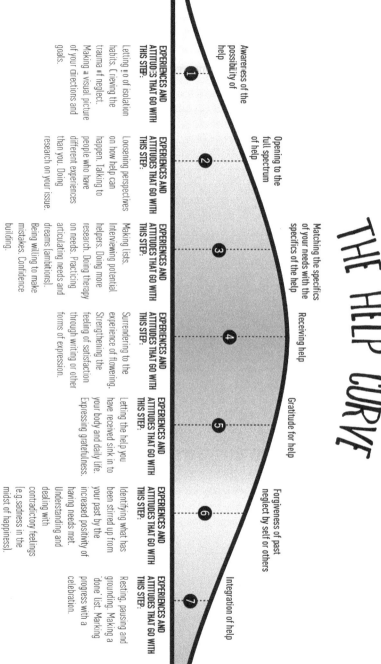

THE HELP CURVE

Awareness of the possibility of help

1

EXPERIENCES AND ATTITUDES THAT GO WITH THIS STEP:

Letting go of isolation habits. Grieving the trauma of neglect. Making a visual picture of your directions and goals.

Opening to the full spectrum of help

2

EXPERIENCES AND ATTITUDES THAT GO WITH THIS STEP:

Loosening perspectives on how help can happen. Talking to people who have different experiences than you. Doing research on your issue.

Matching the specifics of your needs with the specifics of the help

3

EXPERIENCES AND ATTITUDES THAT GO WITH THIS STEP:

Making lists. Interviewing potential helpers. Doing more research. Doing therapy on needs. Practicing articulating needs and dreams (ambitions). Being willing to make mistakes. Confidence building.

Receiving help

4

EXPERIENCES AND ATTITUDES THAT GO WITH THIS STEP:

Surrendering to the experience of flowering. Strengthening the feeling of satisfaction through writing or other forms of expression.

Gratitude for help

5

EXPERIENCES AND ATTITUDES THAT GO WITH THIS STEP:

Letting the help you have received sink in to your body and daily life. Expressing gratefulness.

Forgiveness of past neglect by self or others

6

EXPERIENCES AND ATTITUDES THAT GO WITH THIS STEP:

Identifying what has been stirred up from your past by the increased positivity of having needs met. Understanding and dealing with contradictory feelings (e.g.sadness in the midst of happiness).

Integration of help

7

EXPERIENCES AND ATTITUDES THAT GO WITH THIS STEP:

Resting, pausing and grounding. Making a 'done' list. Marking progress with a celebration.

Sometimes the help, or resource, we need is inside ourselves. If we are caught in helplessness and imagining that the help can only come from outside ourselves in the form of a drug or "magic bullet" of some kind, we will miss the experience of inner unity, inner strength, and self-sufficiency. Sometimes the help has to come from outside ourselves, and if we are "girded up" to never receive help from others (falsely believing it is "all up to us"), we are isolated and often cut off from community. I have found that a mix of inner and outer help is best.

Here's how to practically apply the Help Curve:

1. Choose something you have already accomplished and mark the stages of it on your own visual representation of the healing curve.

2. Choose something that you are in the middle of accomplishing and ask yourself, "Where am I stuck? What is my resistance to asking for help? What kind of help am I missing?"

3. Choose something you have not even started and map out the beginning steps. Mark on your curve each stage as it happens.

4. Look back occasionally at your curves to analyze patterns.

This is not a rigid format. Your Help Curve may look different than mine. Feel free to improvise on this metaphor and tailor it to suit you. If you're wondering how long it takes to complete the Help Curve, the answer (of course) is "it depends." There are different tasks that we need help with. Some can take a lifetime, some a matter of weeks. For example, resolving relationships with parents versus recovering from an acute injury. It depends on your level of access to sources of help, your character, and your social-support system. And critically, it depends on if there are barriers in your way, such as barriers consisting of strong emotions from the past that are stuck in the body. I call those traumas. Another barrier is lack of access to help because of difficult economic circumstances that cause a deficit of time and/or money. Johann Hari writes eloquently about this in his book *Lost Connections*:

> If you are going to develop a community, democratize your work-place, or set up groups to explore your intrinsic values—you will

need time and you need confidence. But we are constantly drained of both. Most people are working all the time, and they are insecure about the future. They are exhausted, and they feel the pressure is being ratcheted up every year. It's hard to join a big struggle when it feels like a struggle to make it to the end of the day.... But as I researched this book, I learned about an experiment that is designed to give people back time, and a sense of confidence in the future.[1]

Hari is referring to a guaranteed universal income. I would add to his list, if you are going to be able to get the help you need to grow, you need a base of support, either community or economic—preferably both.

Some people never get conscious of the curve, going through life according to tradition or by the seat of their pants. Some people, if they do become aware of where they need help, don't ask for it because they are too caught up in the feeling of shame—shame about having needs. Shame is a common barrier. Some people get stuck in passivity when asking and don't get specific enough. Some people will ask and not receive, often because of attachment to trauma identities. These identities are based on true experiences but become locked and exaggerated. For example, two of mine were: 'victim of neglect forever' and 'survival at all costs'. They would narrow my view of the world around me like horse blinders, yet it was terrifying to give them up and truly receive. Eventually I learned to have a greater measure of trust. Toward the integration end of the curve, gratefulness and forgiveness are often blocked by obsession with getting more "stuff" (whatever your "stuff" is), which is often based on traumas of deprivation.

Gratefulness and forgiveness often emerge together, but sometimes those who are excessively grateful are hiding a long-held grudge and lack of forgiveness toward a particular person. I think the most common areas to get stuck on the curve are lack of specificity, receptivity, rest, and belief in a positive future. Of course, it is optimal to pass through the curve with each issue that comes to consciousness, but life often occurs in fits and starts. Any part of it we achieve benefits us.

Many of us need an emotional or spiritual crisis before we think of asking for help—the shock of dealing with pain, death, or illness, or the change of becoming parents for example. Many of us need the intervention of a caring "other" to show us that needing help is okay. Some of us need the security of a job and home.

As you can see from my story, I was an isolated young adult experiencing mysterious physical and emotional events. I was afraid of being "helpless" and equally afraid of being disappointed by potential "helpers," whether they were doctors or alternative healers. I had girded myself and shut off my needs for outside help. I would give the idea lip service, but I had not surrendered my overgrown, non-beneficial defense patterns. I was prevented in reaching out by the barriers of my own traumas and the way they manifested in my body, although I didn't know it at the time.

Looking back, I can say I was fortunate to be learning about the Help Curve in the year I returned from the UK and was struck by unexplained back pain; in the years to come, I needed a lot of help. The late seventies continued to be a challenging time in my life.

By the end of 1975, I had received my landed-immigrant status and lived in five different houses in Toronto in two and a half years. The last place I settled into was the house in the Annex, the university neighborhood. I had found some musician friends and hung out with them, envying their easy musical abilities. But slowly, I was re-inspired in my own music and began to write some songs. I had a great deal of talent in my developing healing work, but it was hampered by "acting out," relationally and sexually.

During these years, I had abortions—three altogether. I rationalized my reactions to the pregnancies. I was young, scared, sick, and reluctant. My sexual acting out had produced them, and underneath, I half knew that I needed help. These emotional events were making me conscious of my need for help, but I couldn't admit it fully, to myself or anyone else. I was working a lot, and I when I wasn't seeing clients, I would keep myself busy with activities, and with men.

Acting Out

Acting out is a term coined to describe our behaviors when they are controlled by unconscious impulses connected to buried trauma and attachment wounds. They don't make sense to our friends and family and usually make a mess in our life. The term is commonly applied to children, but adults absolutely act out as well. It can look like binge drinking, blaming, trying to control other people, or many other unhealthy behaviors.

––––––––––

In those years, I was seeing two men, which caused me some stress. Stanley was a theater director I'd met in my Tai Chi class, and Lawrence was a carpenter who had built a massage table for me. In 1977, I wrote to my mother asking for help with my love life:

> *I feel these days more and more like you are my friend (without denying you are my mother), so I want to share with you something very difficult I have been going through. It has to do with Stanley (primary lover) and my friend Lawrence. Between Daddy's visit and your visit, I began falling in love with him. This was very confusing, because I still have a deep relationship with Stanley. It didn't make sense and yet it was happening. I've had a terribly hard time admitting I have some kind of commitment to Lawrence. Stanley has also had a hard time. I have been through many guilt trips, fear, etc., and when I have courage, I examine myself—trying to see if I am avoiding deep relationships or long-term ones; if I am acting irresponsibly, if I really need a change, if Lawrence is more suited to me for a long-term sexual relationship, and so on. It is frightening for me to think about being without either of them, and yet I know the situation has to be more defined because this chaos and pain is a waste of time and energy. I hope I can become more patient and loyal through this. As Stanley says, "Put myself out to people." I seem to recollect that you always tried to help me with that too. I am sorry I have been so stubborn.*

Her reply was less than satisfying for a young, searching soul who had a deep mystery on her plate:

Your dilemma over Stanley and Lawrence may seem confusing but it is not unusual—changing causes some pain but growth has its rewards—eventually. My feeling about you and Stanley is that there is an animus thing that is hard to overcome (the ghostly lover syndrome) and that the difference in your ages could be hard as you continue. Lawrence seems sensitive and makes you laugh. I would like him to come out here and meet everyone and find out more about him.

My mother struggled with depression and probably her mother did as well. The depression went unrecognized, and they just found ways of surviving. In a letter to a boyfriend, my unacknowledged depression came out in low self-esteem and worries about my dog, Karuna. I was attached to Karuna but so busy with work and self-development that I had a hard time taking care of him. My Australian friend Alda could see this and criticized me. I had difficulty with criticism, and it fed my depressed, sad feelings. I went as far as feeling I didn't deserve to have him. Because I was attached to him, this seemed like a heartbreaking idea.

Often, when I was in these moods, I would do Tai Chi to help myself switch out of it. Usually this was a reliable method but sometimes I would just go deeper and transfer my low self-esteem to Tai Chi class. Did I deserve to be there if I wasn't going regularly? This particular time must have been really awful, because I write, "The room began to turn grey and I struggled to maintain a shred of positivity while feeling totally in the wrong place at the wrong time."

I wrote this song to help myself:

> Child in the wilderness crying
> Trying to find your way through
> I'd like to show you the road that you're seeking
> But I'm just as lost as you
> Child in the wilderness crying
> Your sorrow's your only wealth
> You hear a sound all around you
> And you dance to that music yourself
> Dance to that music yourself

Chorus
Some of us live in the garden
Some of us live in the sun
But some of us live in the shadows
Strangers to everyone
Child in the wilderness crying
You're wasting your lonely tears
If they could fall with mine
We'd make a river and sail right out of here

Still I moved forward, using my insight to identify that I was limiting myself and resisting help, even though I had that "quietly dying inside feeling," I reached out to a friend and told him I loved my work, and called it "my saving grace" but revealed to him that the ridiculously long hours working had left no time for the spiritual and physical pursuits that nurtured and gave me energy. I told him about my inner critic and how it was triggered by others' criticisms. I asked and received advice on how to keep a better balance and kinder attitude toward myself. I was learning how to genuinely ask for help from my friends.

Shortly after moving into the Annex house, my relationship with Stanley blossomed, and though it was rocky at times (he had an ex-wife and child, and I was acting out sexually), overall it was a supportive relationship, and he decided he would take on my voice and see if he could teach me to sing. He began to coach me with the best of intentions but without fully understanding the interrelated damage to my ear, face, vocal folds, and singing voice—not to mention my self-esteem. He was used to working with theatre students and really pushing them into emotional spaces to get a performance. That method didn't work so well with me. I would freeze up or get very emotional. He did lots of theatre exercises, but I still could not sing easily. This confused both of us. He had me work on an impossibly hard song for my voice, Puccini's "Remember Me." My memory is of constant struggle to get and hold the notes. Stanley was a good man, but I ran from our relationship. I couldn't relax into his support. I had many short-term lovers, overlapping relationships, and so on. I began to worry that something was wrong with me.

I still couldn't figure out why I could sing the songs I wrote but had such a hard time with other people's songs. I felt shame and did not really talk about it. I just wrote more songs. I now understand that I wrote songs that skipped over the notes I had trouble with (the holes in my voice). I did not write melodies that had slow sustained notes in the break areas of my voice. "Crescent Moon" was one of those songs. It was an ode to my inner child and an acknowledgement of my (mostly unconscious) feelings of isolation that no amount of men in my bed could solve. I chose to write it in waltz time, which is a comforting rhythm—the rhythm of many lullabies. Even then, at the age of twenty-four, I had an intuition of how music could both heal me and reveal me.

> Crescent Moon cradle yourself
> In the dark night sky create a harmony
> Wandering one cradle yourself
> In the dark night of the soul create a melody
> To touch your misty shadow side
> Changing always changing ebb and flow of moon tide
> Wave of sorrow, fountain of laughter, changing always
> changing water.

I met a bass player in 1979, and he offered to record some of my songs. It was difficult, because I didn't understand the fluctuating nature of my vocal disability and some days I simply couldn't sing very well. He was generous with his time and support, but I wasn't very proud of the result because of my singing—I wanted to sound like the singers I heard on the radio—and did not share the recording with many people. However, I did have the songwriting bug and continued to write with a faint hope that someday I could perform and rely on my voice not to let me down.

Late one afternoon in June 1980, I was having a nap in my third-floor bedroom of the communal house. I heard the phone ring. Heather, my roommate, came running up the stairs, and I knew something was wrong. She said, "Your sister is on the phone." As soon as I heard Martha's voice, I knew something awful had happened, though I never guessed that it would be my father. I took for granted that he would always be there for me and depended on his phone calls and supportive nature; I was deeply attached to him. She told me he had died in a car accident while he was driving from Vancouver to Seattle. Apparently, he had fallen asleep at the wheel.

I went into severe shock and grief. He was my rock, and now he was gone. When I went out to Seattle for the memorial, everything felt strange. My mother was very tense, and I felt disconnected from my sisters. I wrote a song in an attempt to soothe myself and called it "Father's Song." One of the lines in it was "Warm strong hands sharing his love." I was adrift without his hands.

I tried to talk with my mother about Daddy and about my operation. She broke down and cried. I comforted her, but she did not reveal anything or invite me to say more about my experiences. I felt disappointed, and after several attempts, gave up trying to get emotional comfort or information from her.

In the wake of my father's death, I was searching for connection. I was trying to befriend my body. In the process, I attended many new-age events, and even went to an African dance class. That experience was quite difficult. Moving in rhythm with other people and having to learn specific steps and movements revealed the lack of coordination in my body. I couldn't keep up and felt great shame and grief. I left and never told anyone about my attempts to dance. I just wrote a song called "Dancing in My Dream."

I knew I needed help, and I was slowly learning how to ask for it. I saw a pattern developing in my unhealthy relationships with men, before and after my faux marriage. Everywhere I turned, I encountered blurred boundaries with men, breaks in my female relationships, a voice that I couldn't rely on in performance, and a tendency to conceal and deny when it came to shameful secrets—a tendency that would flip on so quickly I wouldn't catch it. Although I was slowly getting my footing in Toronto, I missed Eagle Island … and missed my father most of all.

While I had developed more legitimacy in my massage practice, I still did not fully understand the emotional releases that my clients were experiencing, and I was working almost all the time. I craved healing releases for myself too. I tried many forms of bodywork, like polarity therapy, Rolfing, bio energetics, and got some relief, but I didn't have anyone to track my progress or help me name the barrier that stood in my way on the Help Curve. I remained confused about why I wasn't getting better until I recognized and began to understand the traumas in my early years.

Innate Intelligence Letter

Dear Kristi,

I know you are feeling confused and sometimes depressed with nowhere to turn to. You are committed to personal growth and that is a good thing. However, the shaming words of others—Alda, who shames you about not spending enough time with your dog; Stanley, who shames you about your "selfishness"; spiritual teachers who criticize your awareness; David who invited you to leave the Center—affect you too much. This is because of the hidden shame of your disability and the shame you carry from your parents. Remember your father spent time in jail, and even though it was for political reasons, he must have acquired shame there. And your mother was shamed by her family when they rejected her choice of your father for a husband. Even though they were supported by good friends in the Quaker community they belonged to, no family members came to their wedding. So, it was rather inevitable that you had a difficult first marriage.

You are doing well in the counseling community, but you need to have a therapist of a more traditional sort too. Also, I see signs that you need supervision in your work. You operate under the idea of having to do things by yourself way too much. Watch out for that "little red hen" mentality. This habit comes from your ancestors and your trauma. It is a survival habit and born from deep disappointments. This can and will be healed. I encourage your instincts to ask for help.

It is good you are teaching Tai Chi and doing it every day. Your meditation support group is effective for your growth. It is good to have a place to go and talk about your spiritual progress (or lack of it). The spiritual practices calm your nervous system and keep you grounded. The quietness of meditation is a good way for you to be with people.

It is good you are singing. Singing also helps to calm your nervous system and gives you a platform to express yourself on. Carry on and believe that your efforts will go somewhere.

Love,

Innate Intelligence

P.S. Your interpretations of the dreams I am sending you show growing self-awareness. You are understanding that dream images represent different parts of yourself and that they express emotions you don't allow yourself to feel in your waking life. You are developing your understanding of the "observer" self—the part of you that can step back and analyze. It's too bad you did not have a therapist to help you follow up on your insights.

Kristi as a baby. This is the only photo that shows her ear before the operation.

Kristi in family photo age 4, far right.

Kristi age 4 with her full smile but already showing the protective left side posture that would become chronic post-operation.

Kristi's mother during college. You can see the scoliosis she tried to conceal with expert clothing design in the tip of her head to the right.

Four of the Magraw sisters on the back porch with a bucket of clams they dug. Kristi is on the right (age 8) and she must have had a cut on her foot because she is the only one wearing shoes.

Kristi's childhood home surrounded by poplar and apple trees

The one room school house and swing set. Kristi attended here first through eighth grades.

Mail boat leaving the dock. Mail was the social hub of the island three times a week

Meredith, Kristi and Alison playing on the beach pre-operation.

Birthday party dress up. Kristi on bottom left, age 8.

Kristi with her sisters, (pre-operation) smiling confidently, at ease and happy in her world.

Kristi's parents pre-operation, shining with confidence.

Kristi post-operation trying to hide her left ear and face.

Kristi post-operation refusing to 'smile for the camera'. This photo was taken by a family friend and framed. Notice Kristi's protective defiance, her awkward hand position and the crooked placement of her jaw. I believe that the event of this photo sowed the seeds of shame.

Kristi's father several months after her operation with the look of sadness in his eyes.

Kristi's mother several months after Kristi's operation smiling with her mouth but not her eyes.

The old wagon that Kristi, Linnea, Melanie, Martha and friends played fantasy games in.

Kristi's eighth grade graduation on the school porch with the play set behind us.

Six summer seersucker suits sewn by my mother and one unhappy Kristi (far left) on our way to the 1963 family reunion. In my mother's expression you can see her worry about me.

This photo was taken before the family moved to town and is one of the few photos that show the left side of Kristi's face.

Kristi (second on the right) with her mother, sisters and Aunt in her teenage years.

Kristi as a teenager—
practicing concealment of her face.

Kristi with her faithful dog Karuna.

Kristi (lower right) with friends at an anti-war rally when she is a teenager.

Kristi in her 9th grade choir trying to 'fit in'. She is seventh from the left in the front row.

Kristi during her performing years (1980's)
Notice the Synkinesis on the left side.

Kristi performing at her first wedding in more
ways than is obvious.

Kristi performing at her favorite folk club in Toronto, singing acapella.

Kristi performing at a folk club with friends in the late 80's.

Kristi performing at a garlic festival on Eagle Island 1987.

Kristi about to go on a songwriting cruise in 1994.

Kristi performing at the Kerrville folk festival.

Kristi playing at house party with her friend Diane.

Kristi recording a demo with her friend Debra.

Kristi with her First Ave Songwriters group, 2002.

Kristi leaning on her guitar, as she often did, at the close of a folk festival.

Kristi giving a treatment in her Eagle Island studio in 2019.

Chapter 5
Trauma and Its Aftershocks: PTSD and Dissociation

There'll be days when hard rain falls
Nights of darkness and pain
Many years of questioning
But I have the power to change
To change my tears to laughter
From here to the sweet hereafter
To change my mind
To change my harsh words to kind
As I plant the seeds of tomorrow

———————

Trauma is like an earthquake in our lives. It shakes up our grounding in our bodies, emotions, social relations, and worldview. Unless we regain our solid ground, the aftershocks continue and our pain is buried.

During my twenties, I was living with the aftershocks, feeling them each as painful and confusing symptoms that seemed to come out of nowhere. I felt like a needy person who was an unpredictable mess, and I was lonely. What I was missing was a way to understand the earthquake, or even how to look squarely at it. It was difficult to remember my hospital experience, and not because I was young but because the earthquake had shaken up my access to that event as a memory, and because there was a layer of silence around it.

I experienced two traumas: the physical one during the surgery to the tissues of my ear, face, stomach, and leg, which then caused post-traumatic stress disorder (PTSD) and dissociation from my body; and the emotional trauma of looking different and not talking to anyone about any of this, which led to the trauma of social isolation.

This is how I understand it now; at the time I did not have the words for my hospital trauma and resulting PTSD. Back then I just suffered; now I know the facts. Here's an excerpt of a letter to my parents, written in 1976, when I first asked them about my trauma:

> "I had a fantastic night last night going to a lecture on Ortho-bionomy given by an osteopathic doctor from England…. He was very funny and packed full of information; I listened with every-thing I had. He was demonstrating a technique called 'spontane-ous muscle release.' He also looked in the irises of my eyes and said I didn't discharge poisons properly through my skin and that I had a drug residue from the past. I wanted him to do a muscle release on me. I asked him twice. I hung around until the end waiting…. I got very anxious. I felt like a dog hanging around people who have food … wanting it so badly but not daring to ask again directly. Finally, I left very upset. I went to see a friend, and after telling him the story and laughing, I felt better….
>
> Mama I was wondering what it was like when I was born—your feelings during pregnancy and after I was born. I would also be interested in any memories you could share around the time of my operation. I am interested in your memories too, Daddy. I am attempting to clearly remember and restore these areas of my life."

My next letter to my mother describes my response to her reply:

> I felt kind of silly that I'd asked you such a complex question in a letter and I didn't really expect you to answer. The important thing was for me to ask the question to open the subject. The answer will come when the time is right. I really appreciate your efforts though."

What I interpret from this is that my mother had pushed aside my questions, and I felt shame for having asked.

Many people use the word "traumatic" to describe something that happened to them and mean unfortunate, scary, or difficult. In my usage the word, "traumatic" refers to an event that has lingering and damaging effects to your body systems, and which is difficult to feel peace about, because in an important way, it isn't finished and it continues to impact your life on a regular basis.

Back in the sixties, doctors didn't think about or treat trauma in the same way they are beginning to now. The nature and after effects of trauma are becoming better understood, thanks to research, popular writing on the subject, the mindfulness movement, and better training for medical specialists. When I grew up in the isolation of PTSD, no one knew what "PTSD" meant. If they did know the term, it was used for soldiers and people who had been in violent accidents. In fact, trauma can affect any of us, not just those in extreme or uncommon circumstances.

For me, trauma has a broad definition: It is any shock to the system—physical or emotional—that is not recovered from and continues to produce states of overwhelm. It is any painful event or series of events that leads to PTSD and dissociative states. It is compounded by unconsciously ignoring or numbing the body, not talking about the event, or feeling shame about the event. This lack of recovery produces a pull to the past, emotionally and physically. For clarity, I have sorted this "pull" into four different categories but often they overlap and mix.

» **Trigger:** This refers to an environment, event, or person that reminds us of something in the past. This word is used for a continuum of experiences that range from very mild painful memories to more traumatic ones, and at times can lead to a flashback.

» **Flashback:** This happens when we are suddenly, vividly re-living a past event, with sensory impressions and body sensations. A flashback is usually short but can lead to a regression.

» **Regression:** This happens when we find ourselves feeling and acting as if we were younger than our actual age—often the age of our traumatic event. This can be a conscious or unconscious process. Memories and emotions can emerge from any of the traumatic times. Regression is not as sensory as a flashback and, done consciously with healing intentions in a therapeutic setting, it can be valuable. Unconscious regressions can last longer (hours instead of minutes) and can influence our actions over time, often leading to a repeat.

» **Repeat:** This is my word for a longer pull to the past that usually involves behavioral patterns over time. Repeats occur when the external present somehow reflects the themes of the past trauma and our behaviors revert to those of the traumatic time. A repeat is quite painful and confusing, and it is important to resolve it as quickly as possible.

Trauma repeats can have a huge impact and will slow down the progress of developmental and personal growth. That is what happened to me. For example, the three abortions in my early twenties were repeats. I referred to the first one in my journal as a "death and re-birth" experience. The conscious reason for the abortion was that I was not totally sure who the father was, my steady boyfriend or my new lover. I did not tell anyone of this confusion—not even the two of them. My steady boyfriend supported me as I went through a spiritual ritual of letting go. I was very nauseous during the short pregnancy, and this frightened me deeply, though I did not understand why. Now I think that my PTSD got triggered by the nausea, and I had flashbacks to my first operation when the fear of forgetting who I was got entangled with the event of vomiting. To my psyche, the struggle to not vomit with morning sickness seemed like a matter of survival, and the relief I felt when the nausea left must have been like a re-birth—from the clutches of flashback hell. I couldn't talk about these abortions, and in fact, "forgot" about them until reading my journals while researching for this book. I believe that the forgetting was because of the accumulated shame and confusion and a habit of silence, both inner and outer.

However, during these years, the healthy instincts were starting to gain strength as well. Here is an example of how I began to decrease the silence within myself through the use of inner dialogue, as recorded in my diary.

I had had a stressful week with musical performances and some reactivity to clients. I was feeling a weird kind of tiredness so when the cycling teacher said, "Increase your resistance." She meant make it harder to pedal. I had an immediate thought: "I don't want to." I wondered at the strength of my reaction and started repeating the phrase to myself. A client whose resistance bothered me came into my head; then I thought of a student and how her resistance to identifying her hurt publicly led to her not getting her needs met. I began to cry quietly—still pedaling and sweating. The internal statement changed to "I don't want anyone to see or hear me," and a full-blown gestalt understanding flew into my head. It was so fast as to be more imagistic than verbal: I knew I was coming into contact with the part of me who was still ashamed of being disabled. She (that part) had a habit of ignoring the details of my voice and face/hearing just like my mother did. Then, like my two clients, I felt meta-shame. I realized how I was re-creating my suffering by playing out the story of my past within myself. I knew that it was crucial that I begin to "listen" in detail to my voice and feelings so that I could give the right kind of assistance to myself, as well as ask for specific help from my music teachers.

Subsequently, I was able to do this. The next week, I had a similar experience in the same class, when I had the thought, "I can't keep going." I then thought, "Just do the best you can." This began an inner dialogue and led to a picture of me struggling in isolation. My inner statement changed to this: "I can't keep going when there is no one at the end of it to greet me." I began to cry again. Memories of isolation at points of difficulty in my life cycled through as the pedals went around. I could feel the specific weak muscle in my buttocks that was carrying the story of isolation. I was able to keep going using the contrasting statements of "I can't keep going" and "Just do the best you can, I'm here." I was able to complete the class at a good speed.

A pioneer and expert in the field of trauma and trauma therapy, Dr. Bessel Van der Kolk, in his book *The Body Keeps the Score*, explains why silence so often surrounds trauma. His study on where in the brain flashbacks are played out showed (among other things) that Broca's area in the left hemisphere, which controls speech, decreased in function during trauma flashbacks.

"All trauma is preverbal. Shakespeare captures this state of speechless terror in Macbeth, after the king's body is discovered: 'Oh horror! horror! horror! Tongue nor heart cannot conceive nor name thee. Confusion now hath made his masterpiece!' … Even years later, traumatized people often have enormous difficulty telling other people what has happened to them…. Trauma by nature drives us to the edge of comprehension, cutting us off from language based on common experience or an imaginable past."[1]

Dissociation is one of nature's ways to help us survive. It is the "freeze/collapse" stage of defense that occurs when an animal or human feels there is no escape from or ability to fight the predator, abuser, or life-endangering situation. In the hope of saving our life, we temporarily lose the "life" in our body and mind as disconnections multiply. Our frontal lobes lose connection from our Limbic (emotional) system. Our left brain loses connection to our right brain. Our actions become more unconscious, and we lose connections with people around us and the meaning of our life. All our energy is pulled deep into our core as we freeze and collapse.

When we're in a dissociative state, we will likely have a pale face, squinty or flat eyes, weak limbs, and a concave chest. We will exhibit spaced-out speech or actions and a lack of ability to think clearly or make decisions. Our memory storage capacity is altered, our narratives become fragmented in the moment and on into our future. As Van der Kolk puts it:

There could be only one explanation for such results: In response to the trauma itself, and in coping with the dread that persisted long afterward, these patients had learned to shut down the brain areas that transmit the visceral feelings and emotions that accompany and define terror. Yet in everyday life, these same brain areas are responsible for registering the entire range of emotions and sensations that form the foundation of our self-awareness, our sense of who we are. What we witnessed here was a tragic adaptation: In an effort to shut off terrifying sensations, they also deadened their capacity to feel fully alive.[2]

Many of us do partial dissociations, as I did from my left side and in particular my left ear. Sometimes dissociation is situational and only occurs under certain circumstances. For example, mine mainly happened in noisy situations and hospital settings.

After many years of intuitively understanding my nervous system and working on it, I now understand my vagus nerve and my trauma states at a more comprehensive level. Particularly helpful was the Polyvagal Theory developed by Stephen Porges.[3] Research into the science of the vagal system, and into treatments that might help it, is ongoing. What follows is my best understanding to date. The Autonomic Nervous System (ANS) is the part of the Central Nervous System (CNS) that we don't consciously control. The vagus nerve is a huge nerve that "wanders" throughout the body and is a major part of the ANS. I was introduced to the power of the vagus nerve by my osteopath and have been working to consciously strengthen it for several years. (See chapter 9 for more.) The term "state" in this context means an overall mind-body event. We recognize these states in our language with phrases like, "I'm in an up/down mood" or "I'm flat today" or "I'm as nervous as a cat on a hot tin roof."

For many years, the traditional way of explaining the nervous system has been to divide it into two contrasting systems, the parasympathetic (rest and digest) and the sympathetic (fight or flight). That is the way I was taught, and the way I explained it. I could never quite figure out where dissociative states fit in, even though I knew the signs of them well. The newer way of looking at it, originated by Porges, divides the system of two differing states into three and explains where dissociative states fit in. The dorsal vagal branch of the vagus nerve is an evolutionarily "old" branch of the vagus nerve. It contributes to immobilizing us in life threatening and highly stressful situations and evolved primarily for survival purposes. It mainly affects the viscera below the diaphragm. The ventral vagal nerve—which is unique to mammals (evolutionarily more advanced) and which originates from a different place in the brain stem than the dorsal vagus—affects structures above the diaphragm, among them the heart, the facial muscles, the head, the voice, and the middle ear. Working via these structures, it helps us to socially engage, rest, and renew, and from birth onward these activities in turn strengthen our ventral vagus system.

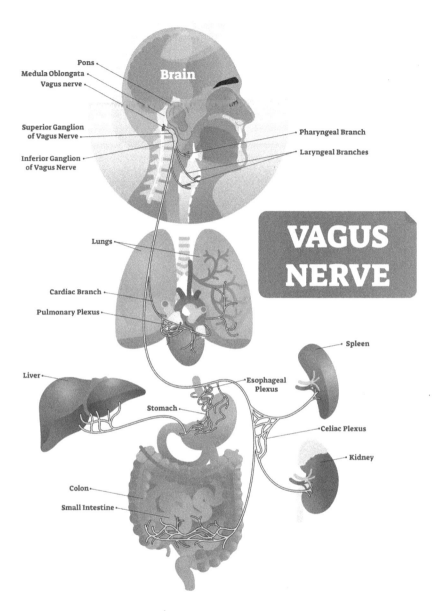

The third part of the system is the sympathetic nervous system—mobilization for defense—and is activated when we are in "fight or flight" and at other times, to wake us up or spring us into action. In trauma survivors, it is common to be triggered into these defense states too often, and as a result, to have body breakdowns, such as adrenal fatigue, digestive problems, and hypertension.

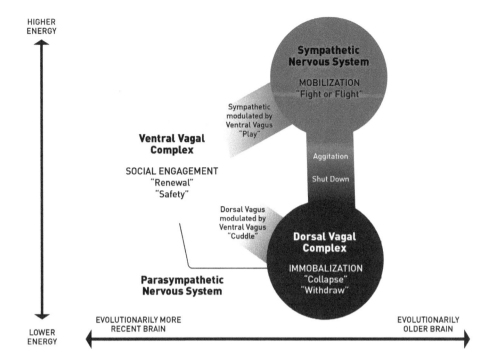

The ventral vagal system is myelinated (stronger and faster) and can regulate the other two systems. For example, when the ventral system regulates the dorsal system, we have immobilization without fear, which can manifest as cuddling. When the ventral system regulates the sympathetic system, we can have mobilization without fear, which allows us to engage in competitive games and play in a friendly and explorative way.

Dissociation is explained by the activation of the dorsal vagal system, which allows all mammals to go limp when they are in danger of their lives. It shuts down organ-renewal systems (such as digestion and absorption) and withdraws blood from the periphery of the body. Humans also do this in events that are perceived as overwhelmingly dangerous situations. Such an event causes partial blood withdrawal from the face ("she turned pale with fright") and shuts down the autonomic nervous system ("she was paralyzed with fear and her mind went blank"). The body becomes numb.

When the dorsal vagal state persists over time, it creates dissociation. This persistent set of mind-body phenomena can have devastating consequences. However, at the time of the traumatic event, the employment of the dorsal vagal system is often the best survival mechanism. It is not a conscious decision but a nervous-system reaction. It is important not to judge oneself or others for what the body has done but rather learn to discern when it has happened and to recover using the ventral vagal system. In my case, the ear operation felt life threatening, and though many parts of my nervous system remained normal, the nerves and tissues around and in my ear and throat went numb and limp—contributing to my long-term vocal disability. Sound confusion and overload, which is common for one-eared people and people with a dampened ventral vagus nerve, would put me in a fight-or-flight state (sympathetic nervous system) and then into a dorsal vagal state, at which point I would withdraw from social engagement.

I gravitated toward activities and treatments that would bring me back to a ventral vagal state (social engagement, relaxation), such as singing, dancing, playing guitar, therapy, acupuncture, and many kinds of bodywork and exercise. But too often, because of my tendency to try to "prove" my worthiness (while internally judging myself) by overworking and over-trying, I would fall into chronic, reactive dissociation (dorsal vagal) and begin to have wandering pains, loss of voice, depressive and discouraged feelings, and as you can see from my story, social isolation.

One of the most important things I have discovered along the way is how to identify when I am in which state (dorsal vagal, ventral vagal, or sympathetic nervous system) and find techniques to bring myself back to a ventral vagal state. Positive self-talk—often speaking out loud to myself or writing to describe how I'm feeling, how my body and nervous systems are feeling—has been very effective for me. Being verbal helps us become aware of our current state, accept it, and consider how we might want to change it. For those ventral vagal states, I often use words and phrases such as content, comfortable in my own skin, at ease, right amount, and belonging. Each person has their own way of describing it. For the combination of ventral and sympathetic, I use words such as playful, powerful, sparky, energetic, and dynamic. For the dorsal and ventral combination, I use words such as cuddly, quiet, still, relaxed, and close.

Equally important was to have names for my uncomfortable states. For the excessive sympathetic state, I use words such as antsy, hyper, restless, irritable, explosive, panicked, and nervous. For the dorsal vagal, I use words such as heavy, numb, flat, cold, discouraged, no motivation, not on this planet, going away, crashed, and weak. If we have names for what we are sensing in our bodies, it helps us to change uncomfortable states. It is useful to find your particular words and metaphors. This process helps us listen to and change what happens in our bodies, and it is one of the underpinnings of the Magraw Method.

With the concepts of the Polyvagal Theory organizing all my observations, I could easily go after a ventral vagal state and find activities that would reliably bring me back to it. For homeostasis (balance) of our system, we need a little of all the states, but too much of the time, because of trauma or tendencies in our family of origin, we get stuck in a default state. We don't reliably return to the ventral vagus state of social engagement but instead linger in the sympathetic fight-or-flight or dorsal state of dissociation. This causes feelings of loneliness and isolation.

I have found that transforming trauma is as much about seeing and acknowledging the instincts for thriving as it is to see how we were injured. The story of my life illustrates this basic principle. Trauma is still something I'm working on healing every day, but the aftershocks are lessening in severity. Note by note, I am finding a way to wholeness and belonging.

Ways to Work with Trauma

Before I describe more of my PTSD experiences, I am going to give you a sense of a "way out," so you can have something to anchor you as you follow my story. While everyone's experience will be different, and the support and guidance they need will be different, several things are common to how anyone works with and heals from trauma:

1. As new research is showing (see Van der Kolk, Damasio and Porges), the body and mind are not separate. I understood this concept early on from reading Georg Groddeck's *Book of the It* and from his idea that our unconscious manifests itself in our body.[4] I further developed my thinking of the mind-body as a circular process through study of the Chinese Five Element Theory. Simply put, our thoughts, emotions, and actions affect

our body, and the state of our physical health affects our moods, emotional states, and actions.

2. We need to understand that trauma states, which are difficult to see when they are your own and manifest in ways that are hard to predict and treat by traditional means, can get triggered and create a "repeat." A repeat must be managed with awareness, patience, self-compassion, and courage. Often healing them requires professional support.

3. We must undertake to do our best to stay present in the body and in the moment, with an ability to tune in to our narratives of both illness and health without getting caught in them. I call this "keeping the body in mind." Presence and moderation need to be practiced often, especially when we are triggered, or in a flashback, regression, or repeat.

4. Eventually, we must establish a customized and creative approach to long-term healing. That approach will be different for everyone, and we are likely to need some help along the way.

There is no one way to help people who have been traumatized. Each person, trauma, and PTSD experience is different. And each road to recovery is unique, although there are many things in common. Here are some questions—worded from the therapist's point of view but equally valid if worded from the client's--to help specify where to begin:

1. In choosing help, in relation to the timing of the event, is it a recent trauma or a long past one? Is it a recent one piled on top of an old one?

     If it is a recent trauma, quiet, kindness, and comfort are the most important ingredients. Peter Levine, in his book *In an Unspoken Voice*, explains this well.[5] He says that allowing the person to shake or cry while in physical contact with themselves (a self-hug) or with someone else (holding a hand) is useful to prevent the "freeze" reaction and helps us stay present.

     If the trauma is old, guiding the person in and out of the memory, practicing separating the past from the present, finding a safe space or spiritual part of self for inner guidance, and locating where in the body the old trauma is stuck is useful. Bodywork can reveal and heal old trauma. If the trauma is a combination of new and old, it will take longer to resolve. It is important to address any feelings of shame involved because, after repeated traumas, shame accumulates.

2. In choosing help in relation to a person's cultural background or any other visible difference from the people around them, ask if they are familiar with therapy or bodywork. Do they have a spiritual base? How do they self identify? Have they experienced cultural, racial, gender or disability trauma?

   It is always important to find out what techniques a person feels comfortable with. For example, if it's praying they know, or dancing they choose, pray or dance with them or find someone who will. Find out if they prefer one-on-one or group experiences and if the gender, racial or cultural background of a practitioner is important. Ask them what aspect of their trauma is most important to them. Traumas of identity/belonging are often what I call the 'drip, drip' kind because they accumulate over years of repeated injury to the sense of belonging, which for a human being is traumatic and shame inducing.

3. In choosing help in relation to the physicality of the trauma, is it to the head? Is it relational? Sexual? Is it hospital based?

   If the trauma is a head injury, such as a concussion, rest and nutrition come first. Little else should be done at the beginning (there is some disagreement about how long the rest period should be) and then neurofeedback, cranial sacral, osteopathy, or brain retraining exercises could be considered, depending on the person.

   If the trauma is sexual or relational (such as physical abuse), someone trained in relational psychotherapy is important. If it is hospital based, more medical help may be necessary, and it is important that the original trauma is addressed emotionally before more medical interventions. Employing good physical care, such as acupuncture, massage, osteopathy, and many types of movement therapy, also work well to heal medical traumas.

4. In choosing social support, does this person have economic security? Is the trauma natural-disaster based? Or is it based in lack of connections? What kind of loss is involved?

   If people aren't secure in their housing or job, it is very important to address that first. If the trauma is connected to a natural disaster or war and involves loss, a grief counselor is a good option (after securing their physical well-being). Also, David Berceli's Trauma Release exercise (shaking) is very helpful.[6] For war survivors, support groups and appropriate help for pain (non-drug based) is good. Social reconnection is an important part of the help needed to solve traumas of natural disasters or war.

5. In choosing the appropriate strength of help, what is the person's nervous system able to handle?

   Everybody comes into the world with a different nervous-system tendency, ranging from very sensitive to very tough (no judgment is implied in either of these extremes). Sensitive people need very little input to produce a change; tough people need a considerable amount. Assessment of the degree of sensitivity is important before choosing the timing and amount of technique to use. Some survivors are reactive (different than sensitive) after their trauma. Stabilizing the nervous system to counteract reactivity is good. That can be done by working with the vagus nerve system and by paying attention to doing the "right amount" of the "right thing."

6. In choosing the best individual help, what type of practitioner would work best for this person?

   The relationship of the practitioner to trauma survivor is at least half the healing. We need to feel recognized and respected to recover from the shame and isolation that trauma produces. It is important that the therapist has done their own work on their trauma no matter how small it is deemed to be. This can deepen the therapists understanding, prevent burnout and projection.

These questions need to be considered before applying any technique. Secondly, always remember that the trauma pattern wants to pull us back in time in an ineffective attempt to resolve the traumatic event. Building an effective path back to the present is one of the main tasks of healing.

There is some disagreement among trauma practitioners regarding emotions and reviewing the past. I think this is because of trauma survivors' differing needs. It is still hard for practitioners to remain objective and not get attached to a certain technique or approach because of their personal experiences. I have had this problem myself, as well as thinking that what is good for me is good for everyone.

One of the main points of disagreement is about whether to focus on the trauma until the person becomes desensitized to it or not to focus on the trauma at all, but rather to work on building strengths and a set of skills the person can use to remain in their body and in the present. A second contentious issue is whether or not to go deeply into a person's emotional memories to release them. Some people think it's preferable to confront emotional memories directly, while others advise containing emotions and working on regulating and grounding. I believe that different people need different things, and I proceed slowly, checking in with the client frequently to discern together which method and practitioner is the best for any given person and their situation. I have seen all the approaches work, and I have seen them not work, depending on many factors.

A third point of disagreement among practitioners who do trauma therapy is about the prevalence of dissociation as an "aftershock" of trauma that makes the healing process uneven and sometimes a long stop-and-go process. People differ in how they like to understand and work with these "aftershocks." My advice is to practice a non-judgmental attitude toward self and others as you find your way.

Re-connection is highly important in trauma recovery. What follows is a series of questions—worded from the client's point of view but useful for therapists as well--with my answers to clarify the process of asking and receiving help. Ask yourself the same questions and discover your own answers.

1. When did I first notice evidence of asking for help with trauma in my adult life?

   I started asking early but was too shut down to receive. The first time I remember asking and genuinely receiving therapeutic help was at my first psychodrama workshop in a small women's group. It was after my father's death, and I was grappling with my feelings toward women. I revealed that I disliked women, didn't know how to relate to them, and that I needed help to shift this. They were compassionate and did not judge me. They helped me begin to see where it came from: fear I couldn't compete in feminine pursuits because of my facial disability and a lack of trust in my mother.

   I got better at receiving help once I acknowledged the depth of my neglect trauma around my face and ear and was able to forgive doctors and parents (for the first but not the last time). This forgiveness allowed a deeper clarity. I began to discern effective help from useless help.

2. Did I have a bad childhood experience of asking for help?

   Yes, countless times with countless people, I did not get the help I needed for my ear, face, and singing voice. The adults seemed confused by me. The doctor did not help as promised. Alternative practitioners were often just as blind and unhelpful.

3. In asking for help with my trauma, where do I commonly get stuck?

   My awareness of my needs and problems is ahead of my ability to relax and receive fully. Forgiveness (especially self-forgiveness) is also difficult due to a low-level bitter mood (connected to neglect of my disability and inherited family habits) that prevents me from resting and integrating, instead, pushing me to start at the beginning of the Help Curve with a new issue before I have fully finished the first one. I have an image of myself rushing and tumbling through life, breathless with "doing" as if to make up for an unnamed crime.

4. Did I have anyone who modeled dealing with trauma close to me?

I didn't have anyone until I moved to Toronto and got involved with the healing community here in the 1980's. Now it is easier to find people and public models (books, speakers, teachers) that we can look to as examples when we get stuck.

I have found that transforming trauma is as much about seeing and acknowledging the instincts for thriving as it is to see how we were injured. The story of my life illustrates this basic principle. Trauma is still something I'm working on healing every day, but the aftershocks are lessening in severity as I regain my solid ground.

PTSD Is Like Emotional Scar Tissue

After a trauma has passed, PTSD can form in the unacknowledged and unreleased feelings in the body. This becomes a holding pattern that stunts and inhibits forward movement.

Curiously, the holding patterns of PTSD have similar qualities to the physical scar tissue that forms after cuts or abrasions. It can be comforting to accept that PTSD is an injury, even if it's not as visible as a scar on the skin. Here are several similarities I've discovered:

Physical Scar Tissue	PTSD
» Inhibits the natural movement of ligaments and muscles as it tightens and hardens with the passage of time.	» Prevents the natural movement of emotions as it hardens defense patterns with the passage of time.
» Causes range of motion in joints to become smaller.	» Causes the range of life choices to become smaller as the "no go" zones become bigger.
» Pulls the rest of the body out of alignment, causing pain far away from the site of the original injury.	» Pulls us out of alignment with our true direction causing "soul" pain and a life unfulfilled.

Healing physical scar tissue is a process of patiently softening the adhesions and resuming natural movement patterns. This process requires constant upkeep and often the intervention of bodywork. PTSD requires a patient unraveling of the root trauma and then a concerted practice of living outside of the trauma story. Often our physical scars carry the story of our emotional trauma, but PTSD can also be a hidden scar on the emotional body and the soul that prevents us from knowing our purpose and connecting with people.

Music has helped me to soften both my PTSD and my physical scars. However, it also can trigger traumatic memories. For example, before I sing, I feel afraid that I won't be able to. When I sing, I feel afraid too, getting breathless and panicky when my voice really comes out. It was confusing when I began to feel these contradictory feelings. I finally figured out that there were two traumas being expressed. One was the loss of my singing voice at a young age, and the other was the physical trauma to the muscles of the larynx and pharynx, which I had partially shut down ever since. Full-voice singing makes me feel those muscles, and consequently, the trauma stored within them. The "scary to sing" feeling is gradually going away.

The following story is an example of the right technique for my trauma applied with the right practitioner to produce a deep "repair" (see chapter 8) of my facial shame and PTSD, thus helping to awaken the nerves and tissues.

By the time I found Jeanette Han, my acupuncturist, I was approaching burnout from my main defense behavior: being a workaholic. Jeanette had been a skilled practitioner in China, specializing in sports acupuncture. She came to study further at McMaster University and was working in the back of a tiny herb store in Chinatown to make ends meet and save money to bring over her husband and son. Jeanette's skill and innovative approach took my body and face to another level of health.

First, she told me firmly that she could help my face, but only if I worked less. I wanted help and felt shame that I worked so hard. She motivated me to begin cutting back. I stopped teaching at the Kikkawa school and cut back clients and volunteer work.

She used many techniques. One of the most spectacular was making a warm mask of beeswax and herbs that she applied to my face before putting in the needles. She said it was a "womb for my face." I liked the idea of my face being born again. She would look carefully at my face when I came out from the "womb" and celebrate the changes. Her enthusiasm at each little detail of improvement was just the "mother repair" I needed, because my mother's guilt had prevented her from really looking at my face in any detailed way. Her needle work with my damaged facial nerve was truly amazing, and I achieved the eye closure I had begun earlier in a facial re-training program. Plus, my whole face came alive and many of my organ systems became healthier. I credit her work with keeping me strong for many years. Jeanette was a major influence for change and help for my trauma.

PTSD and My Ear Confusion

One day in the 1990's, listening to music on headphones, I thought my hearing was coming back (I was used to my voice coming back so why couldn't my hearing come back?) because I felt a sensation in my ear. This hope and confusion lead to a long journey of receiving surgery for a hearing-aid implant, which did not help my hearing but instead led to Eustachian tube and sinus plugging—worsening my hearing for about a year. This was extremely traumatic—definitely a repeat with frequent flashback episodes. It was especially long lasting because I isolated myself and retreated from family and friends. In the end, I managed to speak up to the doctor who had performed the operation (and who tried to persuade me to go further down that road). I learned a hard lesson: Get more advice and do more research. But it came at a cost.

In a letter to the ear, nose, and throat specialist, I expressed what I had learned, which was a way for me to both share what I saw as useful information with a specialist and speak up for myself, in an effort to heal my relationship with the medical system.

> *I believe I am not the only person who has a different hearing experience and listening problems, as well as the emotional trauma that goes along with that. Of all the professionals I have been to see regarding my ears and face, my family doctor, two audiologists (who educated me on the plight of having one ear), and a physiotherapist have been the most helpful in that they listened carefully to the data I presented, noticed where I was lacking information, and were able to find unusual solutions suited to my needs. I am*

writing my story down in the hopes that it might help audiologists and ENTs listen better to their patients with one-ear deafness, Eustachian tube blockage, facial paralysis, and low frequency sound sensitivity.

During the recovery period from my implant, I began to have flashbacks when I was being massaged. I started coughing and knew it was a memory of my early anesthesia experience. I felt again the terror of waking up during the middle of the operation, feeling the searing pains in my stomach and ear. I remembered my power being taken away from me, being stuck in the hospital with no people I knew and no touching. I saw myself shutting down because of fear of death and fear of neglect and experienced more waves of mistrust and sorrow. In another bodywork session, I imagined a repair scene where someone from outside the family helped me and my mother get emotional nourishment and understanding. This calmed the flashbacks.

Generally, if I got lost in my past, I found my way back to the present, but depression was building. On New Year's Eve 1994 I wrote:

Spent tonight alone—bath, TV movie—thinking about why it is that I am alone. I want to face realistically where I am now in my life: not with a partner, not in community or with family. Wondering why I bring into my life people who are retreated from life—especially with their bodies. I think it's because they represent a part of my body that was frozen at age nine and my mind that was forced out during those long operations that made me feel I was not allowed to participate in life or deal with what was happening to me (being cut).

No Good Place to Work or Play

Around this time, I had a short-lived dream of teaching mind-body techniques based on the Five Element Theory at a college acupuncture program in the US called The Tristate Institute. I made what I thought was a really good proposal, and they turned me down. The disappointment was crushing. I had grown tired of teaching small groups and wanted to do something bigger. I was sure I was rejected because I didn't have a degree. More shame. But what I did have was the beginnings of the Magraw Method—a slow and deep unfolding of an understanding about trauma, rooted in my own experience and shared with my clients. At the time, however, I was feeling very untethered. I lived in two different shared accommodations, and my rooms were problematic in different ways (too small, too noisy). I also didn't have a good office space.

Notes Lost in Nashville

Around this time I started going to Nashville for songwriting workshops. I was hampered by my plugged condition. I couldn't sing and sometimes I really couldn't hear. I loved the instruction and inspiration of the teachers, but in the fast-moving and loud social situations, I was lost.

I drove down by myself—a thirteen-hour drive. I would be exhausted when I arrived. I would get lost in the winding streets of Nashville. I would often cry in frustration. By the end of the workshop, I would be very tired and facing the long drive home. One time, I got lost in Michigan just before the border crossing. That time I really broke down but somehow made it home. I remember the feeling of coming into Canada, which was always reassuring and familiar; my body could relax.

I was doing some songwriting, but I was at that uncomfortable time of learning when nothing seemed good enough. I was also feeling not good enough in other ways: as a daughter not able to heal her mother, as a wife not able to stay in a marriage, as a woman who could no longer attract men. The song "Broken Wing" by Martina McBride was my personal anthem.

In the process of this intense trauma repeat, I mentally threw out all the music I had accomplished with Karl (my second husband, more on this in chapter 7). I didn't look at it or listen to it for many years. This was a big loss. The titles of the songs I was writing at that time are revealing: "I Will Comfort You," "Pocketful of Shining Stars," and "Yesterday's Child." My confidence in my own voice was so low that I had other people sing my demos. And once they sang my song, I stopped singing it. Therefore, they did not have as strong a healing effect as my earlier songs had. I also was missing the support of a good teacher or vocal coach. I studied a little finger-style guitar, but it was slow going. I did not play my guitar very much. I had a deep desire for a musical mentor.

"I Will Comfort You" expresses what I was longing for. I performed it at the funeral of a close family friend, and then did not sing it again:

> When you're feeling too weary to walk
> And your destination's so far down the road
> When you wish you could fly on the wings of a hawk
> I will comfort you
>
> When you look at the life you had planned
> And you ache with the passing of time
> When you're lost and confused please understand
> I will comfort you
>
> Chorus
> I will kiss you at the break of dawn
> And when the day is through
> I will hold you while you dream
> I will comfort you

I learned layered lessons about my trauma during those years of my informal trauma-recovery school. Here is a short list:

1. I learned to name and admit my trauma.

2. I learned where the frozen places in my body were and awakened them through body work.

3. I learned about relationships—how trauma affected them and how to have functional, connected, and intimate ones.

4. I learned how to advocate for myself and articulate what I needed around my one-eared status.

5. I learned the importance of having a "narrative," including new inner realities that I was creating in therapy.

6. I learned to support myself and find supportive teachers/mentors for my musical talents.

7. I learned how to stay healthy.

A last story to illustrate my progression of awareness and agency in healing my trauma. A diary entry clearly illustrates the lessons above:

> I am having some difficulties in a musical situation. I am afraid that I won't be recognized for what I can do and for my special needs. Through a dream image, I realize that my mistrust has its roots in the 1963 family reunion trauma. I call my therapist who does a technique called "Havening," which is a combination of nervous system calming, naming the trauma and changing beliefs. My starting place for the session is lack of trust that I will be recognized. As we proceed in the memory, the main emotional theme of the eleven-year-old is, "I guess I don't matter." I release the grief and move into a repair scene, imagining that one of my uncles notices that I am having a hard time and holds my parents to account to find out what the matter is. My mother and father, awakened to their daughter's need, turn to me and ask me what would help. I say, "I need help with my song. I need to prepare it with help and have someone sing with me." They say, "Yes, your song matters, and you matter to us." In session, I am receptive to this new reality and anchor it in my body. The mantra I take from this session is "I matter." Subsequently, I am able to speak up more clearly about my musical needs in the group in which I was having problems. I gradually become more known and people look out for me.

Innate Intelligence Letter

Dear Kristi,

I know you are feeling shame and loneliness after your challenges of the last several years. I want you to remember that I am here. Reach out during your meditations and Tai Chi and feel my presence. Try to be less isolated and tell your friends and family how you are suffering. It will ease the shame. Your mother's example of a life lived with secrets is not your destiny. Soon you will understand why she couldn't tell you the truth as much as you tried to get her to. It is not your fault. You were a good daughter and you can let go now. It is good that you let your sisters take a turn in caring for her. You can let go of that responsibility.

About your hearing-aid implant: We all make mistakes and wish for miracles. That it didn't work and in fact harmed you is a lesson you won't forget and will bring you a rare level of humility. Forgive yourself. Soon you will be receiving the right help and it will work. Your music will come back. Have fun when it comes around.

About your romantic relationships: You are learning about attachment problems and still have a long way to go. That is okay, because attachment problems take the longest to heal for everyone. You will get through it. Love yourself and your music, depend on your friends. Explore yourself using holotrophic breathing, dreams, the tarot, and transformation games. Tell your therapists the truth about your actions. Apologize to your ex-husband Karl and anyone else who was affected by your behaviors. Remember you are human and will hurt others as you were hurt. Every bit of love counts to counteract the pain that is inflicted or received. Practice loving more.

Be clear about who you are and what you need. It's good to advocate for yourself. Keep your head up and don't settle for a smaller life. Keep dealing with your underground anger and fear.

Tune in and you will feel and hear me.

Love,

Innate Intelligence

Techniques for Keeping the Body in Mind

Healing only happens in the present. Bringing awareness to the experiences of the body—physical and emotional—is a great way to access the healing potential of the present moment. Your body is a mirror of your inner experiences; as you learn to listen to your body, you can begin to use it as an instrument of truth and a vehicle for healing.

Each of us has countless triggers that cause dissociation or anxiety and pull us back into the past. Habits emerge from various sources in our past, which block us from keeping our body in mind. The techniques I have collected and used often over the last thirty years work well to circumvent those triggers and habits so we can stay in the present and connected to our body.

It is important to apply the technique that fits us best at the appropriate time and in an effective amount. (I call this the "right amount" principle.) In other words, not everything works for everybody and sometimes issues of timing and amount are important. The key is to experiment and to listen carefully to the signals your body gives in response to your actions. If you have difficulties staying in touch with yourself while practicing any of the techniques, it may not be the one for you, or you may need the help of a witness or professional. Having a witness can also enrich the process of discovery.

That Was Then, This Is Now

Fear and fight-or-flight body states produce an automatic channel back to the trauma. So does being in a dissociative (dorsal vagal) state, when we are most vulnerable to flashbacks. Regressive mechanisms in the brain work very quickly. Suddenly, we go numb in our body or we are in a state of panic. We feel that we are reacting instead of acting or are in danger of giving up on our needs. Sometimes we feel we need the very activity that triggers us. For example, needing to cry with someone but then feeling overexposed or, needing help, but the help triggers a fear of dependency that is linked to danger. It is common to have this tension between need and triggers when recovering from PTSD.

When in a fight-or-flight, or triggered state, the tool of "That Was Then, This is Now" can bring us back to the safe present. It can be done anywhere and anytime and is particularly useful for regulating trauma-exploration activities.

What to Do

While gently pressing the middle of your palm (an acupuncture point connected with the heart) with the opposite thumb or placing your hand over your heart area, say out loud, "That was then. This is now." Notice any reaction in your body. To reconnect, you might touch one or two areas of your body that have these reactions, but this isn't necessary. You may also choose to touch an area of your body that you know has grounding effects.

Then say, "The dangerous event is not happening now. My body is just remembering." Look slowly around your environment, noticing your neck movement and resting your eyes on objects. This promotes a ventral vagal state and helps you to orient and identify that you are safe. Remember to breathe evenly and deeply. Notice any changes in your body sensations. Then say, "This is how my present is different (name the ways)." Pause, breathe, and notice. Then, "This is what makes my 'now' safe." Pause, breathe, and notice. Cycle through these phrases while continuing to press the middle of your palm (or touch your chest or other grounding area of your body). Ground into your feet. Keeping the words simple is best for this exercise.

What to Expect

As your body returns to a ventral vagal state (relaxed, present, engaged), your breathing will become more even, your shoulders will relax, you may sigh, swallow, or yawn. You will feel the possibility and availability of help or contact with others. You will be in connection with your present environment and able to problem solve as your frontal lobe reconnects. I have found that this works reliably for many people. The only time I would not recommend doing it is if you find it boring or have big resistance to any kind of "technique."

Stop Action

We all have unconscious compliance patterns, which is just a fancy way of saying we all have emotional and physical behaviors that we don't have conscious control over—internal or external messages that tend to drown out our own voice. When we're in a compliance pattern, we often feel incompetent and discouraged. Knowing that these patterns relate to our trauma and are difficult to change can help us have compassion for ourselves. People who have been physically or sexually abused or have had medical traumas often have more compliance habits. We say yes when we need to say no and we don't speak up. We either allow things to be "done to" our body without comment or we are caught in habits of over-defending our body, such as in hyper-vigilance. Even people without invasive traumas often put up with something they *don't* want to get what they *do* want. Many who have had the trauma of neglect have urgency habits. ("If I don't get it now, it won't happen.")

The Stop Action technique can help to create safety, empowerment, the "right amount," and the "exact thing." It allows us to be present in our body and discern what it truly wants. It is designed to be used by you or with a practitioner. In combination with the "That Was Then, This Is Now" technique, it allows us to regulate the amount of stimulation taken into our body. Thus, we prevent re-traumatization, over-stimulus, and dissociation. We learn to ask for the right amount of the right thing. I use this technique with every new client.

With a little explanation for your practitioner, you can use it in many therapeutic or medical situations. For practitioners at the beginning of a therapeutic relationship, it is an invaluable technique for gathering information from your client at the body level.

What to Do

If you are beginning an activity that involves only yourself, for example a yoga or meditation session, a swim or a gym workout, do the activity for a few minutes and then, out loud, say, "Stop." You may not have the urge to say stop. Say it anyway, as this is a training technique. Move off your mat or out of the water and analyze how you felt just before and just after saying stop (thoughts, body sensations, and so on). This analysis is done in a kindly manner by your internal "witness," who can hold the information without judgment. Record your observations. Then say out loud, "Start," and begin again. Follow with another stop. Stop and start several times until you gain an insight, for example, "I felt like I shouldn't stop, because I had so little time." Or "After I said stop, I felt my shoulders relax." If the stop produces positive results, it does not necessarily mean that you should stop the activity completely, but it may. If you have a negative result from a start (for example, an anxious stomach), ask yourself for understanding about what the activity might be triggering, about whether you should not do it or how you might do it differently to feel safer.

If you get positive feedback from your body on both the stop and start, proceed slowly because there may be a "right amount" that is not very much. If you feel highly anxious when you don't do the activity, it may be that you have an urgency pattern. Ask yourself, "What am I afraid would happen if I didn't do this activity?"

If you are applying the technique in an action (for example, a role play), move out of the space of action for the stop. If you are lying down or closing your eyes, open them and sit up for the stop. If you are engaging in a therapeutic technique such as EMDR, go into conversational mode to debrief and discuss. If you are in a verbal exchange with a therapist or friend, ask to change the topic.

When you use "Stop Action" with a practitioner, tell them that you need to stop the action occasionally to be able to feel what your body wants, that you will direct them to start again after a few minutes and that you would like to talk about how it felt to stop. Then begin the action. For example, if it is a massage, after a few minutes say, "Please stop." The practitioner should remove their hands and say, "Thank you." Notice how you feel, such as relieved, afraid they will be mad, like you didn't want them to stop, like you wouldn't have enough time to get what you want, increased calmness, and so on. Discuss with the practitioner how you felt before and after the stop. Then ask precisely for what your body wants and resume the activity. Notice how you feel to be in charge of what happens to your body.

What to Expect

If the practitioner feels that your body needs a particular technique, and you are reluctant about it, negotiate for a safe approach and the right amount. Also consider that they may not be the right practitioner for you. Trust yourself and don't stay with something or someone that doesn't feel right. Some people need a very gentle approach, and others a more definite or deeper one. Even gentle techniques can be contraindicated if they are a trigger. At the same time, it is also good to ask yourself, "What does this remind me of in my life? Is this too much of the same old thing or is it scary because its new?"

If you feel yourself going numb or dissociating in any way, this is a definite signal to do a Stop Action on whatever activity is going on. If the Stop Action does not provide any information, this is a good reason not to use it. If you have a feeling of resistance to the technique, you may stop or investigate whether a protective part is operating. If this is the case, acknowledge that it was useful in the past but may not be needed now. Often this can resolve the resistance quickly. The information and personal strength that emerges from doing Stop Action can be invaluable.

Handling Emotional Overload Using Metaphor

We all experience emotional or mental overload at times. Mindfulness is the currently popular and good technique for gaining perspective and peace despite the overload. But it doesn't work for everyone. Sometimes the mindfulness focus triggers too much body sensation and becomes uncomfortably intense. If someone is in a dissociative state, often nothing valuable happens.

When your observer self is having difficulty showing up, using meta-phor is a good option to decrease the amount of disturbing thoughts, emotions, and intrusive memories. If you feel overwhelmed, flooded, jammed up, or simply that something is too much, use this technique. It can help prevent burnout. This exercise is based on the psychodramatic technique of bracketing and tends to work better for visually oriented people, but it can work for others, especially if guided. It is usually good to do it in a quiet room but can be done anywhere when necessary.

What to Do

Close your eyes, unless you prefer not to, and begin by asking yourself, "Where is the 'too much' feeling in my body?" Then imagine a vessel or receptacle outside your body where you could put some of the stuff that's too much. The vessel should be constructed so things can't fall or leap out. A lid, a stopper, or a magical force might keep things inside the vessel.

Spend time imagining your vessel, allowing enough time for the image to become vivid. Then focus on the area in the body that holds the "too much" and name it with a word, a color, or a substance. For example, "My feelings of depression are like a grey veil." Once you have given the excess stuff a name, use your hands and make a gesture that shows how you move that stuff to your vessel (for example, in a pipe, a strong wind, a tube, a canal, a roadway, and so on). Then close the vessel. The gesture may feel a little silly, but it is an important step in making the picture real. If you can't seem to get the stuff into the vessel, imagine someone (or an animal or an energy) helping you. Pause and see or sense "too much" in the vessel at a distance from your body. Say out loud, "The stuff is in the vessel, and I am here."

Repeat this process several times, then notice changes in body sensations. You may feel lighter or clearer. Remind yourself that you are not leaving anything important behind, that whatever you put there will be dealt with, just not now. You may want to make an agreement about when you will get back to the material in the vessel.

What to Expect

When the uncomfortable sensation in your body has decreased in intensity, proceed with the activities of your life. If you start feeling the difficult emotions or thoughts again, stop and drain more stuff into your vessel. If the technique feels irritating, investigate your resistance or choose another activity. I have used and taught this technique for many years and have found that it brings relief and a decrease of agitation and dissociation for my clients.

Chapter 6
Keeping the Body in Mind: Development of the Magraw Method

I am sliding into silence
The emptiness of no husband, no children
The dulling of melancholic wishes and unrequited dreams
But I have a body and it is angry
My jaw yells, "Give me more, God!"
My liver grunts, "Can't get no satisfaction."
Hands in tiger claws I fight my demons of "hard done by"
Back to the words
Back to the music
Back to the rewards of "what is"

Pamela, a middle-aged social worker, came for bodywork on referral from her Jungian therapist. She said she didn't remember her dreams and felt there was something missing because of this: a connection with her inner self. I said that we could work with a technique I called "body dreaming," where she would relax into her body and allow it to produce a stream of images—free-form and random. Then, following the stream of images/metaphors, she would interpret them according to what was going on in her life. Because each stream began with tuning in to an ache, pain, or tension, it taught her to be more generally in touch with her body sensations. She could feel her sensations change as she connected them with insights about her life.

In the "body dreaming" sessions, she had some repeating images, such as steel plates in her legs, steel balls at the root of a tree, steeling herself against something. She wanted to play with the repeating image, to see if she could change it. She changed the steel to silver: still protective but softer. Slowly she began to explore what the "something" was that she was steeling herself against.

I remarked that she hadn't cried yet in a session, though we had talked about sad things. As I was working on her tight jaw, I asked her if she ever cried. She told me that she hadn't cried much since her grandfather died when she was seven years old. He had died of a heart attack away from home. Her mother received the call, and Pamela remembered watching her mother tensely holding herself together as she talked on the phone. When her mother told her that her grandfather wouldn't be coming home, Pamela cried. Her mother said, "Don't cry. Your grandfather wouldn't want you to cry." She was not allowed to go to the funeral and did not cry anymore for her grandfather. In the session, we talked about finding an alternative to her mother's message. She came up with "My grandfather wants me to cry." Although she was a little teary at the end of the session, she did not fully cry.

Then Pamela went on a trip to her hometown. She was visiting with her good friend and her friend's husband. As they were sitting around the table, Pamela uncharacteristically talked about herself and the session about her grandfather. Her friend said, "I remember seeing you play in the yard after he died and wondering about you. Now hearing what was going on for you, I feel like crying." The husband said to her in his quiet voice, "You need to cry." Again, Pamela felt teary and close to her friends, but she couldn't quite cry. As she reported to me, she wanted to cry, but her throat muscles were too constricted, as if she had a boulder blocking the tears. She said, "My mind was willing, but my body hadn't caught up yet." However, their validating response strengthened the new message she was giving herself about crying.

After she told me the above story, she said, "Last night I went to a lecture about Zen Koans. The Koan we were discussing was: You are hanging by your teeth from a branch. Someone asks you, 'What is the meaning of life?' and you have to decide whether to honour their question and let go, fall, and get hurt or to keep hanging on. Now I have tension in my jaw, as if I am still hanging on to that branch!"

I began by working on her jaw, neck, and face—a common place to steel against grief. I coached her breathing and encouraged her to make sounds. I also gave her lots of space and quiet. Later she said that, in the quiet and with the sounds, she could tune in to the trust that we had built over many sessions and that helped her to move toward the grief. She saw the image of a padlock on her right jaw and noticed that her left jaw was softer. She said, "It hurts when you press, but it feels good and feels right. She continued making sounds. I could hear in the tone that she was breaking through the boulder in her throat muscles. I gave her repeated permission to make whatever sounds she wanted to. She told me later that she was picturing her friends and her grandfather as she cried for the first time in years over the loss of her grandfather and the loss of her emotional self. She said, "It's been too long to be locked up."

When the crying subsided, she said, "I feel peaceful, and I can see that the branch of the Zen Koan has snapped, and I let it drop out of my mouth. Now my jaw can relax, and the boulder has dissolved. I feel a refreshing, cooling stream flowing over it." As I massaged her feet, she said, "Now I'm on a cloud above a red sand beach in Portugal. It's fun and peaceful. I feel less cloudy, because the cloud is not in me. I am on the cloud." She had been able to use her body dreaming metaphors to begin healing the old grief about her grandfather. When she stood up, her whole body looked soft and released.

The Beginnings

In Seattle, the winter of 1971, the seeds of my healing work were planted. I went to a class of free movement led by dance pioneer Anna Halprin. She was an innovator and used dance to help people with emotions and social awareness. This class was an introduction to finding emotions and memories in our bodies. We would do free movement with music and then draw a picture that expressed the feelings that came from the experience of our body moving. I remember how startled I was to see anger—a red and black scribbling—in my drawing. This was my first conscious encounter with my unconscious mind.

On Eagle Island in 1972, I read Georg Groddeck's *The Book of It* and was further inspired by his idea of an "it" in our body that would "speak" through various symptoms. I began to explore the practice of talking and listening to my body.

I went to a yoga class and met a hippie called Soaring Eagle. After the class, he offered to work on my feet. I had a headache, so I said yes. By pressing on my big toe, he made my headache go away. I was very impressed and learned reflexology from him. This was the beginning of my interest in the nervous system. Emotional expression and relief from pain were big motivators for my growth as a body worker. I was passionate about seeking healing and believed that I had to heal myself in order to become a better healer—to give from as full a cup as I could muster and to listen and respond intuitively and empathically to the person in pain instead of applying any rigid technique. I always experienced a technique thoroughly before I used it on my clients. If I saw evidence that contradicted an opinion I held, I would change my opinion. My ideas were unusual and somewhat ground-breaking for that time.

These body "adventures" would provide the inspiration and building blocks for my future work. In Toronto, I participated in some new healing techniques, including Rolfing, which reminded me of the bio-energetic groups I had done back home.

Gradually I developed the Magraw Method, a synthesis of Eastern and Western physical techniques combined with metaphor, dream work, and various facilitation techniques culled from psychodrama and bio-energetics. My studies in Shiatsu and acupressure had given me an opening into the use of metaphor as the bridge between felt sensation in the body and verbal insight. The Five Element Theory from Traditional Chinese Medicine, also practiced in Shiatsu, uses language to bring order and understanding to body phenomena, including what I call "repair (healing) metaphors." I began to use it as a way to think about my efforts to heal myself, and emerging from that, how to treat my clients more holistically.

Eastern methods are different from most Western medical approaches that divide the body phenomena into specialties, with practitioners who do not talk to each other, although this has been changing in recent years. Practitioners of Eastern methods (acupuncture, Shiatsu, Ayurveda, and others) generally learn to look at the body/person as a whole unit. The interplay between body phenomena and emotional phenomena is seen as important in the healing process, though Eastern practitioners can also be as disconnected as medical specialists.

I grew up in a community where alternative practices were commonplace, so naturally, I gravitated toward them. Also, for many years, I was still carrying the feelings of betrayal at the hands of doctors, so I gravitated away from them. However, I gradually released this prejudice and began to see the validity of both and where each approach shines. There is a valuable interplay that can happen between traditional medical practices and what I now call complementary practices. Of course, this can only happen if we stay open, like my Uncle Dick did when he truly listened to his patients and taught doctors the importance of collaboration. At the same time, we need to be open to believing good scientific data, even if it contradicts our favorite assumptions.

Through practice, I proved to myself that, except in cases of actual injury or disease, or complex mind-body conditions, applying a metaphor to our body's pains ("my throat feels like a plum pit is in it") first decreases the pain/sensation and then often leads to conscious verbalized insight ("Oh, I need to tell my friend that I am sad she is leaving") and a complete release of the symptom. Even working with a disease process as a metaphor (while doing medical treatment) can bring understanding that supplements medical treatment. For example, I take antibiotics for an infection, but at the same time explore the stresses that are affecting my immune system. Healing is never a straight line, a miracle, or a "one size fits all," but giving the body a language with which to speak heals and enriches.

Metaphor is a good tool to help us "keep the body in mind" because it is a way of naming and of evoking the thing named. Metaphors also help to identify patterns that have been unfolding for generations in our families and can give useful diagnostic clues.

Metaphors engage us in a process of change. Ancient patterns can be released, because metaphor initiates an integration of the mind and body—and a vivid experience of the present—which gives us the power to know and to change. I wrote about a metaphoric experience to my sister Melanie when I was twenty-two:

"Now, as I was listening to his criticism, I was floating on this strange plane where I could fall into the 'hole' of self-rejection but (in that moment) I saw how that hole had created the self-rejection in the first place. I felt the flow of Chi (energy) in my back and the 'hole' disappeared."

Some metaphors are in general cultural use. "Sick as a dog" is an example. Others are more specific to individuals. Wherever the metaphor comes from—a poem, a song, a painting, a piece of guided imagery, or in therapy—it invites us to interact with it. Metaphor can give the gift of providing us with direct, in-the-moment experience—a bodily felt or expressed feeling as opposed to a thought or purely verbal expression. Metaphor is multi-layered and has many meanings—we take from it what we need. If we return to it at a different time, we may discern yet another layer of meaning in it.

Let me give you an example. Jill had a history of inflammation disorders (skin rashes, headaches, muscle soreness). I had named the pattern of "excess heat" (Five Element term for inflammation) and Jill said the "heat" was made worse by agitated thought patterns she often described as "ants in the brain." During a bodywork session, with my assistance, she explored a metaphoric narrative as I massaged her tight back muscles: "Those muscles feel like a forest stuck together with chewing gum. The 'heat' has melted the gum onto the trees. It is all gooey and nothing can move," she said. "What needs to happen is for the heat to go down. Then the gum will harden and slip off the trees, and the ants in my brain will come down and eat it all up. They will be so full that they will keel over, die, and turn into compost that can be swept down to the large intestine and eliminated." After telling me this metaphor, the muscles in her back steadily released.

The beauty of metaphor is how it expresses a person's current and unique experience precisely. It is flow and narrative. It is a way of speaking the truth even before we know what the truth is. A doorway to direct as opposed to interpreted experience, it embodies our truth. The right metaphor communicates immediately. Metaphor is expressed in imagery, including all the senses—auditory, visual, kinaesthetic, tactile, smell, and taste. The flow of metaphor breaks us out of the limbo of not knowing what we are feeling or thinking. It focuses us on what we are actually going through.

My capacity to calmly stay with clients in their emotional/metaphoric experience provides the container for safety. With this container in place, the client feels free to access intense emotions and insights. Staying with the body is one way to be in directly felt experience (as different from past, displaced, or disconnected experience), and the emotion can release because we have emerged from the 'freezing of time' that trauma creates and can come back into the 'flow of time'. The wave passes through, and the useful insight arrives.

At the beginning of a typical session I ask, "What are you feeling in your body today?" A few minutes can then be spent talking in the language of sensation:

> Client: *I'm having a little headache*
> Kristi: *Where in your head?*
> Client: *Well, I can feel pressure from behind my eyes.*
> Kristi: *Is it a sharp pressure or a dull pressure?*
> Client: *Sharp and piercing*
> Kristi: *About as big as a . . .?*
> Client: *A nail! Somebody is hammering a nail in there.*

At this point in a session, I or the client can choose different paths to go down. We might go on a past-history path:

> Kristi: *Does that somebody have an identity?*
> Client: *Yes! They are shadowy, but critical.*
> Kristi: *What is the criticism?*
> Client: *"Why can't you see what you're doing? Why don't you do what I tell you to do?"*
> Kristi: *And who said that to you?*
> Client: *My teachers in primary school.*

Or, taking a more open-ended, body-focused direction, we can go along the path of body sensation, perhaps toward emotional release:

> Kristi: *And what is that hammering like?*
> Client: *Well, it's very surprising. Like "something" is trying to get my attention.*

> *Kristi: And where in your body does that "something"*
> *come from?*
> *Client: I feel a pressure in my stomach too.*
> *Kristi: What is the quality of that pressure?*
> *Client: It's going up. Up to my head like a rocket! My stomach*
> *is yelling, "I'm angry!"*

Moving the body is another way to access the power of metaphor:

> *Kristi: How does your body want to move now?*
> *Client: I want to wiggle my feet.*
> *Kristi: What is this movement like? What is it telling you?*
> *Client: It is like a bird. They want to fly. It's telling me to be*
> *more free.*
> *Kristi: What part is having a hard time moving?*
> *Client: My arms. They need to learn from my feet and start*
> *expressing what they want!*

The client will respond according to his readiness to work in the body. If he is not ready, he will feel few sensations and have some difficulty describing them metaphorically. If this is the case, conversations that help him say who he is in the present are useful, as he may be in a dissociative state. If he is in a state of "fight or flight," he will feel many sensations but may have difficulty naming them. If this is the case, slowing the whole process down and doing calming and grounding is good. If he experiences ease in finding sensations and translating them into metaphor, and if he finds relief in expressing himself in this way or easily makes a connection with events in his current life (for example, "my boss is a pain in the neck"), then he is ready to begin the challenging but rewarding work of changing the body using metaphor.

Movement Can Bring Insight

In a bodywork session, Sally, a visual artist, could feel a sensation going up her leg, along the liver meridian. She said her lower legs felt heavy—heavy with details, "Like when I was at my last job, having to take care of all the details—I couldn't fly." During those years, she made dozens of pictures of birds; they all got to fly. When encouraged, she kicked vigorously, while vocally expressing her anger. During a pause, Sally identified a desire to paint a picture of a big bird flying and realized that this was a picture of action she needed to take in her life. I explained to her that the Chinese believe that the liver, which is part of the "Wood" Element (in the Five Elements Theory), influences our body's capacity to move and our ability to act. The information strengthened her resolve and made her feel that her body was wise. Sometimes we miss the body's wisdom, because we aren't paying attention to its language.

Deciphering signals and metaphors is never a straightforward path, because the body's story has many twists and turns, leaps, and sudden changes as part of its inherent makeup. It is important to have a good bond with a client, so that moments of dismay or confusion can be navigated smoothly, making efforts to follow the client's cues rather than enforcing a rigid program or my own beliefs/interpretations.

It is equally important to discern if there is a pattern at work in the client's urgency or suppressive behaviors. For instance, a state of fight-or-flight is the norm for some abuse survivors. Their attempts to solve their problems can be accompanied by urgency, which only replicates and ensures the persistence of this state. In this case, it is best if the process counters the pattern and leads the client to slow down.

In suppression patterns, the expression of the root emotion, such as fear or grief, often defaults to the preferred displacement, such as resentment or depression, which prevents finding solutions and thus promotes staying stuck. If this is the case, it is best if the client is consistently encouraged back to the root emotion.

Working with metaphor creates a vividness that can continue to support a change (indicated by insight) over time. By taking the time for a "metaphoric conversation," a more holistic (inclusive of more parts of ourselves) form of healing can occur. A longer-lasting pain-free time can result—a feeling of confidence and competence in the body.

I found that my songwriting skills, combined with my psychodrama-storytelling skills, came in useful in coaching my clients to follow their metaphor-based narratives. It takes patience and imagination to do this, but the rewards are wonderful. After a client finds "the heart of the matter," I can lead them to discover healing metaphors. These will be remembered for long periods of time, because they are so vivid. This vividness helps the mind-body have a better ground to grow from. Metaphor provides a surprisingly quick and accurate summary of the state of the body. Working with metaphor has been effective in my practice and could be an invaluable diagnostic tool for doctors and other healthcare professionals.

Diaphragm bouncing
Can't stop laughing
Shoulders
Want to be crying
I know now what it means
To breathe deeply
And it's just all right
Everything
I have made a connection
With myself
Questioned and responded
I have seen myself
Be powerful
I feel as if
I have moved
The entire earth

—A first-time client

An Emotion Named Is an Emotion Tamed

Emotions, when they are in a flowing healthy state, are like waves. They rise up and then go down. They move us and help us to know ourselves.

Many people are afraid of their emotions, sometimes with good reason. Unregulated or acted-out emotions can create havoc in relationships and within our self. However, there is also much danger in the repression of emotion: body tension, relational problems, lack of energy, tissue inflammation, and lack of self-knowledge. Using my body's pains and signals (rashes, nerve bumps, indigestions, and so on), I worked on resolving this thorny issue of what to do with emotions. There was little to guide me. What I discovered was that naming emotions in a safe circumstance released the muscles in my body and gave me self-knowledge that I could put to good use in relationships. You will see this principle working through many of my stories. Continuing my theme of different strokes for different folks, however, there are circumstances and people for whom emotions work differently. Please employ caution when using my techniques and follow the steps closely.

A Practical Approach to Anger

In the sixties, in the time of primal scream and encounter groups, the emotion of anger was glorified and expressed without context or guidelines. Now, in the time of anti-depressants and increased awareness of abuse, anger is often vilified. I would like to put forward the idea that the emotion of anger—when it is balanced with compassion and in service of the goal of connection to others and health in our bodies—is a useful, natural energy.

Anger can be helpful in several ways. This may sound radical to people who have had trauma at the hands of another's aggressive or displaced behaviours or grew up in a family where anger was forbidden. However, if we hook our angry emotions up to the ventral vagal system by looking in each other's face (see chapter 5), anger can serve the intention of engagement with others and a deepening of relationship. With the use of humor and play, it can enliven us. A good example of this is play wrestling or other active games.

When we do structured anger release, it can bring us out of a collapsed or depressed state and lead us into productive action. Anger can also help us to find our "truth," if our listener is calm and doesn't interrupt. Dealing with our own anger makes it easier to listen to someone else's without becoming reactive.

It is also useful in helping us develop healthy boundaries and a relaxed "no" to put to good use. Many people are afraid of their own or others' anger, but we all have anger at times. If we get to know it in ourselves, it is much easier to regulate and put to positive use instead of having an outburst, a tense "no," or passive-aggressive behaviour. I have found that knowing my anger allows me to be clearer and more direct in communication and less avoidant of confrontation and challenge. Perhaps most importantly, it helps me be less inflamed in my body and mind. In the Chinese Five Element system, anger is associated with the liver organ. Originally, I used my liver symptoms (itchiness, eye problems, burping, and irritability) to guide me toward my store of suppressed anger. Also, making our liver healthier can prevent angry and irritable states.

An important thing to remember in dealing with anger is to be aware of the state of your nervous system, and whether you feel present/calm/connected enough to set boundaries. Being present instead of dissociated is an essential ingredient in resolving anger. Try slowing the angry expressions down to micro movements or slow motion or do lots of "Stop Action" exercises. (See chapter 5 "Technique for Keeping the Body in Mind".) Laughing will create an internal "at ease-ness," and so will knowing the full volume of your anger in a safe setting.

The Dark Side of Anger

Anger is a confusing emotion, because it is so often hooked to fear, aggression, helplessness, and displacement. Any of these non-beneficial hook ups can lead to violence. Displaced anger means shifting into anger when you are feeling another emotion. For example, if it is not okay for you to feel sad and cry (as is the case for many men), that sadness will be felt as an agitation that can transmute into anger. Displaced anger also means taking the anger you have for one person and transferring it to someone else. For example, you are feeling angry with your boss, but it is not safe to express it, so you bring it home and take it out on your partner.

When we often default to the state of fight-or-flight, we experience irritability and the frequent urge to fight our way out of a perceived scary situation. This anger from a disconnected place is hurtful to others and us. It can be manifested as anything from critical remarks to physical violence. Drugs and alcohol congest the liver, and when it is congested, we often experience excessive anger.

Sometimes, if we have brain injuries, early childhood trauma that creates radical attachment disorder, PTSD, or other mental illnesses, the regulating mechanisms in the brain are not fully developed or have become injured. In this case, we need expert support and "protection." We need an environment where our emotional self is not going to get rejected as we learn to regulate our anger.

Steps for Dealing with Anger

1. Find a supported, protected place—mostly this means with other people, but for some being out in the woods or in a car is also good. Supported and protected means you will not hurt or disturb yourself or others. It also means being connected to your heart or your spiritual self.

2. Keep in mind that anger is very physical, and determine a satisfying, sacred, or funny way to move your body. (If you need them, use props such as a punching bag, paper to tear, or sticks to throw.)

3. Speak your angry truth loudly and fully, using whatever words you want until you laugh or cry or do both, feeling some kind of peak and release. Then try to express it without the language of insults or put downs (simple swearing is fine) and see how that works. Over time and with experimentation, I found the most effective language was clean and simple, such as "I feel angry about___" or "Stop doing___." If you feel frightened, remind yourself that these are just feelings, and there is no hurtful action taking place.

4. Ask yourself if there are any triggers to people or events in your past. Speak the anger to the situation where it belongs. It is important to find the "root," especially if you are dealing with chronic anger.

5. If you are using a role play to do a one-way expression to someone who has hurt you, consider reversing the role and receiving the anger you just expressed, then pause and notice if you feel differently toward them and yourself. Role reversal helps to give you a fuller perspective. You can do this step inside your head or by moving your body to two different locations,

but it is helpful to do it with a therapist or in a group setting. (See chapter 8, where I present psychodrama.) What is effective will be different for each person. If you absolutely need to express anger directly to someone, make sure to have the support of a therapist or a well-defined structure to keep it safe for both people. If the other person does not feel safe with your expression, there could be further complications, such as shame, shutdown, and lack of resolution.

6. When your body feels somewhat free of the tension of anger, come into awareness of any new sensations in your body and observe the natural relaxation process. This may be enough. If you wish to spend more time to calm your nervous system, try conscious breathing or listening to music. If you do not feel free of the tension, try vigorous exercise, journaling, or seeking professional help.

7. Often anger comes to help us change, so planning for that change can help to calm and resolve anger.

A Practical Approach to Fear

Fear and shame (which often go hand in hand) are the trickiest emotions of all, because they affect our nervous system so directly and because they can easily go underground/unconscious.

Is fear ever useful? I have asked that question many times, because I have had to work so assiduously to calm my excessive fear. It can be—as an emotion of caution—to prevent us from taking risks that might cause harm to ourselves or others. But fear caused by trauma and stored in the body can easily trigger us into a state of fight-or-flight or a dorsal vagal collapse. When we fall into one of these, the fear becomes a mood (unmoving) and we are restricted from fully living.

The less time I spend in fearful moods and uncomfortable ANS (autonomic nervous system) states, the happier and more productive/creative I am. Each person will have their own way of resolving and releasing the fear. Here is what has worked for me:

Steps for Dealing with Fear

1. David Berceli's method, which he describes in his book *Trauma Release Exercises: A Revolutionary New Method for Stress/Trauma Recovery*, allows the body to shake out the residues of fear states.[1] This is a very useful tool, because you don't have to name the fear to begin addressing it. You have all seen animals shiver when they are afraid—usually after a stressful event. This natural movement helps to disperse the excess adrenaline accumulated during stressful events, thus allowing their nervous system to shift out of fight, flight, or collapse into a ventral vagal rest and engage state. Then they just get on with their lives. We can do that too, through allowing our limbs and torso to shake and therefore disperse fear after scary events or gently release us from numb states.

2. Face or name the fear, either directly, as in "I am feeling afraid of X," or metaphorically, as in "The fear in my stomach is like X." Finding the balance between time spent in the witnessing mind and time spent in the experiencing body allows our frontal cortex to connect with our limbic system and communication is restored.

3. Doing other nervous-system calming techniques, such as self-massage or breathing or mindfulness, can also help to alleviate fear states.

4. Exercise has a role in calming chronic fear states, but it needs to be the right exercise for you. Everyone is different. Here are a few to try: aerobics, yoga, Pilates, working on fascia (with a ball or roller), and dancing.

5. If the fear has an attachment trauma at its root, then positive visualizations or actual connections with people or animals may help to soothe you.

A Practical Approach to Grief

Is grief good? Can it ever be too much? When should I cry? Are there different kinds of crying? How should I behave when someone else is crying? These are some of the questions often asked around the emotion of grief. There are conflicting answers depending on your cultural conditioning: Yes, you can cry when your parent dies. No, you can't cry if you are a man. Yes, you can cry if you are a child. No, you can't cry above the age of sixteen. No, you can't cry if you lose a personal item. Some people never cry. Some cry at the drop of a hat. In my work, I have taught many people how to access their ability to express grief. I have also taught people how to regulate their floods of disconnected grief.

Tears can come for many reasons, and when we are not afraid of the full experience of grief, we can allow the variety and magic of this emotion.

The key to having a positive grief experience is connection, with others, with self, or with spirit. The aspect of connection helps grief to flow and have its natural peak and resolution. But connection does not mean being intrusive to yourself or the person you are witnessing. The emotion of grief needs room to breathe—a quietness and non-interference that allows it to flow. Some people have had their crying smothered or hijacked (as in "you think that is sad, listen to this"), and as a result, will shut down if someone tries to hug or get too close. Other people who have strong defenses against crying had a difficult experience when young of being disconnected and unprotected while crying. This can be scary for a child and often leads to statements like "If I start crying, I will never stop." In my experience, crying "in connection" and "with space" resolves the grief feeling and I return to a better, more joyful place. As well, shared grief can help people to become more deeply bonded.

I have found that real tears will bring me out of a dissociated state fairly reliably. Other people need to get connected to the present first and then cry. The process is different for each person. I cry to let go when there is nothing else to be "done." I cry to move my stuck energy, which I can then re-direct with intention to change the source of my grief (where possible).

The Dark Side of Grief

When grief is hooked into anger (bitterness) or a dorsal vagal state (depression, melancholy) or fear (anxiety) or all three, it creates what many people call a "balled up" feeling in their stomach. This is evidence of the connection between our nervous system (polyvagal aspect) and our emotions. Accumulations of unresolved chaotic emotions such as this are very uncomfortable, and human beings will do almost anything to avoid them, for example, with addictive behaviors and dissociating and displacing. If we ignore the "ball," it can turn into a mood—a longer wash of low-level, unconscious feeling. Stuck grief can create a malaise in the body—a stopping of forward progress.

We need to bring ourselves into connection, movement, and self-reflection, to ground and sort out the accumulated ball of emotion. Sometimes, letting grief wash through without mental pushing or pulling until insight arrives is the best way to do this. Sometimes focusing on feelings of protection and comfort are the best ways to begin.

Steps for Dealing with Grief

1. Connect with a friend or therapist, reaching inside to your adult or spiritual self or by listening to music you like. Sometimes holding a friend's hand or having an arm around your shoulder will facilitate the feeling of connection. Sometimes, just having someone near but not touching is better. Remember, quietness and patience are the best facilitators, so tell your person (or inner self) what your preferences are and that they don't need to "solve" anything.

2. Do self-massage or other nervous-system techniques to switch your ANS out of dorsal or sympathetic domination. Crying works better when you feel comforted, engaged, and with your ventral vagal system operating (see chapter 5).

3. Allow your whole body to participate with sounds and sobbing. Weeping silently is also good, but sometimes there is grief stored in the diaphragm and pelvis, and the resolution is more complete if we have what most people call "a good cry," during which we don't hold the body back from expressing freely.

4. Location and positioning are important. Find a crying tree (or river or lake or other place in nature) for a feeling of comfort

and connection. Or perhaps you have a crying chair or a room in your house that feels secluded—it's important not to be interrupted. You can lie down on your back, front, or side to enable the full release. You can cry into a hole in the ground or looking up at a mountain. If you have a habit of closing in or collapsing your body in grief, try remaining upright with your eyes open. If you have a habit of "steeling" yourself, try surrendering and collapsing in a heap. Working to counter our defense habits can bring a different level of grief release. Take time to find your place and position for best crying.

5. Name the grief. Sometimes this occurs before a release and sometimes after. Either is fine, but it is important to put words to feelings. Doing so can bring you into a place of perspective and suggest actions to take. However, it is also valuable to explore wordless grief and not to categorize it. Slowly move into any action phase. Wait until well after the release. Right after, spending time focusing on your senses through color, music, or other playful activity, is good for the integration phase.

6. Sometimes, especially with childhood grief, it is good to first cry about the pain and then create a repair scene and cry with relief.

7. Lastly, do something creative—a drawing, poem, or craft that helps soothe you and give meaning to your sadness.

The Body Speaks Loudly

The mystery of the connection between our body, brain, and mind is longstanding and often confusing. I have sorted out the event of pain into three main branches:

1. **Acute pain:** This pain is caused by tissue processes (cutting, breaking, bruising, inflammations, infections, and cancers). This pain directly connects to an injury, surgery, or disease.

2. **Chronic pain:** This pain is based in the nervous system. Chronic pain happens when the brain forgets to shut off the "danger" signals from an originally acute pain or from a reactive nervous

system that can get irritated by very slight stimuli. It can also come from weakened, imbalanced muscular efforts due to nerve/brain level disconnection.

3. **Mind-body pain:** This pain is related to trauma or emotions. It may operate as a distraction from unbearable feelings or as a signal of surfacing emotions or memories of trauma. Mind-body refers to the intersection of mental/emotional and body/brain processes. Though the scientific work on this is just beginning, I and many others have been working with these phenomena for years.

One of the main questions I have faced in my own body, and in the practice of helping others, is this: Are the symptoms and sensations of pain I am experiencing rooted in the mind-body, in the nervous system, or in the tissue processes of my body? How do I discern which is which? I often think of myself as a detective listening carefully to the clues or using my "eagle's eye" to get perspective on the whole situation.

The Eagle's Eye

The Eagle's eye is a metaphorical name I use to describe a state of perspective. In neuroscience, it occupies a part of the brain called the medial pre-frontal cortex (MPFC), which is activated in meditation and other contemplative exercises. It receives messages from the thalamus, which mixes together all the incoming sensory information and passes it on to the amygdala (home of our alarm system) and the Pre-frontal cortex. Bessel van der Kolk calls the MPFC, "the watchtower." He says, "Being anchored in the present, while revisiting the trauma, opens the possibility of knowing that the terrible events belong to the past. For that to happen, the brain's watchtower (medial prefrontal cortex), cook (Thalamus), and timekeeper (dorsal pre-frontal cortex) need to be online."[2] Sensations of pain can be a form of flashback to the past. It is important to develop a good connection with your "eagle's eye" through self-knowledge and mindfulness.

Pain is in the brain but not just "in your head." Our nerves send messages to the brain. Some of these messages indicate tissue damage, and the brain sends out pain signals to alert us to be careful. This is good and normal in the case of acute pain caused by trauma to tissues. Within a fairly limited time after injury (three to four months), these danger messages settle down. However, in chronic pain situations, they don't.

Danger messages can be stimulated more slowly as well. Scar tissue and muscle stiffness/weakness from lack of use or disconnection will send messages of pain to the brain, and in this case, it can be more complicated to sort out the balance between the actual tissue problem and the reactions of a sensitive nervous system.

It's like a radar system. If there are a great many signals showing up on the screen all jumbled, false "enemy near" or "rock ahead" alarms may be sounded. For us, the more stress happening concurrently with the pain, or because of the pain, the more confused and reactive our personal radar system will become. We can mistake clouds for enemy planes or large fish for rocks. In a normal nervous system, the technician comes, turns off the alarm, and re-sets our radar system. We feel relief.

As authors Adriaan Louw, Sandra Hilton, and Carolyn Vandyken describe in the book *Why Pelvic Pain Hurts*, "We now know that changes in hormones, blood pressure, touch, illness, stress, anxiety, and movement are all capable of setting off the alarm system, activating danger messages and alerting the brain. As a result of these danger messages, you may be convinced 'something is wrong' and your brain will produce pain to grab your attention and get you to seek help. The good news is that these sensors change every few days and can be influenced....You can turn down your extra-sensitive nervous system."[3]

It took many years to re-interpret my body pain as a signal of need (in modern terms, a "friend request") instead of an "attack or disaster" with no solution (like my ear and operation). It was through self-massage and listening to my emotions that I discovered that, if I listened, the pain would speak words. Now when my body sends me friend request in the form of pain or dysfunction, I do my best to listen calmly and learn from everything.

This ability has come through the hard work of developing body awareness and perspectives on different types of pain. I make vigorous efforts to stay away from extremes, such as "I have to just ignore that pain signal." Some of us take drugs to block the pain, and at times, this is the appropriate thing to do. Some of us just decrease our movement or brace our body to avoid pain. Some of us dissociate parts of our body (numb them) and carry on until we have a really dramatic pain event. This numbing is a nervous-system response to not being able to get away— like an animal's freeze state. The numbing /dissociating habit decreases blood flow to organs and muscles and becomes a difficult pattern to shift.

Another extreme is "I have to worry/obsess about that signal." This is the nervous system in hyper Sympathetic Nervous System (SNS) mode, which brings adrenaline and cortisol to the forefront and mobilizes the big muscles at the expense of the smaller muscles. This dynamic contributes to weakness in small muscles, inflammation, and organ dysfunction. In this state, I overly focus on diagnoses, allow the pain to take too much attention, and engage in non-beneficial behavior loops, such as physically worrying the pain through excessive self-massage and exercise (although these things are pain relievers in the right amount). Using a tense state to try to resolve a tense state doesn't work very well.

Somewhere in between these extremes is the "right amount" of focus, intervention, and allowing healing its own course. The "right amount" is different for each person. For me, it is the place where I can gently pay attention, notice what makes it better and worse, and try out experiments of movement, release, and getting help, including medical tests. Understanding the different kinds of pain signals that our bodies have is useful in sorting out a treatment approach.

What to Do with Pain

When we are injured, pain is a signal of the need to heal. In that case, the pain is relevant to the tissues hurt, and with the correct medical or alternative intervention, it resolves fairly quickly. It signals us to be careful of that part of our body until the tissue is strong again.

Chronic pain is a habit the brain has fallen into. We need to teach the body and the brain that there is no tissue in danger now. This often happens with people who are sensitive to sensation in their body. The inflammation and pain that is produced by a chronic brain/nerve loop habit usually stays around one area, often previously injured or compromised in some way. Movement and exercise are the most reliable way out. Mindfulness meditation works for some people. Practicing changing how we think about pain is useful for others.

The other type of chronic pain is a mind-body pain, and it will move around from location to location or from symptom to symptom—sometimes disappearing completely for a period of time. Dr. John E. Sarno, in his book *Healing Back Pain: The Mind-Body Connection*, calls this type of pain Tension Myoneural Syndrome (TMS).[4] ("Myo" refers to muscle and "neuro" to the brain.) According to Sarno, when there is no diagnosis of cancer, fracture, or infection connected to a chronic pain, it could be caused by the mind-body system. The pain is real, but the solution is not a physical treatment. Sarno believes in the "Knowledge Cure," as in knowing if your emotions are building up pressure, knowing if there is a past unresolved event that was triggered, knowing if you are meeting your deepest needs, knowing if you are in conflict with yourself, knowing if you have an investment in not moving your body, and knowing if you have an investment in "not knowing" in general.

Years before I heard about TMS, I realized that there were pains in my body telling me about what was bothering me on an unconscious level. They would come and go in mysterious ways and often pre-occupy my whole mind. I had TMS and didn't know it—no one had coined the term yet and no mainstream healthcare providers gave much credence to the theory that physical symptoms could be coming as a result of "invisible" causes. My pain was a distraction from matters of importance that needed handling.

An example of the latter is my early experience with my "crying point." I was nineteen and spending a year on Eagle Island. I thought that this was "the place I was meant to be." Then a persistent pain showed up in my right shoulder. I decided to try an experiment with this pain. I went down to the beach, a comforting and solitary place for me, sat on the warm, grey driftwood and asked my shoulder, "Why are you hurting?" As I focused on this question, I began to feel increasingly emotional and soon I was crying deeply about family matters, feeling isolated and stuck on the island. I realized in that moment that I actually needed to go out in the world and make my own way. I realized I had not cried for a long time. When I finally dried my eyes, I checked my shoulder. Magically, it seemed to me, my pain was gone! This event of facing "what the matter was" as a way of dispersing physical pain has been one of the bedrocks of my own healing and of the Magraw Method.

Different techniques can work to resolve mind-body pain. Sometimes an emotional release (crying, yelling, shaking, and so on) will move the pain. Sometimes an acknowledgement of the "truth" will do the job, and sometimes, it requires taking action to move your life forward to make a TMS pain release.

This was the case when the shoulder pain returned on my trip to a folk festival to perform in a contest twenty years later. When I was nineteen, the pain went away after I paid conscious attention to the area. This time, I tried a crying release, but that didn't work. I tried self-massage and stretching. No luck. The pain left only after I had taken the stage and performed. It may sound strange, but the pain in my shoulder was "cured" by my performance. I had to push through an emotionally challenging situation and connect to my self-confidence to move the pain toward resolution.

When I say mind-body (particularly in relation to pain), I am referring to the unconscious emotional processes that play out in our autonomic nervous system, causing pain or other symptoms of discomfort. If this sounds confusing, first consider how the autonomic nervous system (ANS) works. The ANS is always engaged and at work. It is indirectly influenced by our state of mind and mental imagery, not by conscious will. It also is affected by physical things such as hunger, thirst, and arousal. The Sympathetic Spinal Nerve Chain, which is another name for the Sympathetic Nervous System (SNS), controls the fight-or-flight responses that are part of our survival mechanisms and provides the energy we need to become alert. This part of the nervous system helps prepare the body to wake up, run, or fight by decreasing blood flow to the smooth muscle (think intestines, urinary and bowel functions) and increasing blood flow to the musculoskeletal system for waking or survival purposes. It also raises blood pressure and opens the lungs to increase oxygen intake. It uses up energy.

The ventral vagus nerve system (VNS) contrasts with the SNS, and it restores and saves energy. It decreases heart rate, restores digestion, increases urinary output, lowers blood pressure, and diverts blood back to the skin and the digestive tract. It soothes the mind-body. The dorsal vagal branch often goes too far and kicks in not only when we are actually in danger but when we think we are in danger. All body functions slow down and blood is withdrawn from the periphery to the core. It is harmful to stay in the dorsal vagal state for long but a good option in real danger situations.

In normal human functioning, these three systems balance each other, providing homeostasis: a balance of arousal and relaxation and a feeling of well-being in your whole body. But what happens if the sympathetic system gets stuck in the "alarm" position and fails to re-balance after the stressor event is over? We recognize this in the expressions, "I'm stressed out" and "I can't relax." These states of a SNS working overtime can be at the root of many physical disruptions, including inflammatory processes, oversensitive nervous systems, adrenal fatigue, sleep disturbances, and critical self-talk. What if we get captured in the "freeze" of the dorsal vagal system? When we talk about being stuck, helpless, powerless, and our energy keeps "crashing," we have likely succumbed.

Many clients who come to me for bodywork show symptoms of one or all of the above. I often have to teach them to regulate their SNS and vagus systems, strengthen their adrenal system, and rebalance their ANS before we can proceed further with healing.

If we have experienced an early or radical disruption of homeostatic processes in the body due to illness, neglect, or trauma, causing a dominance of one part of the ANS over another, the resulting dysregulation itself is a form of trauma, because it disrupts attunement and attachment processes in relationships. We need to be in an engaged ventral vagal state to bond with our caregivers. And being in engagement with others can help strengthen our ventral vagal system. Dysregulation and disruption in turn produce more trauma in a body that is already prone to reactivity to emotions and inner-body sensations.

For example, the following scenarios can produce disruption of attunement when we are young and in consequence trauma: a child in a hospital setting dealing with needles and drugs (my experience); an adoption process; an ill or depressed parent; a child born prematurely with time in an incubator; or severe childhood illness. In fact, anything that disturbs the child's physical development, the attunement that happens in early childhood between child and parent, and the gradually learned emotional regulation processes can qualify as a trauma. Attachment processes can also be disturbed in adults by sexual assault or accidents, but if given the right treatment, usually resolve more quickly.

Pain as Distraction

Dr. John Sarno says that many common pains are an unconscious attempt to distract ourselves from unbearable emotional truths.[5] When inner conflict or anger becomes untenable, we play it out in our body systems—mainly the ANS. The tension of inner conflict and the fear that our "bad" feelings will separate us from loved ones keeps the nervous system stuck in overdrive. Inflammatory processes begin producing discomfort and disease. Many doctors call these symptoms medically unexplained symptoms (MUS) and often prescribe placebos. They are reluctant to go as far as Dr. Sarno does, but there is a growing recognition of mental/trauma causes for physical ailments—prescribing anti-depressants for muscle pains is evidence of this. However, it is still common to encounter an attitude of dismissal of the after-effects of trauma in the medical profession.

When investigating to see if Tension Myositis Syndrome (TMS) is the source of your problem, it is essential to be thoroughly tested to rule out a mechanical cause, such as a bowel obstruction resulting in a stomach pain or a tumour causing a headache. Once those possibilities are ruled out, and it is clearly a case of the ANS gone rogue, the process of uncovering what caused the unhealthy suppression of feelings can begin. The lack of awareness of negative feelings can shift and finding the "emotional truth" of a difficult experience or circumstance becomes easier. Then the process of meeting true needs can proceed.

———————

Among the many books I read in the nineties, I found myself particularly fascinated by Candace Pert's book, *Molecules of Emotion,* because her research indicated that the body is very connected to the subconscious mind, and that it communicates via neuro peptides, which in turn are influenced by how we think and feel.[6]

"I've come to believe that virtually all illness, if not psychosomatic in foundation, has a definite psychosomatic component," she writes. The "molecules of emotion run every system in our body," creating a mind-body intelligence that is "wise enough to seek wellness" without a great deal of high-tech medical intervention.[7]

I believed that mind, body, and brain were one unit, and like a family, had either painful conflicts or valuable conversations. I was determined to have and teach others the latter. I wanted everyone to be happier in their bodies. But what combination of diagnosis and treatment would resolve the situation in my own body or that of my clients? At times it is confusing. Now when I am confused, I always begin with consulting with my doctor first to rule out infections or disease processes. I have learned that this can save time and heartache.

Sometimes, in the process of avoiding the emotional content in a particular muscle system, we don't move naturally and unused muscles acquire weakness. Then lack of blood circulation and muscle imbalance create pain. In this example, I had a neck pain caused by a pinched nerve that became so bad it affected my arm. There was no specific injury, just a gradual buildup of tension. Once I had sorted out enough of the emotional components to think clearly, I still had to deal with the tissue aspect of my pain. I went to a physiotherapist, who applied traction and gave me neck-strengthening exercises. I also took pain killers for a month. My return to normal functioning after this combination pain event had to include strengthening the weak muscle area and getting over a fear of moving my neck as an adjunct to the investigative emotional work.

With a less long-standing symptom (for me headaches or muscle pains), I found I could quickly discern what the inner conflict was that was causing the symptom (or check to see if I was dehydrated or under slept) and disperse it within a few days using emotional investigation or better self-care. However, if there was scar tissue involved, it took me longer, because the tissues had become stuck together in adhesions and they required loosening through manual therapy or exercise. In addition to this loosening, I would have to face the traumatic content in the original injury. This could take up to several months of effort. Each of the seven scars I have on my left side has required different combinations of emotional investigation, fascia and scar tissue loosening, and exercise /postural work to resolve the pain. With every journey I took into resolving my own pain, I learned techniques and attitudes I could use to benefit my clients. This was the Magraw Method.

For example, I began to notice that, if I treated someone quickly after an accident—calming their nervous system, having them tell the story in several different ways and working on the heart meridian points (acupuncture theory connects the heart to shock), they would regain good functioning sooner than people who had no treatment after their accident or injury. If the shock is addressed, the tissues can move through the natural swelling/pain cycle and the release of an emergency ANS state much more quickly. In the Magraw Method, I have developed a pre- and post-surgical protocol of dealing with emotions and shock to speed up the physical recovery process.

Stories from the Frontlines

The Magic of the Psoas Muscle

Darlene, an office worker, came to my office clutching her back and walking crookedly, saying, "I don't know what happened! My back just suddenly gave out!" I asked what she had been doing the several days before the onset of pain. "Well," she said, "I haven't been sleeping well, and I got my bike out (because it's spring) and took a long bike ride and worked in my garden. I should be feeling great from the exercise." I asked her if she knew about an important muscle called the psoas. Like most people, she had never heard of it. I told her it was often implicated in lower-back pain.

We began the session with her in a comfortable side-lying position, and I described the origins and insertions of the psoas; the lumbar (lower back) vertebrae, the inside of the hip bone, and the inside of the femur (upper thigh bone). I helped her to visualize what these muscles could do—raise the leg, bend the torso, stabilize the core. Then I said, "When these muscles weaken from sitting (as you have been doing all winter and at your job), and then they are called upon to deliver through sudden activity, they can twist and pull in odd ways that puts stress on the back muscles." I then proceeded to give her my psoas treatment, which involves a felt awareness of how the psoas tension is connected to the back by pressing both the back muscles and abdomen at the same time and coaching Darlene to notice how she felt. After a few minutes, she said, "Oh, I feel the back pain decreasing, but you are hardly pressing there, how can that be?"

I said, "Notice this tense line of muscle in the front. As it releases, your back can come back into its normal alignment."

The session proceeded with my physical techniques and her growing awareness. When she got up from the table, she was able to stand upright and the pain had decreased. She said, "But how do I keep it from happening again?"

I gave her some psoas releasing and strengthening exercises and suggested that she go to a Pilates class, because they specialize in core-balancing exercises. I also suggested that she get more sleep, as lack of sleep negatively influences the psoas and lower-back muscles. This was a straightforward case of understanding muscles and their function in order to heal the pain.

Changing the Nervous System Can Change the Mind

Carrie, a regular client, showed up for her session looking wild-eyed and disheveled. She said, "I just ran into the back of someone's car when I was parking. I didn't even look to see what damage was done. I was too rattled."

I could sense that her nerves were firing overtime, and that as a result of the shock, she was disconnected from her ability to think clearly enough to make decisions. (When we are in shock, the connection to our frontal lobe is decreased in favor of the connections to our more primitive survival system.) I knew it would be pointless to help her problem solve when she was in this state, and after a kindly acknowledgement of her plight, I decided to do some cranial sacral work. Gradually, as I worked in silence, she calmed and relaxed. When she got up, she said, "I can think now, and I know what I have to do—go leave a note on the car and be prepared to pay for any damage." There was a big difference from when she had arrived in the grips of a triggered state.

A Messy Combo

Of course, my own story continued as well. One summer, my right ear itched in an unbearable way for about a week. This usually happens when there is something going on in the left ear (an infection, a wax buildup) but there was no pain in either ear. Then I woke up one morning, and there was a colored liquid coming out of my left ear. I panicked. My internal danger siren was going off, and I went into survival mode. I checked to see if there was blood or pain—neither one.

I worried: Do I need a diagnosis from a doctor? Is there muscle weakness that needs exercise? Do I need a therapy or a bodywork session to understand what important issue I am avoiding by focusing on body pain? Do I need to practice calming techniques or change my diet to decrease the climate of inflammation and hence pain in my body? Is there a memory of trauma pushing to the surface to be heard? What about a symptom that is not pain? I turned to my "team" of helpers (internal and external), engaged their detective abilities, and we worked together to solve the mystery of my plugged Eustachian tube.

I managed to get a five-minute appointment with my osteopath, so he could look at it with his ear scope. He looked and said there was no blood, but the tissues looked very slightly disturbed. I was reassured enough to calm down and start observing. (The technician had reset my radar screen and my Eagle's Eye could click into gear). No pain, the itching in my right ear had decreased, my left ear was very sensitive to sound, and there was a liquid, crackling sound in it that would come and go. Little did I know that this very annoying sound would last for months.

The next week, I went to my ENT, who regularly cleans out my left ear because it does not clean on its own because of the operation. He looked in and said, "Oh, you have a burst eardrum. I can see the hole." This shocked the heck out of me. I asked him what I should do, and he said, "Don't get water in it. Don't worry, kids get these all the time." I was too shocked to be able to ask anything else or tell him about the noise in my ear. Later, I thought, *My ear drum is implanted. Will it regrow?*

I worried about noise and wind. My sleep was affected. I worked on my Eustachian tube reflexes in my feet somewhat obsessively, and I went back to my osteopath. He said there might be stiffening scar tissue

(I have plenty in the area around my ear) that prevented the flap of skin between the Eustachian and the throat from working properly. Instead of draining, the tube accumulated mucus, which then, having nowhere else to go, burst the drum. This made sense to me. He gave me a gargling exercise that would enliven and loosen those tissues. The gargling helped the heavy feeling around the left ear and the right ear stopped itching. I was feeling better, but the crackling sound persisted.

Was this turning chronic? Was there something I was avoiding? I decided to try the therapy option and did some sessions focused around my ear. I did a repair scene, with my father apologizing to me and acknowledging that the way he and my mother reacted to my ear set me up for confusing experiences. I had a grief release and was more relaxed, but the sound in my ear persisted and periodically I would get excessive drains of mucus down the back of my throat (postnasal drip).

Then, having more emotional calmness, I noticed three things that made it better: yawning, gargling, and singing, which all improved the strength of the ventral vagal branch of the vagus nerve, which has fibers that are connected to muscles of the head and neck. Noise and tense states, which weaken my vagus nerve, made it worse. I took this info to my osteopath, and he said that he thought it might be the fault of the small muscles that attach onto some tiny bones in the inside of the eardrum, whose job it is to dampen sound. Interestingly, these muscles are controlled by fibers of the vagus nerve. His analysis made sense to me and was a relief. But what was this stupid irritating sound that kept persisting? Predictably unpredictable, it kept my radar screen of sensation jamming up, which made my nervous-system alarm go off. The symptoms were feeling endless and attacking. Finally, I went back to the ENT and he "vacuumed" the wet debris from my ear and suggested I use some eardrops (cortisone and antibiotic). After three days, my ear was clear, dry, and making no sounds.

So now I had to revise my analysis. There could have been a low-level infection; the antibiotic would have addressed that. There certainly had been swelling that the cortisone addressed. I was relieved of the symptoms, but would it last? It did, but under stress they would return. I was reluctant to overuse the drops, so I continued my work on the vagus nerve function as an adjunct to the ENT's approach.

This waiting time is what can drive us crazy and make us jump at quick and unbalanced solutions, such as too much physical focus or too much mind-body focus rather than "attuning" to find effective solutions, which often involve a combination of both. The patience it takes to hang in with a recalcitrant pain or symptom until it resolves is hard to comprehend until you have gone through it. As odd as it sounds, I am grateful for the education and stamina that pain has given me.

Music Was My Companion

Music was a major soother of my nervous system, and it helped me no matter what the source of the pain was. Singing stimulated my vagus nerve, which then had better "tone" and could bring a sense of well-being to my body. This soothing effect of music decreased inflammation in my tissues and increased circulation. Music also brought balance to my brain and body by working the left and right sides of my brain. (Melody stimulates the right, rhythm the left). A balanced brain is better at solving problems.

Where did music fit into my experiences of pain? Because music has been both important and traumatic in my life, I can also have pain from avoiding music and from having inner conflict about music. I wanted to sing/play, but I was afraid I wouldn't succeed. This has produced many TMS events. Equally, music has had a strong overall healing affect. It provided a strong motivation to deal with the leftovers of trauma: PTSD and scar tissue. It brought me many feelings of well-being and competence in my body. It brought me connections with others.

There were times when bad musical experiences threw me back into isolation and depression, leading to physical pain. One of these times was in the summer of 2003, when my voice was going downhill after a long good spell. A close friend invited me to do a few songs during his regular gig at an Irish pub. I was playing around with different keys, because I noticed my low range was not doing well. I had pitched my songs higher. It was a noisy afternoon, with conversations being held at a shout level. I bravely took the stage, hoping for the best, but actually the worst happened. My voice gave out, and I missed notes. I am sure I was singing very flat. I could see the audience turning away. It reminded me of the disastrous coffee-house experience when I was twenty. I struggled through, and afterward, I asked my friend what he thought. I could see him avoiding the truth. He very diplomatically said, "I don't think the keys were very good for you." In that instant, I decided I would not perform again for a long time. I stopped writing songs too and began to struggle with mid-back pain.

However, part of me knew there was still hope. I wrote a song called "Save Me for Later". My friend Suzie wrote the music. It is a blues love song, an unconscious cry from my singing voice to me, telling me not to give up hope during the "waiting to heal time." Ironically, this song has continued to be one of her audience favorites.

Innate Intelligence Letter

Dear Kristi,

You have been on this mind-body journey for a long time! You have accumulated a large body of knowledge, and the world is now ready to hear it. You have also accumulated confidence in your body processes and your ability to get the right kind of help for it.

I know it has been hard to have re-runs of the trauma, especially around your voice and ear. Just keep breathing and intuiting the next step on your journey. Don't be afraid to repeat techniques or approaches that have worked before. Keep your open mind and your ability to collaborate. These qualities have served you and others throughout the years you have devoted to the practice of bodywork.

Continue to speak up and advocate for yourself as a one-eared person and trauma survivor. People can learn from your story— be bold and tell it again and again.

With respect,

Innate Intelligence

Techniques for Keeping the Body in Mind

You Have the Key

Massaging ourselves in a healing way can bring many rewards. Physically, it improves circulation and decreases pain. It can improve our ability to feel and sort the sensations inside our body and thus improve our early warning system for disease. Psychologically, it is a tangible expression of self-love. We can show our caring to our body, and it responds by relaxing. A few techniques are useful, but simply paying attention and experimenting is enough. Find a quiet room with various pillows at hand to prop your arms. You can also play soothing music. Set aside at least half an hour for this self-massage. Remember, if touch makes you nervous, you may not want to do this technique, or if you want to explore this nervousness, do it with a professional to guide you.

What to Do

Rub your hands briskly together to warm them up. Then, lying on the floor or sitting comfortably, place your palm on your chest over your heart area. Focus on receiving the heat from your hand. Send love from your hand to your heart. Ask yourself, "Where is the tension in my body today?" Let's say that the answer is "my neck." Place your hand on your neck, and using your middle and index fingers, make little circles up and down your neck. This may show you more precisely where tense areas are. If you want to work on a specific point, press where it feels a little painful, breathe deeply, and allow it to relax. Or, press it and ask your body, "What are you telling me now?" Repeat until you have a sensation of release or completeness. After the deeper pressure, you can just hold it with a lighter pressure. This allows the tension to continue releasing. Hold the area for soothing after a release.

What to Expect

The position of your hands and body can make a big difference in how effective the self-massage is. Remember to use gravity, positioning, and props, such as a tennis or lacrosse ball (good for back points). For learning to sense where tension is, practice consistent awareness and use your breath to relax muscular defenses.

The body can store any emotion anywhere, so remember to stay open to your own unique storage system. However, some areas commonly hold certain emotions. Consider exploring the jaw for fear and anger, the face and chest for fear and grief, and the upper stomach and under the ribcage (the diaphragm) for all the emotions.

Body Messaging via the Fascia Train

There are many ways to do self-massage and improve awareness of how our body constantly communicates. This exercise is a variation on self-massage. I have used it frequently to deal with the consequences of scar tissue. Fascia is a membrane-like tissue that wraps around every-thing—muscles, organs, nerves. It has three layers, just under the skin, around muscles nerves and blood vessels, and around the visceral organs. It carries water and fat molecules, making it slippery and moveable. It is called a "train" because it is all connected (some people call it a web). Much about its operation is still a mystery. It is useful to have a picture in your head of what it looks like (let Google help you). Scar tissue makes fascia dry up and knot, creating adhesions. Eventually these pull-on larger structures and affect posture and organ functioning. It is worth it to learn how to soften and renew the flexibility of your fascia.

If you have received massage, reflexology, or acupuncture, you'll have a head start on sensing in diverse regions of your body. If you feel nothing, this technique may not be for you.

What to Do

Lying down or in a sitting position, do a body scan asking, "What is the most significant point or area in my body today?" Or, if you are investigating a scar tissue, start there. Using your finger or thumb or a massage tool, start to circle it gently over the tissues. You can also pinch, lift, and twist the tissue to release it. Experiment and find the best way for you. Continue until you feel a change of sensation not from your fingers (though you may feel that too) but from inside your body.

As you are massaging yourself and right after, be aware of anywhere else in your body that is signaling with a congested sensation, a slight pain, a tingling feeling, or another sensation. It may be close to the first point or distant. Go to that new area next and repeat the process. To reach your back, use a tennis or lacrosse ball or a massage tool. Place the ball where the congestion or pain is and make tiny movements on it with your body. Notice where you feel referral signals (places other than where you are massaging that feel sensations of tension or release). Do the same point on the other side of your back, even if it is not hurting.

It is good to pause often and let yourself feel sensations. Also, if you can simultaneously hold two points that seem connected, they both will release more quickly. This works well with the psoas muscle in the abdomen and lower-back points. Follow the related points until they run out or you are tired.

What to Expect

When overly stiff fascia softens, improvement in movement, both in range and in smoothness, can result. Also, any muscles that have weakened inside a restricted fascia compartment will be free to strengthen normally. Other reliable results are parasympathetic (ventral vagal) responses and an upswing in energy. Fascial release will promote the ability to sleep more deeply. At first, it may be difficult to feel sensations. If this is the case, start with the most sensitive area in your body and have patience, slowly building your ability to sense inside your body. There is probably a reason that your body has shut down awareness.

Bring Your Body Along

Often, we approach transitions in our lives—for example, in relationships, jobs or events—without knowing how our bodies are reacting. Frequently, we ignore our own sensations and signals completely, struggling through the events of our lives and feeling pain from not bringing our bodies along (dissociating or numbing and neglecting). Fear and anxiety prevent us from using our bodies as instruments of truth—as a direct line to our intuition. If we address our needs—as intuited through our bodies—before entering an activity, we can avoid waking up with unmet needs, manifested as pain or discomfort, in the middle of an action.

This technique is designed to assess our readiness for an action we think we may be ready to take by slowing us down enough to notice and interpret our body's messages.

What to Do

Pick up an object that represents what you are moving toward (for example, life goals, people or difficulties of any kind). Then put down the object, move away from it (at least to the far side of the room), and stand as you observe it. As you look, check in with your body and notice where it feels tense and where it feels at ease. Connect with your body by asking

» What is this physical sensation in my stomach/upper back/head telling me about how I feel emotionally?

» Has my body felt this way before?

If no sensations, images, or words come to you, you may be too nervous to feel. If that's the case, try standing further away or hiding the object. Check in with your body again. If your body still gives no signals, don't do the exercise at this time. You may need professional guidance.

If your body gives you positive signals, proceed as follows.

Take one step toward the object and check your body again. Did the tension increase or decrease? If it increased, ask yourself, "What do I need to do, say, or ask for to make it easier for me to move forward?" Maybe you need to eat something before a meeting with your boss; maybe you need to do more research before you write your thesis; maybe you need to ask someone to go with you to the party. Don't do these things in the moment, simply acknowledge them. At the same time, make an agreement with your body that you will do the action before you face your boss, work on your thesis, go to the party, and so on. With the agreement in mind, notice whether your body responds by releasing tension. If it does, take another step forward, stop, and check in with your body again. What are its needs now? With that answer in mind, move toward the object until you feel there are no more steps to take and you can move into the activity, bringing your body along.

If your body's tension does not release, then move a step backward and check in with your body again. If the tension consistently decreases when you move backward and always increases when you move forward, ask yourself if you really need to do the activity. It could be that this is not the right time to be taking the action.

What to Expect

Contradictory voices within you often speak up: one that wants to move forward and one that doesn't. If so, you may need the help of professional guidance to negotiate between them. Or see technique "Decreasing Inner Conflict by Talking to Myself" in "Techniques for Keeping the Body in Mind" in Chapter 8.

You may take few steps or many, and you may not arrive at a finishing point at all. Your original idea about what you need to do may change in the course of practicing this technique. But whatever now seems possible for you, you should do, as you will have made agreement with your body. So that you'll keep those agreements, it may be helpful to write down the body's needs and answers.

Heart Warming

Stress takes a toll on our heart. So does disconnection from ourselves or others. Practicing this technique will help to calm the vagus nerve system, bring us out of a fight-or-flight state, and reconnect with our true desires.

The heart holds intuition, passion, and love. When we are connected with our heart, we feel centered and aligned with our actions. Often, we feel this as a sensation—our heart feels warm, filled, overflowing, or any other metaphor for a good feeling. Each emotion has its gift, even fear and self-doubt (I call this the flowing, healthy state of fear/caution). But when we are swayed by unhealthy levels of fear or self-doubt, internal arguments arise and we become confused and get thrown off centre. Our heart can feel closed, caved in, tight, or numb. When we learn how to connect with our heart using this technique, we also connect with our deepest sense of identity, what we have passion about and touches us, what makes us happy.

Sometimes a critical voice, reflecting a fear, may emerge while using this technique. I provide follow-through questions to help face the fear. This technique teaches us to connect with our heart using the sensation of warmth and then to ask questions to activate alignment.

What to Do

Using your breath to focus your mind, bring your attention to the area between your shoulder blades, as this is a reflex area for the heart. Do not try to change anything, but simply feel what's there. Is the area tight, achy, or numb? Does it feel warm and full? Then bring your attention to the front of your chest. Is it constricted, achy, concave, or numb? Does it feel warm and full?

To increase awareness of the feeling, use one or more of these methods:

» Visualize an image for your heart—for example, the color pink, a heart shape, a light, or a fire—to make it vivid.

» Use words to describe sensations in your heart area, for example, hot, cold, twisting, painful, empty, full, heavy, light. Or, warm, full, light expansive.

» Stretch the chest and upper back, alternately curving the shoulders forward and pushing them back to stimulate sensation and circulation in the heart area.

Next, create an image for the good feeling in your heart. Make it vivid and encourage it to grow. Place your hand on your heart and feel warmth enter your heart. Spend at least five minutes and up to twenty minutes with the sensation of warmth in your heart and notice where else in your body you can spread it to.

What to Expect

You might feel a tightening or a loosening in your heart area or find that the imagery gets darker or lighter. As you practice, you will learn how to interpret these signals. Insights or emotions may arise.

What to Do, Part 2

Having established the physical and emotional connection with your heart, ask questions to activate intuition. After each question, notice the effect on your heart. Perhaps record your insights.

» In what specific way is my heart uncomfortable? (The answer might be physical, emotional, mental, or issue-related, depending whether you are doing an open-ended exploration or trying to make a decision.)

» What does my heart need to grieve or let go of?

» What did I learn (about a past event), emotionally, physically, practically, or spiritually?

» What am I learning (about a present dilemma), emotionally, physically, practically, or spiritually?

» How does this experience, emotion, or thought, align with what I know of my heart's desire?

» What is the smallest step I could take, under the direction of my heart?

Anchor your new awareness in metaphor. When you have found the right metaphor, say three times, out loud, "It is in my heart." For example, you might imagine the action or thought as a flower and plant it in your heart; or you might imagine the action or thought as a color or warm sensation and breathe it into your heart.

What to Expect, Part 2

Most often, this technique brings positive feelings and an easing of discomfort and confusion, but if focusing on sensation is frightening or generates obsession, pause and sit with the resistance to see what you can understand about it, and then if it persists, seek help before continuing. Sometimes fear will surface. Name the fear, do a "That Was Then, This Is Now" separation (see chapter 5 "Techniques for Keeping the Body in Mind") and then say, "I am doing the best I can." To release tension and bring back a sense of openness and presence, say this a few times while taking deep breaths.

Then continue with the metaphor you have placed in your heart until you feel finished.

Chapter 7

The Haunting:
The Ghosts of Attachments
Keep Appearing

The little girl cries for her mother
Heartbroken
She cannot understand
Why the tie has come untied
But now a new mother is taking up residence
In the centre of her being
She brings calm in times of uncertainty
Warmth on a damp grey winter day
She tells the girl what she needs to learn
And when it is time to let go
The girl feels light and easy because she knows the mother is here.

When my mother was dying in an adult family home in Seattle in June of 2000, I wrote a song called "I Can Let Her Go." Because of the chance rotation in the twenty-four-hour bedside vigil of my sisters and me, I was the only one of us sisters there when she passed. I sang the song to her. I was ready to let go.

I was also ready to face the truth about her life. When it comes to 'truth' in attachment narratives it is important to remember that within a family or community each person's experiences and memories are different. What follows is the story of my attachment truth. Whatever the source, no trauma is easy to recover from, but I discovered that my attachment trauma was the most tricky and difficult. At the beginning of my healing work, I did not have a therapist to look at the various dimensions of my medical trauma. I naively thought that once I had accepted my face and ear, I had done the hard work of therapy. I had done hard work, just not all of it.

What followed the work of accepting my disability involved turning my attention to my family, especially my mother and my relationship with her, which I did during the years when she became ill with Parkinson's. I was brought into confrontation with my long-buried attachment trauma. Often associated with attachment trauma is "core shame," which is an early belief that we are intrinsically "bad" because why else would our parent disconnect from us? I tell the following stories in the hope of giving you a head start on seeing and resolving your own attachment issues.

Originating in the work of John Bowlby, Attachment Theory helps us to understand how we relate to one another and how we grow into mature human beings.[1] Attachment Theory has become the main approach to understanding how early social development can affect us as adults. It explains many of the underpinnings for our complex interactions with others.

In infants, behavior associated with attachment is connected to needing the parent close for survival purposes. Infants become attached to adults who are sensitive and responsive to them, and who remain consistent caregivers during the period from birth to two years of age and into childhood and adolescence. During the latter part of this period, children begin to use these familiar figures as a secure base to explore from and return to. Parental responses lead to the development of patterns of attachment, which in turn lead to "internal working models" that guide the individual's feelings, thoughts, and expectations in later relationships. Separation anxiety and grief following the loss of an attachment figure are normal and natural responses in an attached infant and often not addressed. After the early years, there are further developmental stages and potential attachment traumas as the child grows into adulthood.[2]

There are different types of attachment styles: secure attachment, avoidant attachment, anxious attachment, and disorganized attachment. Evidence of these attachment patterns shows up in how children ask for attention, in interactions with peers of all ages, and in romantic and sexual attractions. We also show them in how we respond to infants or children, people who are ill, or the elderly. It's a big subject that I can only touch on here.

Cradling

In my research, I read a curious fact with huge implications on understanding my relationship with my mother. Regardless of whether mothers are left- or right-handed, they tend to cradle their babies on the left—as high as 80 percent of mothers choose the left. "This may be an evolutionary trait that allows sound to enter the infant's left ear, which means it will then be processed by the right hemisphere of the brain, the center for the emotional part of the language. The earliest communications may be pure emotion with no literal meaning—the right hemisphere, which develops first, is stronger at interpreting the melodic tones of baby talk that mothers and fathers use when holding newborns.... This right-to-right communication begins the emotional bond and ensures the importance of first nonverbal and then later verbal interchanges to the bonding process."[3]

When I was a newborn, the figure eight of cartilage and flesh in place of my left ear couldn't receive all these melodic tones, and my right ear was muffled against her body. My mother and I missed out on that right brain to right brain emotional feedback experience, which affected our bonding process for years to come. One source of my attachment difficulties arose in my early years when my mother was distracted by relational difficulties in her life. She later made me her "favourite," and this required me to be there for her instead of her being there for me. After the operation, when I needed a steady mother, this was especially traumatic. My experience of my mother was of an off-and-on presence, as well as of someone I was supposed to help. These factors caused an insecure-attachment style. I was untrusting and often pushed away people who loved me while clinging to others who were not available.

My parents ascribed to a bohemian lifestyle. I inherited their mindset and during much of my twenties I was obsessed with living a life "free of illusions," by which I meant without the constrictions of norms and without pretense. In part, this was a social/spiritual idea of the times, but it was also a way of being close to my parents by following their philosophy. They wanted to be ahead of their times and not beholden to the political or social dictates of the fifties. They investigated intentional communities, they ate healthy food, they went on peace marches, and they worked on tribal reservations building houses for Indigenous communities. They lived on an island with other independent-minded individuals and had many friends from varied backgrounds.

From my father, I learned how to live on the fringes and be an activist. A family friend remembered that my father once had said to her, "I want my daughters to learn about sexual freedom, but I don't know how to teach them." However, he did make it possible for me to have sex with my boyfriend at a young age by approving the pill and letting us stay for occasional weekends in a friend's basement. I picked up the idea that radical was good. Ironically, at the same time, I was learning from my mother by osmosis about how to be secretive. Inside me, these opposing influences created confusion, and as a result, I created the "illusion" of being an open person while still concealing many facts about myself.

Their striving was admirable and brought interesting people and ideas into our house, some of which guided me in my choice of career. I am grateful for that. And I am grateful that their "seeking" approach to life gave me the ability to wonder, question, and find resources. However, they both came from highly educated middle-class families, and making such a big shift, especially in my mother's case where her Norwegian Lutheran family disapproved of her and her choices, required denial and secrets.

Bargains

In our child's mind, we make efforts to get from our parents the love that we want and need by making bargains such as: "I'll be a good girl/boy, if you won't leave"; "I'll never complain, if you love me" or my favourite, "I'll be the best worker ever so you will always choose me." The problem with these bargains is that they harden into defense systems and perpetuate the fears we are trying to soothe. I used hard work as a way of ensuring my place but was never sure I was really wanted. It took a long time to let the "best worker" bargain go.

How Music Helped with My Attachment Trauma

Playing the guitar and writing songs was an important "attachment activity". I could talk to my inner child and my spiritual self through the music and words. In the 1980s, the inlaid butterfly on the headstock of my beautiful custom-made guitar inspired me to write. It was symbolic of re-found music (a theme in my life) because I had once had a butterfly necklace that I was very attached to that I had lost. I re-found it by placing it on my most treasured possession: my guitar. I would sit for hours hunched over its lovely curves, catching melodies. It was a comfort and a challenge. In many letters I wrote during that time, I berated myself for not practicing, and celebrated when I did. I began taking singing lessons with Gloria, an eccentric but dedicated teacher. I performed at the Free Times café. My dreams were beginning to take shape: I wanted to be a performing songwriter.

My intuition told me that, as I healed emotionally, I would improve as a songwriter. Two years after my father died, I had collected enough songs to make my first recording, with my teacher and mentor Milton on bass and myself on guitar. We recorded in Milton's home studio. I could sing sustained notes then but had not yet had any music or songwriting education to speak of. Most of the songs are recorded too high up in my range. But the very existence of this tape shows that he was a patient and good mentor.

Listening to the recording now, I see that I had talent—both in creating interesting melodies and in the clear tone of my voice. But there was an odd lack of expression. This had been noted by my lover, the professor, in his feedback. I felt ashamed of this lack of expression, not knowing that it was a result of my trauma, my "frozen" face, and my fickle singing voice.

Though I did not know it consciously at the time, singing to my inner child supported the idea of being unified with self. One of the first tenets in attachment-trauma healing is creating a "self-object" to become attached to. It's obvious that I was creating song "self-objects" and acquiring inner strengths by singing them. This gave me enough self-respect and courage to play with other people and begin actual music study.

These lyrics are an ode from my hopeful self to my discouraged self. I knew, even then, that laughter was healing:

> Show me the path where there is singing
> And words of opening a door into a world of being more
> Where can we find the shining temple?
> I want you to make me laugh to make me laugh
> I want you to tell me there's magic.

I still puzzled about my voice, but my new teacher/mentor Don helped arrange my unusual melodies crafted around my unnamed vocal disability. One of my songs, "Dancing in my Dream," was in 12/8 and had sections in other time signatures. Don gave me guitar lessons. We made a three-song demo in a real recording studio, where I had the happy revelation of hearing my voice in a different way. I remember saying, "Wow, I can really hear my voice!" Using headphones was my first experience of hearing my voice from the outside—a much better sound than what came through my left ear internally through bone conduction. This "bad" sound often took over from the normal hearing in my right ear.

I didn't know at that time that my internal voice-hearing mechanisms did not work well—background noises became foreground, and I couldn't hear my own voice clearly. It sounded muffled. Most people have a hard time singing when there is other noise around—hence the use of monitors of various kinds that feed back to you your own voice. However, because of my one-eared soundscape, this common problem was tripled for me.

In the middle of this wonderful creativity and forward movement, I became involved with an actor who was alcohol addicted. I got tangled up in rescuing him and his son and working very hard to support all three of us because he would get work only occasionally. I was a classic co-dependent. When he left me for another woman, I languished in sorrow. He came back, but it wasn't the same. My music suffered. It was hard to pull out of this disruption. I wasted time and energy in worry over him. During this time, I wrote the song "Nobody Wants Me Around":

> Tonight we have agreed he's to be free of my need
> But jealousy strikes as I want to be dancin'
> Jealousy strikes as I want to be singin'
> Where is he now?
> Tonight, emptiness weighs me down
> Tonight, nobody wants me around
> Memories slip to the dark of the moon
> Who am I now? A wallflower that waits to be chosen
> A young girl without her first love.

Instinctively, by identifying that work might be some kind of defense pattern, and that I was somehow missing my life, I wrote these lyrics to my workaholic self:

> Make the time, take the time
> To rest from your busyness
> Touch a curly kale leaf, hear the rustling corn
> Smell tomato vines, thank a marigold
> Play and find yourself, have a lazy daydream
> Let the shadow's story emerge from the night.

A Time of Relational Healing

As I was breaking up with my second alcohol-addicted boyfriend, I decided to sell my house and take a year off work. I moved into a tiny apartment in the west end with my elderly dog, some boxes of old letters, my guitar, and little else. I rented a friend's treatment room for the few clients I kept on. I did this pared-down work schedule for close to a year, until I moved in with Karl, my new boyfriend. I met Karl at a Zen Buddhist event. I liked the chanting, and once again meditation put me back on my centre. I could feel his kindness, and I was so happy that he was a musician and could understand my musical dreams.

During my year off, I learned that I felt uncomfortable not working and that focusing on my music was harder than I thought, even when I had the time. Even if I wasn't officially working, I would give away my time to others. As I continued to examine the roots of my over-work problem, I discovered influences of the protestant work ethic coming through both family lines. I worked on the legacy of my father's unrealized dreams.

Karl and I bought a house and got married. I started to smile in photos. I now had some important things to smile about, and I was accepting my facial asymmetry at a deeper level because of the emotional healing I was doing in psychodrama. I felt better about myself, and my music blossomed. In turn, my music fed me and healed me. In the marriage, I felt secure and loved, so I could finally relax, and that enabled me to be more creative. I wrote many songs, some with a teacher and most with Karl. He helped to arrange them, and I discovered the joy of collaboration again. I studied voice with Donna O'Connor, and she sang backup on gigs and recordings. I performed at small clubs around Toronto with various musician friends. Karl and I did some recording.

Songwriting was an important emotional outlet, and I loved to play with words. It was the one activity that I could totally lose myself in and that allowed me to take a break from my worried mind. Everything I was going through influenced my writing.

I wrote several protest songs. The best one, titled "Giving Up the Gun," was an attempt to get inside the mind of a gun-carrying man. Another is an examination of who has power over the land and what is done with it. The chorus asks, "Whose dream is this land, who's dreaming, who's getting the nod from God?" There also was a lovely power of music, power of the feminine song that celebrated life, "Dream Weaver":

> In the rhythm of a sweet mountain song
> She heard your heartbreak your secret longing
> She cast the threads of your dreams to be
> A tapestry of love set free
>
> Chorus
> She's a spirit of silver moonbeams
> Old dream weaver (she) brings your dreams
> She's a lover of magic and mood
> Old dream weaver (she) makes your dreams come true

In the wailing sound of a country blues
She held a mirror to your darkest muse
She healed your fear and let you shine
Revealed the power of love's design

In the harmony of an old swing tune
She had you dancing under the moon
She helped you to feel your heart come awake
And wove a dream you will not forsake

Chorus
She's a spirit of silver moonbeams
Old dream weaver (she) brings your dreams
She's a lover of magic and mood
Old dream weaver (she) makes your dreams come true

My guitar had the voice I wished I had—lovely, clear, reliable tones—perfect for finger style playing. I took lessons and practiced and composed in our cozy little house. Even though I sometimes performed my songs, my voice was still a stranger to me. Why could I sing some songs and not others? Only one of my vocal teachers mentioned that the variability of my voice might be related to my ear and suggested I get a hearing aid, but I didn't carry through on that experiment for many years.

Karl was a jazz guitarist and had studied music at York University. I admired his musicality and he mine. Being with him gave me the confidence to study jazz with a jazz pianist, Fabio. He introduced me to the American standard songbook (so many great melodies!) and taught me many useful musical skills. I was a member of a woman's jazz trio being coached by him. Oddly, I was the singer, not the guitar player. I think this was because my guitar was an acoustic steel string and not well suited to jazz—plus the other members didn't want to sing. With some difficulty, I learned to sing many of the standards from the American songbook mainly choosing up tempo ones with short notes. Even though progress in my singing was sporadic, and even though my sustained notes had started to deteriorate from years of straining, the singing kept me physically and emotionally healthy because it led to social connections with other musicians and singers. I had a place to belong.

However, meditation, exercise, music, and psychodrama were not enough to halt the encroaching physical dysfunction and emotional acting out that began in the early nineties. I still had not solved the problem of keeping secrets and being isolated in my disappointments. I was still confused about the nature of my disability.

Attachment Repeat

The denial of attachment feelings and consequent "acting out" ran deep in my history. In my twenties and thirties, I had multiple relationships happening at the same time. I did not look at the consequences of my infatuations with married men. I thought that, if I talked openly, I *was* open, but although I struggled to be, I didn't know how to be truthful. It took me a long time to learn what "real" was.

Then, in my early forties, when my "best helper" identity was shaken by my mother's illness, the reoccurring attachment pattern of unrequited love echoed. The context: I began to work harder. Karl and I took in a boarder to earn extra money, because he was making a musician's wage at the time. I was secretly angry at having to share.

In the fall of 1990, I began a program at Sunnybrook hospital for facial retraining using bio-feedback. It was administered by the physiotherapy department and involved an assessment of the degree of my Synkinesis—a nerve-wiring error that causes muscles to move together that shouldn't, for example, blinking your eye when you purse your lips. They assessed the degree of weakness in my facial-expression muscles. I was very excited to have this possibility of further development of my face and also of a "repair" experience of help, instead of harm, in a medical setting.

My first session was a revelation. I became aware of how disconnected I was from certain muscles and how starved I was for precise attention to which muscles worked and which didn't. I loved the machine that told me exactly when I began moving muscles together in Synkinesis, instead of normal coordination. Finally, I could begin to sense my facial muscles and know my expressions. The homework was good too. I was instructed to use a hot water bottle on my face for ten minutes before exercising in front of a mirror. The warmth was comforting and gave me permission to comfort myself in a way I had never done. The mirror provided the challenge of once again "facing my face."

The encounter with my face was emotionally rewarding but also exhausting. I went faithfully once a month for a year, and then they told me they were terminating treatment. They said I had made progress and should stop coming to make room for others. This was very upsetting to me. I knew there was more work to be done, and I was not sure I could do it without the machine guiding me. I wrote a letter of protest but to no avail. Instinctively, I knew that I had not had enough repair of my earlier experience of neglect or enough muscle training, but this intuition was not matched with the mandate of their program, which was to put as many people through the program as possible. I was triggered back to my trauma mindset of "something is wrong, but no one is going to help me." This was the beginning of a long slide into challenges and repeats (a trauma trigger that causes acting-out behaviors or defense mechanisms to return).

My loss meter was on high, and then my dog, who I was quite attached to, got very ill and we had to put him down. We immediately acquired a cat, who I also became attached to but who, after a short time, was run over by a car. I was inconsolable and felt responsible. This incident probably triggered the abortion traumas, but they were so deeply buried I did not make the connection. In response, I began an emotional affair with man who looked like my father and who was unavailable (married, as was I).

In the eighties, after my father's death, I had acted out sexually and pushed away stability in favour of unrequited and transitory love, usually with men who were charismatic or alcohol addicted. In addition to the losses mentioned above, now my mother was dying, and I was entering anticipatory grieving. I was in another "repeat," in which I recreated the attachment break I had with my mother at the time of my operation that had resulted in intense loneliness and an addiction to being unrequited.

I was married and had better control over my actions than previously. However, the pull of the pattern was stronger than my mental understandings. I kept my unrequited longings secret from everyone, including the object of my obsession, to a degree. It didn't stay very secret—I had too much of my father in me. Like him, I couldn't keep a secret very well. Some people in my circle could see that I had a crush on my friend. I felt ashamed but driven to find ways to spend time with him. We never acted on any of my fantasies, but they created a disruption in the social field around me much like my father's actions had done at times in our family and community. I wasted so much energy and time being tense and feeling longing for what was impossible. I still loved my husband and didn't want to hurt him or leave him. I experienced a storm of inner conflict.

A Good Man Is Lost

I feel sad that I was haunted by my dynamic with my mother and the chaos of the secrets both parents carried. I was locked into caring for my mother and resisting her influence at the same time. I was unconsciously following in my father's footsteps while at the same time idealizing him. At the height of this inner conflict, Karl became quite depressed for his own reasons. In one of my journals, I mention feeling like he was "work" and that maybe I had my experience of him entangled with my experience of my mother. I think this was true. And the power of the projection on him was too strong for me to resist. My feelings were beginning to surface in my body with a new intensity, stimulated by acupuncture and psychodrama. At the same time, I had high expectations of myself that I could help my mother face her increasing disability, even if I couldn't cure her disease.

When my mother had begun to show symptoms of Parkinson's in the early eighties, it took a long time for the diagnosis and naturally, because I was a body worker, I wanted to give her treatments. On my scant time off, I would go to Eagle Island and give her many massages and try to get her to deal with emotional issues. Of course, the treatment was limited: I was her daughter and she kept secrets from me. I would also ask her questions about my trauma, but she still felt such horrible guilt about my operation that, if I brought it up, she would collapse into tears and not be able to talk. One year, she wrote:

It's your birthday and I wanted to let you know I'm thinking of you and remembering what I can of happenings and feelings about your "formative" years. Yes, I did feel some frustration when you were uncommunicative—and those times were also complicated by the heavy feelings of guilt I had around your operation and the consequences. But here we are now having grown beyond that hard place and I can say that I feel grateful for the closeness I feel between us.

After this, I completely put aside my need for her to talk with me openly and calmly. I treated her like a client, not a mother. She felt close to me, but I did not trust her. Giving to my mother the support that she had not given to me was emotionally difficult but at times rewarding.

I optimistically and naively thought that she wouldn't have to take medications and when, at the direction of her doctor, she finally did start medication for Parkinson's, I felt ashamed and embarrassed because the drugs helped her—more than massage and herbs did. I never talked about this with her but resolved to be more open to the possibilities of medication being helpful. I could see that I had been operating from my trauma-influenced point of view toward allopathic (Western) medicine and drugs. That "doctors and medications are bad" was one of my fearful beliefs that had been with me since my medical trauma. This was a philosophical turning point for me—turning toward collaboration and combining various approaches. I wanted to use the most effective methods for my family and clients and didn't want to be a zealot about anything.

In the end, I left my marriage. I was distracted by my unrequited longing for the impossible lover, and I felt triggered by Karl's ongoing health problems and depression. I was locked into my insecure-attachment style and running—scared of real intimacy. By 1995, my friendship and "emotional affair" had ended too. I was alone again—a familiar place. Karl was in another relationship; we divorced, and I had to move my office out of the house (I had already moved out). I floated around various workspaces and rented rooms in friends' houses. I was isolated and feeling "like a drifting seed, lost in the wind," right back in my trauma state.

Because I couldn't get away from feeling overwhelmed by my love-sickness, I moved even farther away from Karl. It was sad, because we had been a good team in many ways—especially musically—and loved each other. When it was too late, I found out how dependent on his emotional and musical support I was. My songwriting went downhill, and I stopped performing.

The House That Healed

When I was forty-four, I found a house that I became deeply attached to. This was the first time since living on Eagle Island that I had formed an attachment to a place and really had a sense of "home." These attachments to "place" that all human beings form are an important way of healing attachment trauma.

The first time I entered my future house with the real estate agent, I knew I had to have it. It was filled with light and quiet. I had no idea how I would manage it financially, but I was very determined, and with the help of a good real estate agent and a take-back mortgage by the vendor, I bought my dream house.

One of the house-warming gifts I received was a bright red tool chest. This was significant, because I had many anxious complexes about fixing material things—afraid they couldn't be fixed, definitely afraid I couldn't fix them, and worried that I wouldn't find the right person to fix them. It was an obvious projection of my ear trauma onto the house. Of course, I was very happy that it was a new house—I was the first owner—because that meant fewer things to be fixed.

Once I moved in, I felt that, like a good mother, the quiet of the house took care of me. At that time, I didn't realize consciously what quiet did for my nervous system; I just knew I liked it. I was experiencing the nurturing power of my house while my mother's Parkinson's was getting worse. We made the difficult decision to move her off the island into an adult family home, with very few residents and good caregivers, in North Seattle. It was such a relief to have her in a safe place. I no longer had the job of being responsible for her direct care, which had meant helping my sisters organize the hiring of caregivers, worrying endlessly about her falling, and puzzling over the medications, not to mention all the massages! I began to have a more normal life, though I spent quite a bit of time in Seattle, driving an old Volvo belonging to one of my sisters, on an unfamiliar highway, from my oldest sister's house to my mother's new residence. Relationally, this was a lonely time. I didn't have a boyfriend and felt a bit distant from my sisters. I think that, each in our own way, we had a hard time with my mother's illness.

I felt relieved when I was in Toronto with my nice bath and quiet house. With this new freedom of a good place to be, I was able to start a new level of self-work. I investigated the roots of my overgrown "helper" (again). I realized that I sometimes helped others when I was the one who needed help—that I had a deep hole of neglect. This was hard to face.

In June of 2000, my mother died from complications of Parkinson's. I felt more relieved than sad. This bothered me, as did my recurring isolation and a new relationship with an alcohol-addicted man. I entered therapy again to try to solve the states of mind and harmful behaviors I kept falling into.

This time around the therapy block, I tried a technique called Eye Movement Desensitization and Reprogramming (EMDR). The name didn't make much sense to me, but the technique (working on changing core beliefs while moving the eyes in various patterns) was very good. It had the effect of unlocking my psyche, and the therapist was willing to work with my dreams, which had always been prolific and full of messages, and which I could now decipher at a much deeper level. Among many other issues, I worked with changing my core beliefs, such as "I am a seed drifting in the wind" to "I am a part of things." Previously, I thought these opposing beliefs were only connected to my disability experience. However, I soon learned that the disturbance of my attachment bonds at an early age also contributed to these beliefs and the defense behaviors connected to them. Through EMDR and my dreams, I did the hard work of long-term therapy. My relationships with friends and family began to improve, but I still had further to go.

A year or so after my mother's passing, I decided to follow up on a story a childhood friend had hinted at. He had very kindly checked with me about the timing of the disclosure, and we had decided that it was better to wait until well after my mother had passed.

My Mother's Secret

In a small cabin on Eagle Island, as the sun was setting over the Canadian islands, I heard the story of my parents' open marriage. I had vaguely known that my father had affairs and felt embarrassed at his clumsy flirting with women when I was a child, but I had no idea (at least not consciously) that my mother had also had affairs and that they had a philosophy to go with it. (Exactly what that was is still unclear.)

She had kept the secret all my adult life. I felt shocked, and later, angry. I felt hurt that in all my questing for the truth, I had been deprived of this very crucial one. Especially as I could see the attachment disturbance it caused and my unconscious acting out around men and relationships. Unknowingly, I had been following in their footsteps. The bare bones of the story are that, when I was in the womb, my mother began an affair with a married man (not the first but the most intense). It was secret from everyone in the family except my father. She had an on-and-off relationship with this lover for many years. He eventually divorced and had several other relationships. I think she always yearned after him and was distracted from me due to heartbreak.

As I imagined what it must have been like for me as a small child, my defense patterns began to make sense. I had learned to cope with uncertain bonding and repeated parental disappearances by becoming indispensable to my parents. I turned into the best little helper any parent could want. Since they always needed a helping hand, it became my way of guaranteeing I was loved (the attachment bargain). I became very anxious about plans. Things needed to happen the way it was planned or I would become upset. I became a reading addict. All these things covered up a deep fear of being abandoned, physically by my father and emotionally by my mother.

Beginning to Break the Attachment Bind

In 2002, the year I turned fifty, I had an experience that began to change my relationship behaviors. I was living with an alcohol addicted man who had a binge-drinking pattern, knowing I was co-dependent but not able to break it off. I went for a trip to Eagle Island, in part to say goodbye to my primary-school teacher Marietta, who was dying of cancer. Another family friend encouraged me to look in the boxes of archives. I found my father's senior yearbook—"well liked, good dancer, and leader" read the caption to his photo. I found love letters from my father to my mother in the months before they were married, and it surprised me to see how much in love with her he was. I found some admiring letters from a close family friend to my mother.

Then, most importantly, I found some notes my mother had made about places she felt safe to cry, in other words, where she felt safely attached:

» the fireplace

» the hayloft in the old barn

» the kitchen stool

» reading "Experiment in depth"

» in Friends Meeting

The list of people and events she couldn't grieve about showed her attachment difficulties:

» a burn when she was four years old

» her sisters (they had difficult relationships)

» with Ann (her best friend)

» Kristi, when little

The first item on the second list, her childhood trauma, explained the last item, which I'm sure referred to my disability, and I felt strangely confirmed that she really couldn't face my face because of not dealing with her own trauma.

I found two letters that I had written to my grandparents when I was a junior in high school. In one I wrote,

> *"I have been quite busy lately with guitar lessons, drivers ed. and working (babysitting). My guitar cracked so I am going to buy a new one with money I have in the bank. Besides taking guitar lessons, I have been playing in this trio (two guitars and a violin). We play jazz and blues."*

My 2002 journal comment was, "Was I lying to myself? Engaging in fantasy? I never played with them—I sold this new guitar so he could buy an amplifier." In the second letter I wrote,

> *"I have applied to Stanford for next year. I hope to be accepted. If they don't, I will probably go to some college in Washington."*

My 2002 journal comment on this was, "Wondering about my memory and my bravado. Why did I bend the truth? Was my core weakened by years of shame?" I never did successfully apply or go to college.

With all this rolling around in my unconscious (in 2002), I had the following dream: I was climbing Mount Crystal (an island landmark) feeling despair. I found a tree at the edge of the cliff and climbed it. Slowly, it began to fall over the cliff. I was not afraid and was able to relax as the tree fell. When it reached the sandy beach, I felt the branches hold me like arms. I felt loved and protected and a dog came and licked my face.

The interpretation of the dream message I recorded in my dream journal: "I am connected and protected—able to go out and express myself."

My Goodbye to Marietta

With the dream in my head, I walked across the field to say goodbye to Marietta, thinking this could be my last visit. She said she had been thinking of me during her clear period at night, when irrelevant thoughts disperse and they become essential and pure. She said she had been thinking that wouldn't it be wonderful if my face could be completely fixed; but then she thought, no, it's beautiful just the way it is. It's alive and moves, and though it is not the same as others, it still brings beauty. Two times she looked at me with tears in her eyes and said, "You are beautiful just the way you are." When we hugged goodbye she said, "You take care of *yourself*."

I felt good about what I said to her too: that I was ready to let go and feeling that I have inside me what she had given me. I told her the tree dream and said she had given me that wonderful feeling of being held and loved. When I walked back home, I had a strong desire to do something different with my life than my mother had. After this visit, when I returned to Toronto, I broke up with my boyfriend who had the alcohol addiction, an important step forward to end my addiction to co-dependency.

Marietta was a "repair mother" for me. Over the years, she had been very encouraging of my musical journey. In a letter, she had written and underlined, "I believe you can do it." I shared my recordings and creative plans with her every time I went home to Eagle Island. I could receive her love more deeply than I could my mother's, and after she passed, I wrote a song in her honor, to anchor the repair in my psyche. I sang "Don't Lose That Smile" frequently for several years.

For my tiny legs, her house was far across the field
But she could see my dreams, knew they could be real
She taught me the secret of following my feet
And how to see what's underneath
When I felt as lonely as a seed in the wind
She'd open up her arms and bring the sunshine in

Chorus
(She'd say) You are so beautiful; don't lose that smile
When the world turns its shoulder, let it go by
Build on the best and let go of the rest
Always remember, don't lose that smile

When she read to us, each story came to life
And when she played those keys, we'd sing all night
She taught us to wonder what lay beyond the stars
And what makes heroes who they are
Even though I lacked some grace
'Round her table everyone had a place

Bridge
It's a way of listening
That gets a growing heart to flower
That makes a friendship in a few precious hours

Chorus
You are so beautiful; don't lose that smile
When the world turns its shoulder, let it go by
Build on the best and let go of the rest
Always remember, don't lose that smile

In therapy, I dug even deeper. I worked with the attachment dimension to my trauma, with forgiveness, with acknowledgment of the cost of my behaviors on others. I was determined not to be like my mother. I also rediscovered what I called "ancestral patterns" and is now often referred to as intergenerational trauma. (See more in chapter 8.)

Old pain and deep patterns do not let go easily. Though I had sworn off relationships with men who had binge-drinking patterns, I slipped into one with an ex-alcoholic (who was in a "dry drunk" stage). I was obsessed, worried, and distracted for three years. Eventually, I realized that the binge-drinking pattern—a man with charisma, sudden disappearances, unreliability, then sudden re-appearances with promises—mimicked my early relationship with my mother and how she must have felt when she was in the grips of losing and regaining her main lover.

Though I had a successful, thriving healing practice, I still yearned to be in a stable romantic relationship and was not. What I really had going for me was a better understanding of the cost of attachment trauma, and the refuge of my quiet home in which to continue to be patient with myself. The house and the understandings were important, as I was soon going to lose my singing voice for the third time.

Innate Intelligence Letter

Dear Kristi,

I know that you are sometimes shocked by your behaviors—the sexual risks, the sudden outbursts of temper, the occasional deep malaise, and the repeats of patterns you thought you had conquered, such as unworkable relationships. I know this is hard for you, because you are also suffering the shock of a change in your world view because of discovering your mother's secret life. Though you had stopped confiding in her years earlier, you thought that she had confided in you. She did tell you certain things, like how she felt having an ill father and having to sew to keep the family afloat financially during the depression. Those were important parts of the story, just not all of it.

I know you fully embraced the role of being your mother's therapist, and she unfortunately, did not stop you from doing this, and she was selective with her truth telling. But you were always her daughter and understandably lacked perspective. As good a detective of the human psyche as you have become, you cannot fault yourself for not knowing, even if the whole island community (or at least half) knew.

The process of releasing the suppression put in place at the time of your operation is speeding up now. It will be stormy for a few years, and then you will find a deeper level of peace. Think of it as a giant healing crisis. In time, you will be able to forgive and let go of both your mother's mistakes and your own.

Remember to trust in your creativity—poetry, songs, dreams, and metaphors. They will feed and illuminate your path. And don't let anyone tell you that you can't use the word "scar" in your lyrics. That is what you know, the anatomy of scars. Of course, you want to write about them.

Yes, you are a wounded healer. That means you are human and have imperfections. You can use those wounds/scars/imperfections with compassion and insight to help others. You will do this wonderfully. Release your shame.

Love,

Your Innate Intelligence

Techniques for Keeping the Body in Mind

The Loving Face

Some of us need to practice the skill of bonding as a first step to healing our relationships. It takes time and patience to develop a mature sense of self (which emerges from healthy attachments) that allows connection and bonding without enmeshment (too close, little sense of self) or avoidance (too mistrusting, closed). The purpose of this technique is to remember a bonded moment with an attachment figure and expand on it, thus strengthening the memory and encoding that moment in your mind-body system. This practice of healthy bonding (along with other techniques) can lead to healing our attachment issues. For most, this is a safe technique, but if you feel too much discomfort, stop and find a therapist to guide you.

What to Do

In a quiet room, and perhaps with music you like, allow yourself to relax and sink into your body (scan your body and notice sensations). Then scan your memory for a face that has meaning to you. It may be one or both of your parents. It may be a pet, spiritual teacher, family friend, or relative. Whoever comes into your mind is right for you.

When you have chosen a face, allow your mind's eye to see it in as much detail as possible. If you are not visually oriented, focus on the voice or touch that goes with that face to make it feel more vivid. When the picture is vivid, imagine the person or animal is smiling at you. Take the smile in. This means noticing how it makes your body feel. Be with the person or animal and allow them to be with you (pause, breathe, notice). You may wish to say things like "thank you" or "I love you" or "please help me." When you have had all the contact you want for now, say goodbye to the face and bring your awareness back to the room. Perhaps write or draw to integrate your experience.

What to Expect

You can expect insights and probably a grief release. Because you are healing the attachment system, your vagus system will also relax. You may sleep better and feel more engaged with people and with life in general.

It is also possible to be triggered (particularly if you have attachment trauma) and have a fight-or-flight response or shut down. If this is the case, seek professional support for doing the technique. To disperse any uncomfortable emotions, exercise or do something familiar and soothing.

Who is Who

The purpose of this technique is to discover which person from your past you are projecting onto your current relationships—the ghost haunting your present. This knowledge gives freedom and is a way to understand the depth and reactivity of emotions. You can do this technique as a role play using a chair or in writing or in your imagination. If you have not done any of these techniques, try all three and see what works best for you.

What to Do

Choose someone you are having present difficulties with and place them in an actual or imagined chair. Do a "speak out," where you just say whatever comes to mind directly to the person in the chair. Then, pausing after each question, ask yourself:

- » What does my body feel like (sensations) when I sit in front of them?

- » What does my body want to do (movement or posture)?

- » Who does this person or this dynamic remind me of?

- » To whom have I said these same things?

- » What does my choice of words imply?

- » What age do I feel when I am speaking to this person?

- » What do I know about my past that might be implicated in this situation?

- » What trauma is being triggered now and how has this person walked into my trauma?

- » How have I projected my trauma onto them?

When you find the ghost (my partner reminds me of my father, for example), talk to the person from your past in another chair. When you are finished, say out loud how they are similar and how they are different from the person in the present. At this point, you can move the chairs apart.

What to Expect

It can be a little weird talking out loud alone, but it is an important part of the release. You need to hear your own voice to be your own therapist.

If you can't figure out what the ghost or past trauma is, it's possible that it occurred when you were pre-verbal or happened to one of your ancestors. Because intimate relationships involve touch and sex, they often trigger traumas from an early age—the age at which we are being held. This infant-level trauma is hard to sort out on your own and you might consider professional help if you continue to have relationship difficulties. However, it is possible to find an energy inside you that can lovingly and calmly "hold" you until understanding arrives, much like an actual mother holds her baby with love, even before she knows what the matter is.

Sometimes simply finding the ghost solves the relational difficulty, and at other times, you need to take the next step and use the "In Their Shoes" technique to solve the relational problem.

In Their Shoes

After you have named the ghost, you may be ready to see the other person's point of view. This is sometimes hard to do on your own but always worth a try. We need to put ourselves in other people's shoes to heal attachment traumas. It brings freedom from projections, learning, and true forgiveness. If being in their shoes doesn't work, it is possible you have more anger or sadness to express from your own role. This is okay. Perhaps try it with professional help.

What to Do

In a room where you can make noise without disturbing anyone or being interrupted, place two chairs or cushions, one for you and one for the person you are dealing with. Name your ghost and then state your feelings. When you have thoroughly had your say, sit in the other person's chair, close your eyes and take on their posture. For example, if they curve their chest, imitate that. If they speak in a loud voice, do that. Say, "I am [their name]." Listen to what was said by you while you were in the first chair and allow yourself (in the other's role) to feel and express. Say everything you can, including guessing at their ghosts, and then go back to your own role and listen and respond. Continue going back and forth until you run out of things to say. Finish with a statement of analysis from your own role, for example, "I think that we got tangled up in this conflict because she reminds me of my mother, and I remind her of her mother."

What to Expect

Role reversal (being in their shoes) generally creates a shift and brings insights that help when you want to resolve a conflict face to face. You may feel a great loosening of tension and flood of insight. If you do several layers of perspective on the conflict—role reversing with each person in a group affected by this conflict—you can gain even more insight.

However, if the technique is frustrating or frightening, you might try a pre-step: visualize the setup of the role reversal (two chairs or cushions facing each other), and then create a statement such as, "Right now it feels too frustrating or frightening to do this exercise. Part of me is not ready. I am willing to believe that someday it might have value for my healing." Practice this visualization a couple of times a week until you feel more open or until the part that is resisting gives more information about why.

Chapter 8
The Drama of Family:
How History Repeats Itself

"The things you experience, she continued, are written on your cells as memories and patterns, which are reprinted again on the next generation. And even if you never lift a shovel or plant a cabbage, every day of your life something is written upon you. And when you die the entirety of that written record returns to earth. All we have on this earth, all we are, is a record. Maybe the only things that persist are not the evildoers and demons but copies of things. The original has long since passed away from this universe, but on and on we copy. I have devoted my miniscule life to the act of copying."

— Madeleine Thien, *Do Not Say We Have Nothing*

Working to heal my trauma in every dimension required me to tune in to my relationship with my mother and father, and to look at attachment trauma. The parallel step was to look back further into my family history at my parents' "stuff"—anxieties, attitudes, and habits—which I was beginning to see that I had unconsciously inherited. Referring to this inherited trauma, Mark Wolynn, author of the excellent book *It Didn't Start With You* says, "With the origin of these traumas in view, longstanding family patterns can be laid to rest."[1]

I first began to understand the phenomenon of what is now called epigenetics through my personal work in psychodrama, and this was affirmed when I read *Children of the Holocaust* by Helen Epstein.[2] I read this book shortly after my father died in 1980. I began a long journey toward understanding the next layer of messages from my ancestors and how they influenced my behaviors and body pain.

My Norwegian Lutheran Ancestors

During one of my annual summer visits to Eagle Island, I went exploring again in the dusty boxes that were stacked on top of my mother's closet. Through my studies in psychodrama, my interest in family history had grown, and although I knew many things about my father's family and had done psychodramas on his life, my mother's Norwegian Lutheran background was a mystery and one I was determined to solve.

As the swallows nesting in the eaves chirped and swooped, I sorted through boxes of random papers, letters, and old bills all mixed together. I was looking for the stories that might help me understand certain patterns in my own behavior, such as a huge fear of mistakes and a Protestant work ethic that left no time for fun and creativity. At the bottom of one box, I found the jackpot: a Bergan family history! Bergan was my mother's family name through her mother. There were photos and a basic history of three generations of the Bergan family in Minnesota after they had emigrated from Norway.

In that first look, I found two particularly relevant facts: my mother's maternal and paternal grandfathers—a doctor and a minister respectively—had been "disgraced" in their professions. On her mother's side, the doctor (Ole Bergan) abandoned his family and moved to Texas after being falsely accused of harming one of his patients (at the same time, his illegitimacy had been revealed by his mother who struck him from the will after his father died). As I learned later from a third cousin on her father's side, my mother's other grandfather, Pastor Lars Markhus, had been involved in a dispute. It was a nationwide controversy over the doctrine of predestination. Pastor Markus took a point of view he had learned in seminary, and which was also the teaching of his own church body, the Norwegian Synod. However, across American Lutheranism at that time there was another faction, which called themselves the Anti-Missouri Brotherhood (Anti-Lutheran Church, Missouri Synod, that is.) They called in an expert to debate with Pastor Markhus. He lost the debate and they fired him, effective immediately.

Afterward, the dispute got carried into court, between the minority who followed him out the doors of his church and the majority who had usurped it. Pastor Markhus was already weak from illness before this. It didn't do him any good to have all that additional stress, and he died the year after. Both Ole and Lars had been successful and productive in their communities before being publicly shamed, but the trauma stories were what my mother knew about (vaguely) and the "failure" pattern was an underpinning in her life, because her parents (my grandparents) had inherited public-shaming trauma, and they also had in common the habit of silence. My mother knew very little about her ancestors, good or bad. I noticed that all the photos of the female ancestors (Norwegian Lutherans) were grim-faced and stoic. I thought, "What a legacy of silence and shame!"

Back in Toronto I decided to do a psychodrama on these ancestors. We gathered for my drama in a renovated basement full of colorful cushions and soft chairs—a carpeted bench along one wall. The group was made up of friends, other psychodrama students and Madeleine, the director. In psychodrama, the protagonist (in this instance me) provides all the story material and the director keeps it organized and advances the action. Using the group members as actors, I set the scene of my present-day situation of overwork and lack of creative pleasure.

Then, moving into the past, Madeleine had me show my mother and my perception of her Lutheran ancestors, which were played by other group members. There was a third location that I designated as "creativity," which I represented with colored scarves. Once the scenes were set, Madeleine had me come back to the present, and we set the role play in action. It became clear that the ancestors' attitudes ("work comes first, always think of others first, be silent about your own needs, sacrifice is good; be careful, don't make a mistake or your life will be ruined") were holding me back and blocking me from my creative pursuits, mainly music.

Madeleine set this dynamic in motion by having the actors hold on to me and instructing me to try to break free. There were four of them, so I had to really struggle to pull myself free. In that physical struggle, I realized that I carried these ancestors in my nervous system. I had to break free to get healed. Finally, I was free, and I ran to my place of creativity. The director asked, "What do you want to say to the grandparents?"

I said, "I understand why you had to make your choices, but I want to choose my own standards. I don't want to carry your fear of failure. I don't have to be in your grip anymore."

Then the director asked, "What do you want to do?"

I said, "I want to be an otter and play." I began to do an otter dance that was very fun and silly. It was a powerful repair to play in my creative space in front of witnesses. My body felt much less rigid afterward, and I had a metaphor for the anxiety in my nervous system. I could name it: "Oh yes, that is the Lutherans trying to recapture my nervous system." After this drama, creative efforts had as much value on my "to do" lists as work.

Strengthening Positive Imagination with Psychodrama

Often, we hear and command ourselves to "Stop being so negative!" or we say, "You are acting just like your mother [or some other relative]. Stop it!" Good sentiments, but the problem lies in the "how" of it. How do we develop the means to see the change needed and then, once we imagine the change, how do we practice it in our minds and bodies? I learned this skill of imagination through psychodrama and role play.

Psychodrama is a kind of psychotherapy in which people dramatically act out (role-play) past, present, interpersonal, or intrapsychic events, often in a group setting. However, many practitioners do one-on-one psychodrama using symbolic objects to represent people, parts of self, emotions, and places. I also do guided visualizations of psychodramas. Psychodrama is known as a powerful way to achieve insight and healing into one's past actions or "story." It exercises the imagination in a focused way.

Psychodrama is often used for young people, and it can be compared to Internal Family Systems (IFS) therapy, currently a popular technique. Jacob Moreno, the founder of Psychodrama, was a contemporary of Sigmund Freud and arrived in the United States in 1925. His methods influenced many psychotherapists and group leaders as well as social scientists of the time. The Toronto Psychodrama Center, where I studied, was founded in 1978 and was quite active in the eighties and nineties with good-sized groups and many workshops. When I entered the world of psychodrama in 1980, I already knew the healing power of touch and emotional release. What I learned from my time in psychodrama, through both the personal work and the training, was that showing/acting out your story (or those of your ancestors) and then creating a "new story" has immense healing power. It's important to note that the concept of a "new story" includes the body, for example, changing my posture and ways of interacting physically with others. It is not pretending that bad things did not happen. In the timelessness of the imagination, we can create an experience that was necessary (but missing) for optimal growth and positive outcomes.

In psychodramas, there are three main sections: the exploration, the catharsis (or emotional release), and the repair. There are four main roles: the protagonist (person whose story is enacted), the double (a person who plays a companion and inner voice of the protagonist), the actors (who play all the other roles in the protagonist's story), and the director (who sets the scenes, keeps the action moving, and holds the overview of the protagonist's story).

The exploration often starts before the action of the drama, in the process of naming the problem or dilemma. Naming the problem can have layers. For example, in the dramas I did on my father, layer one was grieving and remembering my father and how much I loved him. This happened in the months right after his death. Layer two was acknowledging and grieving his absence during parts of my operation trauma, because he would stay on the island to take care of my sisters while my mother came to the hospital with me. Layer three was acknowledging and grieving that he would be gone from the island for work, for weeks at times, when I was a small child. Another somewhat hidden layer was feelings of anger that he had missed many opportunities to protect me. "He was an activist protecting draft dodgers. Why couldn't he protect me?" was my inner child's lament. It had been his decision not to sue after my operation, and I felt shame at the fact of his neglect.

In section two, the psycho-dramatic structure of enacting the unfolding scenes, one following from the other as information emerges from the client's unconscious, is effective for getting to the heart of the matter.

Once I was at the heart of my grief over losing my father, I cried and released emotions in a good catharsis. I was encouraged and reflected in this effort by the director, my double (emotional companion role), and group members. Catharsis is defined as the process of releasing, and thereby gaining relief from, strong or repressed emotions, or the elimination of a complex emotion by bringing it to consciousness and giving it expression—healing trauma by bringing emotions into the light of the present, embodied state. For me, being embodied means feeling the body and its phenomena as a whole. I see it as the opposite of dissociation, which I call a disembodied state.

Section three of a psychodrama is the repair. This is where we can reflect upon and re-imagine events. In order to achieve a deeper, more "real" effect, it was often important to understand my antagonist's (my mother, my father) reality and imagine a repair for their stories, so they could give me what I needed in mine. Once this was done, I could also create and "play" my father as stronger, my mother as kinder, and myself as more expressive and creative. In many dramas, I would have a dialogue with different parts of myself, with my "double" taking on the role of the inner me, the child part of me, or other parts. It was an effective way of acknowledging and resolving inner conflict. I imagined and created many scenes of being encouraged and supported as a musician, and through this imaginative effort, grew into the identity of "I am a musician" despite the trauma of losing my voice.

I have psychodrama and the people in the Toronto Centre to thank for the explorations and repairs that transformed my life. This growth achieved over fourteen years made it possible for me to develop my own healing method and pulled my music out from under the weight of the past.

How do our stories become medicine and not just endless re-runs? For me it was several features of the psychodramatic process that contributed to moving me forward in life. I found that telling my story to a group of sympathetic people, who also shared their own stories, helped me to feel less isolated—thus breaking the stranglehold of shameful secrets. The physical showing of my past "trauma body" improved my abilities to sense inside my body and allowed a release of my fascia (tissue that surrounds muscles), which in turn changed my posture. The end result was helpful in separating my present body from my past one, which had experienced the operation.

The role of the double in psychodrama (defined above) was someone who could put words to my feelings and be "with" me. This would help in the effort to rebuild the trust I had lost from attachment trauma. When I played the role of double, it developed my empathy and ability to read and interpret physical signals. This benefitted my clients and enabled a goal that I had had since my early twenties: to become more sensitive to others' feelings. The repair scenes required me to imagine my way out of old mindsets and belief patterns. Having to visually produce what I had imagined onstage was a creative and transformative exercise. It worked my positive imagination and gave me a new psychological ground to grow from.

What I found after several years of participating in dramas was that the principles permeated my whole life, and I didn't need to be in a drama to recognize an opportunity for repair or the time to reveal a secret. I received the spontaneous doubling that others gave me and gave much of it to others in my bodywork. Using the language of metaphor, I was able to help my clients construct their own repair scenes during bodywork.

I co-led groups with Madeleine for ten years and emerged as a knowledgeable group leader and an aware group member. One of the foundational concepts of psychodrama is that the clinicians/therapists/group leaders must do their own psychological work rigorously, and that this work is transparent to group members. The director is very clear, when she is in a director's role as different from when she is doing her own work, and there are always two group leaders so that one remains as director if the other wants to do personal work. This brings a feeling of equality in the groups. As in, "We are all here together working to get better" as opposed to the ones who have it all together versus the ones who don't. As a director in training, I learned to look at myself and identify transferences (projections of my emotional material on someone else) before they went very far. As a group member or leader, we all learned to temporarily put aside our own emotions/problems when it was someone else's turn. This was a good exercise in emotional regulation. All these practices made me a much better and safer therapist and a better friend and family member.

Transference

Transference happens when we don't see the "other" as who they are but instead project on them qualities of someone from our past—often parents or siblings—or aspects of ourselves we have difficulty accepting. There can be positive or negative transference, and it is stronger when we are unaware of what lies in our unconscious. In the process of becoming mature and self-aware adults, many of our transferences drop away.

I grew socially through the psychodramatic concepts of sociometry and role reversal. Sociometry is the study of how people interact in group situations. It involves looking at choice-making patterns and learning conflict resolution. It helped me to emerge from the social isolation that had followed me since my operation. I could tell the truth about myself and also face the truth of how my actions affected other people. Sociometry is designed to help groups become safe places for members to do deep work in personal psychodramas. Part of sociometry is making a personal sociogram—a visual representation of a social network that depicts how close or distant various people feel, and if the relationship is calm or conflictual. Doing this network analysis pointed me in the direction of many good changes.

Role reversal is an exercise of putting yourself in the other person's shoes and trying to see events from their point of view. Because it is done through the body—you take on the posture, gestures, and words of the other person—the insights that arrive are felt and integrated on a physical level. They feel "real." I have found that role reversal leads to deep forgiveness and tolerance. The theory and practice of psychodrama has a strong social awareness component that appealed to my radical roots.

In addition to psychodrama training, I was attending workshops in "Re-evaluation counselling," a form of peer counselling with a component of social awareness. At that time, there was an emphasis on the oppression of minorities and the internalized oppression—the negative messages from society turned against oneself or other people like oneself—these minorities suffered. In one group, I reluctantly began to reveal my mother's attitude toward people with visible disabilities, and even more reluctantly, my own attitude. In this group, a social worker named Howard noticed this. He questioned me about my fear of dealing with people with severe disabilities—in wheelchairs or with facial differences—and when I admitted that I, like my mother, shrank away from them, he offered to introduce me to some clients of his. Lew and Jean Blancher were a couple who both had cerebral palsy, a condition that happens at birth and creates various motor dysfunctions and speech difficulties.

The day came when Howard and I were to meet them at their apartment in downtown Toronto. I was nervous and excited. I trusted Howard, but I also wanted to impress him with my openness and confidence. However, I was lacking a model for acceptance of people with disabilities. I only had my patterns of avoidance and my feelings of shame. We entered Lew and Jean's apartment at their greeting. Lew was standing balanced on his toes and tipped forward. Jean was in a wheelchair and had a handkerchief for her constant drool. When they excitedly began talking with Howard, and saying hello to me, I could barely understand what they were saying. I felt ashamed of my fear and my hearing incompetence. I admired his ease and camaraderie.

I don't remember if I gave them massage treatments that first time. What I do remember is asking Howard afterward whether he thought I could do this. He said, "If you want to get over your internalized oppression, just being around these very fine people will cure you."

He was right, and I took the challenge. I learned to understand their accents. I learned which of their muscles could relax with treatment and which did not. I witnessed them speaking up for themselves and asking for accommodations. I saw how they gently educated me. I learned not to be afraid of their faces. They did indeed teach me to love the visibly disabled part of myself, and I could feel the increased strength that brought me. I worked with them for ten years, and then mentored one of my students to take over, helping him to get through his fears to develop a rewarding relationship.

Because of what I learned through facing my internalized oppression, I was able to see it in others, such as my racialized clients, and help them to face and deal with it. I am grateful to Howard, who led the way, and to Lew and Jean, who taught me through their strength and vulnerability to be less afraid in the world.

The first verse in my song "Spirit Free" was inspired by Lew's story of growing up with a frightened mother. It was an angry song and quite sophisticated musically. I didn't sing it when we recorded it, because I wanted it to sound angry, and I knew I couldn't get there with my voice. I had my singing coach, Donna, sing it, and the song took off! Deep down, I must have felt ashamed that I couldn't do my own song justice. Still, it was strengthening to vividly name the disability shame and this helped me to let go of it.

> Born with Spirit free, though his body could not be
> He was his mother's shame; she kept him home bound and out of sight
> Afraid the neighbors would laugh outright, she never let him grow
> Before today, you've been hiding us away from the world, from ourselves
>
> Chorus
> In your guiltiness
> Don't you pity us
> Don't you glory us
> See us now for who we are

I continued to struggle with being a workaholic during my psycho-drama years. Some of this was because I needed the "repair" of long-term therapy with one therapist, which didn't come until later. However, in the process of dealing with my ancestry by putting them onstage, I discovered more about the pattern than I thought possible. Now I know that the influence of my mother's unacknowledged scoliosis made her want me to be successful at something. Her investment in my being a good worker and her fear of what the consequences might be from having an obvious facial disability made her discourage me from taking creative chances. Her fear fed into my own of not being wanted, and so I became addicted to people wanting me as a body worker, and I could not say no.

I didn't learn to see her love for me, because we had the trauma of the operation between us—I realize now that it was her trauma as well. It took me many years before I understood that I was using work to hide my feelings of musical inadequacy and being unwanted in general, which was directly connected to my operation and facial disability. I had to do many repair scenes on validating my beauty, my worthiness to receive attention, and the validity my musical capabilities before what now seem like realities finally sunk in.

Not only was I participating in psychodrama for my own healing, I was training at the Toronto Centre for Psychodrama to receive my certification as a psychodramatist. About halfway through my training, I identified that my hearing disability would be a big handicap in leading group psychodramas, as I could not hear everything (because there is often more than one person speaking at a time) and would lose the overview. That's what I understood then. Now I realize that I was also going into a trauma state (fight-or-flight) during the action phase of a drama because of the audio confusion and losing my thinking capacity. It was very frustrating, because I knew the theory and was good one-on-one, but I would lose focus (and feel the stress of triggers to the past) in groups because of conditions outside my control that were necessary to the whole experience—multiple voices speaking at the same time.

Eventually, I quit the training for a year (when I was at the last third) but was persuaded to come back by my trainer and to discover ways that would help me achieve the goal of being a director even with a disability. We devised several strategies: sometimes I would use a director's helper as an additional "ear"—someone who could hear in moments of noise and tell me what was said. Sometimes we would slow the action down or alert the actors to not speak all at once. This effort took an additional six years of training. The big payoff was that being aware and truthful about my disability helped me to stay calm and present in noisy situations.

This success enabled me to develop and teach a communications class at the Kikkawa school of massage, where I incorporated sociometric theory and role play. I hired my actor ex-boyfriend to help me create role plays of realistic clients with difficult situations for the students to hone their communication skills with. It was forward thinking of me to experiment with role play and made for a dynamic class. Subsequently, other massage schools based their communications/client management courses on mine. Now the use of role play is more mainstream, used in many professional training programs.

The Magraw Method had matured into a deep, flexible framework for facilitating healing, and my clients continued to have emotional releases thanks to metaphor and bodywork, and to develop secure relationships with me as their facilitator/healer. I continued to learn new practices all the time.

I developed my one-on-one skills by working with symbolic objects. Symbolic-object work involves choosing objects to represent goals, feelings, events, family members, friends, or parts of self. This representation outside yourself provides enough perspective (yes, I am in the safe present now) and safe emotional release (yes, someone is listening to me now) to stimulate new perspectives. What I understand now, through my study of the brain and trauma, is that stories stimulate the pre-frontal cortex. This is the area of the brain where we have the capacity to understand and choose what is good for us. My training and personal work in psychodrama helped me to choose what was good for me—and my music. The concept and practice of repair opened me up to the experience of getting help in unexpected ways.

I was part of an improv theater group, Sponte, comprising actors and therapists trying to bridge the gap between art and healing. We did music and sociodrama, in which the actors took stories and themes from the audience and did improvisations based on those stories. Developed alongside psychodrama, sociodrama was designed to wake up audiences to social issues. The group was a good creative support. I learned to be less inhibited in a performance setting and was inspired to write songs with socially conscious messages, which we sang in our performances. It was good to be part of a creative group, and it gave me collaboration skills that came in handy in co-writing songs a little further into my future.

Many songs are stories or parts of stories. Most songs have a beginning, middle, and end and lyrically need to support the emotional messages you convey to your audience. Sponte taught me how to do that, and the group experience decreased my shame of showing myself. My psychodrama experience was most instrumental in bringing my shame to light and healing it.

Shame and Its Consequences

The origins of shame are many and varied. It can emerge from sexual, verbal , physical abuse, neglect, unmet needs at any age, learning and school environments, bullying, disability, racism or classism, medical trauma and much more. My original shame came from being born 'different' at a time in society when disability was still a shameful thing.

Shame is a very sticky feeling state. It is static compared with grief, and so I would call it more of a mood than an emotion. One of my clients, a sexual-abuse survivor, visualized it as a bumpy field of tar. Often shame hides beneath well-designed coping mechanisms and only emerges at stressful times or with certain triggers. If we repress shameful feelings, they become more stuck. Shame in one area of my life often oozed into other areas—all on an unconscious level. The way out is facing shame with self-acceptance.

I have done many rounds of work on my shame. I first worked on the shame of having a facial disability, eventually owning my smile and not hiding my ear with my hair but wearing it up so all could see my difference. At this point, I thought I was done with shame, but alas, it was stickier and deeper than I could ever have guessed when I began my journey.

I felt shame about my first marriage, which was a co-dependent attempt to rescue a man with mental illness that mystified my family. I called it a "blooper" but never really discussed it in depth with them. At that time, I also had hidden shame about not going to college. Being in survival stress (lack of money or housing) helped hide that shame. I finally healed that by finding my career and teachers who told me that I had talent—all I needed was training and to learn to trust my motives around helping people. I had more bumps to go over, but I was well launched on a shame-free work front.

I felt shame around losing my voice for the second time in the nineties. My solution was an action: have other people demo my songs and focus my attention on the songwriting. This worked to some degree but the shame of not singing my own songs ate away at my musical soul. I acted out my shame by breaking off from the people who loved me (my husband and my coach, several teachers) and chasing after unavailable men and various musicians.

A Practical Approach to Shame

One of the keynotes of shame is its power to make us hide from ourselves and others. If our primary emotions have not been recognized by our early caregivers, then they often get tangled up with shame. These steps are designed to gradually reveal and release the sources of shame in the body and mind:

1. First, with someone you trust who will not give you advice or push you too soon to forgiveness of self or other, name the shame. The person could be a close friend, partner, or therapist. Groups are good for this too.

2. Discharge the emotions connected with shame through bodywork or other techniques. Give this step the "right" amount of time. For some people, spending time in the discomfort with a witness to ground them helps in the working through of it. For others, it may be too intense to do more than simply name the shame. Choose what is right for you.

3. Using your imagination, construct a repair scene of a shameful moment. For example, if you were shamed by a teacher when answering a question and your schoolmates continued to tease you, which led to a habit of not speaking up in groups, you could imagine another adult arriving on the classroom scene and saying, "Everyone is trying here. That is what is important. We each have different talents and some people need more time to learn. Will you [the teacher] apologize to this child and refrain from speaking your impatience in that way? Let's figure out how to help everyone learn what is difficult for them."

    You could go on to imagine how your life would have been different at key points if that early repair had happened. If the shame feeling is too intense, tell the story in the third person, as if you were watching a movie, and spend little time on the incident and more time on the repair.

4. If it is right for you—and it isn't for everyone—begin to use the word forgive, with self-acceptance of the parts of you that need more healing before they are ready. Sometimes using the word understand is less loaded than forgive. There is no "right" timeframe for forgiveness. It's important not to push it but rather wait until it can be naturally honest. Or decide that it is not the way for you.

5. Take any actions necessary, such as acknowledgements or apologies to yourself and/or others (as in the AA concept of making amends).

When I lost my voice for the third time, it was still difficult to name and deal with my shame. Because I did not have an accurate diagnosis, I became depressed and avoided musical situations and friends in the business. The only project I allowed myself was my guitar-based recording *Everybody Has the Gift*. It was a hopeful project, and in my mind, I produced it to accompany workshops I would be doing on healing. But I was suffering shame and its consequences, including the grief at loss of opportunity, which at that time meant working too much and becoming isolated in a "small corner" of my possible universe. I only did a few workshops with the CD.

Finally, as my voice began healing again, I realized all the things that not singing represented to me: not being part of life, not being attractive, not being successful, and not being wanted except as a helper. Through this naming, I could feel the depth of the angry/hurt shame. It was a relief. On an ancestral level, I felt betrayed by my mother's shame patterns and secrecy. Eventually, through therapy, meditation, and vocal healing, I could forgive my mother and myself for the acting out both she and I had done as a consequence of shame.

Through reading my mother's family history, I came to understand that her family was steeped in shame, and she had carried a heavy load. I truly wish that she could have had the same opportunities as I, such as good therapy. She lived out her mother's shame as I lived out hers. Secrecy was the habit that became the binding. It was hard to learn to tell the truth to myself, but once I began, it was such a relief that I never turned back. With perseverance, I searched for a way out of the secrecy/ shame bind. However, I also spent many years searching outside myself, trying so hard to be a "good seeker" that I would often miss the point.

Mark Wolynn writes:

> "The great teachers know. The truly great ones don't care whether you believe in their teachings or not. They present a truth and then leave you with yourself to discover your own truth.... They understand that where we come from affects where we go, and that what sits unresolved in our past influences our present. They know our parents are important, regardless of whether they are good at parenting or not. There's no way around it: the family story is our story.... Regardless of the story we have about them, our parents cannot be expunged or ejected from us. They are in us and we are a part of them—even if we have never met them."[3]

Now I can see how my shame about needing more attention from my mother, or whoever represented her in the present, was tied into my shame about my face, which was tied into my shame about losing my voice, which was tied into my shame about sexual acting out, which was tied into my shame about my desperate need for touch, which was tied into my body shame, which prevented me from receiving touch.

Self-forgiveness is an antidote to shame, but it has its own timing. It cannot be forced, much as we try. It comes through honesty of feeling and fact. Once the whole truth is told, it comes naturally. However, it is possible to practice forgiveness (and necessary for some people) by honoring (accepting) the resistance to forgiving and observing the consequences of holding on to bitter feelings. Reading my letters and journals has allowed me to see the scope of my shame, but also to see the striving for healing that I consistently engaged in, however clumsy and misguided it sometimes was. I feel tenderness for my confused younger self and grateful for the clarity of my present self.

A Family Repair

After my mother's passing, and with the truth of my early years unfolding, I let go even more. I began to take better care of my appearance. I began to question some of the ideas I had been raised with. I began to wonder why I didn't have more contact with my uncles—my father's brothers, Uncle Dick and Uncle Chuck. These were the same uncles who were doctors, who had wished they could have done more for me when I had my first operation. Uncle Dick was a well-known doctor and psychiatrist in Minnesota. Uncle Chuck was a respected analyst/psychiatrist in Boston. I decided to write them a letter.

I asked them what they had thought and felt at the time of my operation. They were honest and eloquent validating my courage and regretting the difficult disaster of my operation. They had both opposed it and let my parents know that. They were begging them to get a second opinion, but my parents were too proud and convinced that they should take advantage of the special state-paid offer for the operation. When my uncles heard the news that my facial nerve had been partially severed, they were very angry, especially Uncle Chuck. And though they respected my mother, they also said that she was a prickly and defensive woman, and they didn't know how to handle her to get to me. They apologized.

I felt so relieved. At least they had noticed and thought about me. I had grown up with the impression that no one really noticed what I had lost—my smile, voice and my well-being—or how lost I was in a social sense.

In 2004, we had a family reunion. I had written a poem and was determined to show it to my uncles, even though I was nervous. We were gathering in Vancouver with about fifty members of my father's side of the family. My sisters, aunts, and uncles, and all the cousins were there. We took over the hotel at Harrison Hot Springs for a weekend in July.

The poem I had written for my uncles was called "The Elephant." I gave it to them early in the weekend gathering:

Dear Mama,
There is an elephant in our house
And yet you pretend all is normal
I am confused but want to call out
What is this elephant doing here? It's too big
I am scared. Am I the elephant?
I wish we could have talked more

The next day, we were all assembled for breakfast in the large airy room of the hotel restaurant. My uncle Chuck dinged a glass, and when he had our attention, he said, "I think we should talk about the elephant in the room, which has been here for years. That elephant is the circumstances surrounding Kristi's disability and operation." I was stunned, though in retrospect it seems so obvious a thing to do. At that point, I had kept the "no talk" rule begun by my mother for forty years.

I was in a daze, but the conversation went on for a good while with everyone finding out what had happened, guessing why it had happened, and contextualizing it with a good deal of family history. I received many hugs. During the rest of that day, conversations kept popping up about unspoken events in others' lives. Talking about my experience openly had enlivened us as a group. We need to feel recognized to come out of the isolation trauma produces, and I certainly felt recognized by my family that day. Finally breaking the silence was revolutionary for me, and very healing. I wrote another poem, this one called "The Deepening":

> Dear Daddy and Mama,
> I wish you could have felt this unfolding
> of understanding
> Like a rosebud opening
> Spiral petals leading us to the center of our hearts
> Where many sorrows had lain unspoken
> Now washed with tears
> We all begin to shine
> Deep in the bosom of family

This event created a big shift in my ability to advocate for myself from then on. My sisters began to ask if I was in the right location to be able to hear, and to touch me if they could tell I hadn't heard something. I felt more integrated into group settings and was better able to acknowledge my early neglect. I never went back to the "hiding," because I was less dissociated in general and more open to being loved. I had more mountains to climb, but the triumph of climbing this one was sweetly satisfying.

Innate Intelligence Letter

Dear Kristi,

You have been exploring your extroverted self in a most appropriate way. Psychodrama provides a structure for your stories to come out. It provides the magic of metaphor that will enliven your song lyrics. It gives you the concept of repair that is strengthening you and helping you to build on the good parts of your past. You will soon birth yourself from the cocoon of your history and arrive at your "place." Here, life will console you.

You will survive the loss of your father, your abortion memories, and the co-dependent relationships. You will be a stronger person. You will overcome the disappointment of how your disability interferes with your progress as a group leader and a promoter of your mind-body method. Remember that your envy of others will dissolve in the many tears that you will courageously let flow. Your history will take on a softer feeling. A unique niche is awaiting your butterfly self!

You are on your path. Practice forgiving your mistakes and facing your fears. Learn to be even more open to collabora-tion—it is one of your best talents.

Psychodrama will loosen the burden of family history and the shame of disability. Underneath, you will find gems of songs and lovely flows of creativity.

With encouragement,

Innate Intelligence

Techniques for Keeping the Body in Mind

Metaphor and the Body

If we have become separated from our body's reality, learning how to follow body sensations is an important step in keeping the body in mind. These sensations teach us to know our emotions, our body's needs, and how emotional, physical, and sometimes spiritual needs interact. There are many types of body sensations we are hardwired for, including touch, temperature, pain, and balance. Proprioception is the inherent sense of the body's position and motion in space. Interoception is the ability to read and interpret sensations arising from within the body. Metaphor is the tool that I use to translate these sensations into meaning. For example, a heavy sensation can become "heavy like a rock" and then become "the heavy rock is how I felt when [name the event]."

Techniques like this one can be found in many disciplines. What is important in using this one is to stick to your preferred choice of words and to relax into the flow, whatever speed it is. Honor your own way, your own timing of metaphor in the body. If at any point your sensations become overwhelming or too anxiety producing, pause and ask yourself if there is an easier way to do it, or seek professional help. Maybe do a "Stop Action" technique to determine the right amount of stimulus (see chapter 5's "Techniques for Keeping the Body in Mind"). It is possible to become hyper-focused on sensations, in which case shift yourself to a more balanced place with a familiar activity.

What to Do

To begin, find a quiet room or put on some music that appeals to you, then lie down or sit in a comfortable chair. Close or half close your eyes and let your attention slowly shift focus from the outer environment to the inner world of sensation. Place your hands on your body during the metaphoric flow (I'll explain in a moment what I mean by that) to increase it or to steady you through the process.

Begin by identifying comfortable or uncomfortable sensations in various regions of your body. When you find one you want to focus on, gently inquire, "What is this sensation like?" Or "What do I see or hear here?" After a pause, in which metaphors may emerge (the metaphoric flow), encourage more of them with questions such as:

» What is the shape, color, texture, sound, or word associated with it?

» How does it affect my posture? What is this posture like?

» If this sensation/posture were an animal, which would it be?

» If it were a plant, which would it be?

After developing a metaphoric flow, you can begin to ask questions such as, "What emotions are associated with these metaphors? What thoughts? What memories?"

Sometimes you can encourage the flow by imagining you are on a journey or inside a fairy tale. Just keep saying, "What happens next?" When you end the process or the flow stops, ask, "What is the meaning of this story?" There is no particular destination that you have to get to. Simply being with your body sensation and giving meaning to that sensation will develop your body-sensing skills and elicit insights and information from your body for the benefit of your life. One of the main benefits is entering the world of body sensation. It is a wondrous and exciting place and can lead to epiphanies. You can return to normal, thinking consciousness refreshed. To finish your body journey, place your hands on your body and project a feeling of gratefulness to your body. If you are dealing with issues of illness or disability, try projecting a feeling of forgiveness to your body.

Music facilitates a metaphoric flow. Try imagining a path toward and into your body sensation while listening to music you like. Is the path in the woods, across a field, or up a mountain? Use the rhythm to take you deeper inside your body. Then anchor (in a "felt" way) what your body has told you about, using or speaking a key word, a mantra, or something else.

Complete the session by expressing something about your journey in a medium such as song or poetry, gestural movement or dance, drawing, or something unique to you. This will solidify and anchor the body-sensation experience.

What to Expect

I have facilitated metaphoric body journeys with many people and most often they are a safe and fun way to engage with the body. However, many people worry that they will produce a blank when they try to find a metaphor. The event of no metaphors is unusual. But, if no metaphors come forward, it's important not to put yourself down. Do not push. There is probably a good reason for the blank. You may need the safety of another person with you or a professional to help analyze a possible mind-body disconnection. Sometimes the process backfires and produces anxiety. In this case, shift out of the flow and come into conversational mode or do another activity, such as the following technique.

Picture This (Symbolic Object Work)

As children we have done this kind of representing many times. It is natural. Symbolic-object work is a process whereby we use an object—a stuffed bear, piece of art, rock, driftwood, picture, doll, cushion, scarf—to represent something else. This "something else" can be connected with our trauma or it can be connected with our resources (a trusted person, animal, spiritual teacher). In a session, it is often good to connect with both for the purpose of balance.

The object can represent an inner energetic state, a part of self, another person, a place, an animal, or an event. When we represent on the outside something from inside, we gain perspective, insight, increased safety and stability, and control over flashbacks and triggers.

By choosing multiple objects and observing the spatial relationships between them, we can understand more about how close or distant we are to things they represent. When we choose an object to represent a positive message, it becomes a "self-object" (a parental or spiritual substitute). A resource we can become attached to. This resource can then be used for self-soothing at times of distress, for example, the way children use their teddy bears.

When the object represents something we want more distance from, it brings a vivid reality to the unwanted thing, makes it easier to "unchoose it". Engaging the body, the senses (sight, texture, and smell), and the imagination encourages both the right and left brain and the front and back brain to engage and gives us a stronger sense of what is "self" and what is "not self".

If the technique triggers too much performance anxiety or if you do not like to work with different parts of yourself, it is best to not use it.

What to Do

Choose an object that "feels like" the event, person, or part of self you have chosen to work on. It is important that you get up and walk around, pick up the object that your body wants, feel its texture and observe its color and shape. Then describe or write down what it is about the object that reminds you of the situation. Make connections between things in your life and the object's qualities. This will make the choice of object and the situation clearer. For example, you might choose a sharply pointed rock to represent an argument with a friend and realize that it was the sharp tone of voice that bothered you the most. You might choose a soft piece of cloth to represent the comfort you felt with your mother.

Sometimes there is more than one aspect to an event. Pick objects for each aspect but no more than about six unless you are doing a timeline (see below). Each object should receive a short, vivid name that is easy to remember ("that crystal is my intellect; that shell is my defenses; that stick is my ex-partner"). Next, arrange the objects in a way that represents the relationships between them. Closeness and distance are particularly important. Ask yourself: "Is this close enough? Distant enough?" Remember to leave silence, space, and time for your instincts. Let answers "arrive" from your body.

Creating a picture with your objects and reflecting on it may be enough for you. If you want to continue, there are several options:

» Imagine yourself in the role of each object, holding it as you describe what it is like to take on the qualities of that object.

» Play with the arrangement and see how you feel about different possibilities.

» Generate a dialogue between two objects either in first person, in role-play as the objects, or in third person, moving and touching the objects.

» Represent a dream image and use the object to interpret the meaning of the dream.

» Use objects to represent images from a visualization. For example, a safe place or a vision of the future.

» Choose several positive messages, meaningful people, and qualities of self and represent them with objects.

» Bookend another activity, such as movement or meditation, by using the objects as a starting image and then returning to them at the end for any additional insights.

When you are finished, de-role each object by identifying it in its original form, saying out loud, "This is now just a [name the object]" and placing it back where you found it. This step closes the piece and is especially important if you have opened up something emotional. Also, if you use objects from your home, you may not always want them to be symbols. If you have decided to use an object as a resource for soothing, do not de-role it.

What to Expect

Symbolic-objects work is a good way to get to know yourself. You may feel more relaxed because of the emotional regulation achieved by representing. You may feel comforted by the objects you have chosen. Comfort objects help children (and our inner child) to regulate their nervous system when the caregiver is not present to do it (think teddy bear). You may feel anxious about matters you have brought partially or wholly into consciousness. This is not unusual, and it is okay. If this happens, you can bring in your loving witness (see "The Loving Face" exercise in chapter 7's "Techniques for Keeping the Body in Mind"), ask your body what it needs, or seek a practitioner who can help you.

Symbolic Object Timeline

This use of symbolic objects can be a good way of getting perspective on your life or on a particular issue as it played out. If you're doing an exploration of a trauma, identify positive resources along the way as well as the painful events. Though you can do this on your own, it can be richer and is sometimes essential to be done with a therapist or close friend.

What to Do

Choose a beginning and end of your timeline and objects to represent these in the same way as above. Then go through the important events in between the two points and represent them—not too many and not too few. You can always add as you go along. After laying out the objects, write or talk about them. You can choose to do this in chronological order or not as your intuition guides you. You may become overwhelmed by information. If so, return at another time. This is okay. Any amount that you do at a time is fine. It is better to put the emphasis on feeling rather than completing it all at once.

To close the work, go to the object that represents your positive present self, look back at the rest of the timeline, and make an over-view comment.

What to Expect

You may have insights and a sense of narrative flow. You may feel stuck, in which case you may want to try movement or bodywork as a warm up. You may feel emotional about certain times or objects you choose. If it seems boring or uninspiring, then this technique is probably not the "way in" to your unconscious.

Decreasing Inner Conflict by Talking to Myself

It is common to have self-critical, non-productive, second-guessing talks with ourselves. These "critiques" cause stress, body pain, and procrastination. In psychodrama, I learned a better kind of inner dialogue—one where fears and traumas could be revealed and solutions found so my life could move on. The different voices within are called "parts" and often represented by objects, although the exercise can be done entirely as a visualization.

What to Do

The first step is to achieve a vivid naming of the parts of self that are in conflict. Using objects or visualization, name between two and four parts (any more than this becomes unwieldy). Then develop a guide or teacher part that can give perspective during the discussion. Next, give each part time to speak out its point of view, including its feelings. Try not to interrupt yourself with comments from other parts. You may need to do several rounds of this step. If there are two parts in acute conflict, alternate between them to uncover any ghosts (parental or other figures) that may be carried by the part of self. Once all that is done, go access your guide for advice. Having heard the advice, go back to the roles of the conflicting parts and assess if they are satisfied. It is best if the solution brings some satisfaction to all "parts."

What to Expect

When inner conflict is resolved, stress symptoms are often relieved—body pains and inflammation disperse, and we feel calmer. It is easier to find a course of action. If you get stuck in the "parts" dialogue, you may need professional help. Sometimes it is easier to keep track of the themes if someone is helping you. Doing this exercise in written form can also be helpful.

Four Corners for Emotional Intelligence

In my definition, emotions are mind-body energies that move us. Feeling states and moods may not. It is important to know the difference and to have a centered place from which to observe emotional phenomena and to return to after an emotional release.

This exercise is designed to do that. The place at the center is for grounding in the present—my twenty-eight-year-old definition of grounding is "a physical sensation in my body, often a pleasant warmth, a feeling of my Chi dropping that is a round feeling, a sense of rhythm and slowness in the way I do things, a better sense of priorities and a cessation of worrisome thoughts." We can then be in a place from which to negotiate with defense systems (which most of us have around one emotion or another). If you have a chronic flooding of emotion, if you are dissociated, in a flashback, or if there is a need for calmness and struc-ture (healthy suppression), it may be a better choice to work with a professional or wait until you're more stable.

What to Do

In a good-sized room, designate each of the corners to one of the primary emotions: fear, sadness, anger, and joy/love. There are many combinations and variations of emotions, but these are the main "movers." Place a cushion at the center of the room to represent your version of grounding in the present, Innate Intelligence, Eagle's Eye, frontal lobe, and so on. Then choose one emotion (the easiest) and begin to explore it with gestures, movement, and sound. For example, anger might be stamping, fear might be shaking, sadness might be moaning or sobbing, joy might be laughing. Sometimes you have to fake it to make it happen. If you feel resistance or lack of engagement, step to the side and have a discussion with your "center place" about what the matter is. Depending on the outcome, either go back to that emotional corner or move to the next. Repeat with each of the corners, and when you are done, go to your center place and ask yourself, "What have I learned about my emotions? What have I learned about my defenses?"

This technique can be deepened by doing it with a facilitator or in a group setting.

What to Expect

Your body may feel more relaxed. You may feel more energized. You may have many insights about your history with each emotion. It is good to take notes on what you discover. You may feel more agitated. If this is the case, try taking a walk or doing something that you know is soothing to your nervous system.

Chapter 9
Riding the Brainwave:
A Sea Change

At the heart of listening
Music changes everything
And comes alive in our body
The art of listening is like peeling an onion, unfurling a sail, the sun opening the petals of a rose. There are layers of effort releasing spirals of energy that circle to reveal hidden truths about the one listened to and the listener. I have tried to teach the art of listening with ears, with hands, with eyes, and with heart. Have I been successful? Only further listening will tell.

—Haiku by Kristi Magraw/Robin Freeman

When my body hurt, I listened. I tried to pay attention to all the levels of messages—from the mechanical to the traumatic to the ancestral to the spiritual. The pains in my tissues were good guides to truth telling. My body wouldn't stop hurting until I found my truth and acted from it. It was a gradual process; there were no miracles, only solutions. In the nineties, I was realizing that the connection between what I called "brain level" work and trauma therapy was essential. Neuroplasticity was a term not yet in use, but I wondered why some people could change easier than others, and I noticed some changes were more permanent than others. There was no one to guide me in this intuition, but through a psychodrama colleague, I heard about The Listening Centre.

Going to The Listening Centre in 1996 and 1997 changed my life and my relationship to my disability. I began to understand the brain effects of having only one ear, and the mechanical problems that came with ear strain and bad sound. In those years, I was still deeply involved in therapy groups and spiritual pursuits, but the physical and physiological pieces of the puzzle became the most essential. What was so life-changing was, first of all, being recognized and allowing myself to be seen. The staff recognized me, named my mechanical symptoms, and explained that what I was dealing with was common. If it's precise (not just a dismissive "everyone feels that"), being seen and told you are one of many goes a long way toward healing. My allowing myself to be seen was a sign of progress along the Help Curve.

My music motivated me to stick with it. I wanted my voice back, and I wanted it to be reliable so I could make my art, which was also my primary way of self-therapizing, expressing, and soothing.

I couldn't figure out why my singing voice would randomly come and go, which had been the case for almost three decades. It was bad magic that my voice left and good magic that it came back. No one knew that I felt as if I had lost something as important as one of the other senses. In an interview following her high-profile loss of her singing voice for a period of seven years, Shania Twain put it well: "I think of singing as a sense like hearing or sight. I was grieving. It was a real loss."[1]

I resonated with her analogy, and I remembered a less than helpful ENT, who had said to me, "Well, you can talk. We only treat people who can't talk. You are okay; just don't sing." His confirmation of my invisibility had made my heart shrivel and my dreams shake on their vine.

Who Will Listen?

In 1996, when I first walked through The Listening Centre doors, I was isolated and desperate, not sure that anyone or anything would be able to help me. My Eustachian tubes were swollen and plugged as if I had a very bad head cold, making the world seem far away. I didn't know why, and I couldn't get them to unplug. I was used to not hearing through my left ear, but I couldn't hear from my right ear either! It felt like I was in a giant bubble of cotton batting. At the time, no one in the medical profession could advise me on this condition. I went to several ENTs and they all said, "We don't have a good solution for Eustachian tube problems." I had difficulty projecting my speaking voice and sang with a shaky strained sound. My promising start as a songwriter was at a standstill. My existence seemed jerky and dissatisfying.

I had been putting off going to The Listening Centre. I wanted to wait until after I got a hearing-aid implant, thinking that it made sense to go there after achieving as much hearing as possible in my left ear. I'd had disappointing experiences with the hearing-aid implant. I had used the implant in musical situations—bombarding my ear and brain with sounds, thinking that it would stimulate my musical abilities, but instead they were getting worse. Now I know that this was because there was an overload of low-range sounds and a deficit of high range entering the left side of my head. This stimulated my survival system connections in the limbic area of the brain, bringing on a nervous state instead of making connections to and within the musical area of the brain. That was a failed experiment, to put it mildly.

On a sunny afternoon in March 1996, I showed up to The Listening Centre anyway, with hope that there was something they could do for me. As it turned out, there was. Although it was no panacea, the treatments there did help me, and I returned for boosts over twelve years.

The Listening Centre

The Listening Centre is a private clinic in Toronto, established in 1978. Paul Madaule is the director. His approach is based on the work of French ENT Dr. Alfred Tomatis, who found that receptive and expressive communication, attention span, learning ability, social behavior, self-regulation, activity level, motor function and coordination, and musical capacity, especially singing, are all related to how we listen. Tomatis, the son of an opera singer, developed his approach as an effort to help professional singers (including his father) in Paris. He formulated the theory that many vocal problems were really hearing problems. With the Tomatis Method, or Audio-Psycho-Phonology (APP), he made a major distinction between hearing and listening. While hearing is the passive, involuntary function of sound perception, listening is active and voluntary. When well-developed or well-trained, the listening function allows us to focus on the sound information we need and leave out, or protect ourselves, from those sounds we don't want to hear. His theory that the voice only produces what the ear hears is the basis of his research and his method.

———————

Recognition and Revelation

I had my preliminary interview with Paul Madaule, director of The Listening Centre. He told me about the physically, mentally, and emotionally draining effects of too much low-range and not enough high-range sound. The list of these effects validated my experience in the world—musically frustrated, agitated, obsessive, lacking a feeling of contentment, tired, depressed, and perceiving myself as disconnected. He told me I couldn't do the program until my right ear cleared by at least fifty percent. After this stunning recognition of my reality, I was able to make headway on my worst symptom, the swollen Eustachian tubes, with homeopathy and emotional-release work. I was motivated to do this work. I wanted my musical voice completely available to me.

Finally, the swelling and plugging had receded enough to proceed with my first fifteen days at The Listening Centre. The Listening Test—a modified version of a standard hearing test—at the center was similar to the ones I had had in many dark and claustrophobic sound cubicles. The beeps, the straining to hear, the embarrassment of knowing I was supposed to be hearing something and not, and the frustration of the white noise used to mask the sound in my right ear so the left ear would hear on its own were all familiar.

The difference was in the person who administered it and the careful analysis made afterward. Sophie, the listening therapist, was reassuring and informative. After some other coordination and lateral-dominance tests and careful interviewing about how I perceived different things, she showed me a graph of my hearing curve and said, "Ideally it should be a smooth curve, lower on the low and high-range sounds and higher [meaning better hearing] in the conversational range." The graph was meant to help me understand how I perceive the world through my ears and what kinds of problems this was causing in my life. As I looked at the dents in my right-ear graph and the deep valleys, even canyons, in the left-ear graph, I felt my heart sinking. "Can it ever change?" I asked.

"Yes, to some degree," said Sophie. "That is the goal of doing the listening-training program—to help the ear and the brain become more coordinated and developed in areas that they haven't been. That may be reflected in a change in the curve."

My heart jumped up with hope. I visualized a smooth curve and a glorious rescue.

This fantasy was partially disappointed when I had my second interview with Paul. He said that the program would not be able to help my left ear, because there was not enough hearing ability in it, but that they would work on my right ear to try to help me feel more balanced. This might result in a smoothing out of the curve in the right ear.

He explained that my hearing loss had impaired my listening ability, and as a result, I had a lack of brain development for certain musical abilities. While I knew that my hearing affected my music, I had very little understanding of the role the brain played in that relationship. I knew the brain was the source of much magic, but as a body worker, I had a lot more experience with the nervous system than with the brain itself. This was during the late nineties, before the ground-breaking research about neuroplasticity was released and before the boom in pop-psychology books on the subject of brain function, attention, and other brain patterns.

Referring to Sophie's notes, he pointed out that I also had "vestibular coordination" problems. He said, "The vestibular system is part of the inner ear, and it controls body movement, balance, and the position of your body in space. This would explain your difficulty in hand and eye coordination. An undeveloped Vestibular system also makes sports and musical instruments hard to negotiate and can make dancing and social interaction frustrating."

"That's me," I said. "I always wondered why I couldn't catch a ball, and it explains that jerky feeling I live with as well as my frustrations with playing and singing." He identified that my listening curve indicated some difficulty in expressing myself, whether it's emotions or creativity.

This was crucial new information for me. A problem of emotional expression not based in trauma but in listening function. According to my own process of discernment about whether a symptom is mechanical pain or mind-body pain, I realized that this mechanical blockage was related to my frustration as a songwriter.

I was overwhelmed by the accuracy of what Paul was saying about my experience without even knowing me. Being recognized led to personal revelations about my challenges as a singer and songwriter. Looking back, I can see how important the validation of my reality was to my healing. I now believe that, in addition to asking about someone's mental/emotional reality, it is important we ask about the way they perceive and comprehend the world. The validation (the naming) of my sensory reality was making me feel a part of the world again. I was relieved by the realistic approach he was taking to what could improve and eager to try.

Naming

The first naming I had was from The Listening Centre. The second was "vocal tension dystonia sometimes called spasmodic vocal dysphonia." Having a name for a problem I had struggled with for years helped me to explain to people why I couldn't sing and being able to talk about it more easily increased my sense of belonging. The speech therapist who gave me the diagnosis had only a few techniques, and I wasn't aware of a dystonia community yet, so I was still left somewhat puzzled as to techniques that would help it, all of which came much later.

The next naming was Microtia (one undeveloped ear) that came through my friendship with Kristy, my young kindred spirit, who also had been born with Microtia. I was introduced to Kristy through a mutual friend, and when we met, I gasped in recognition! There in front of me was my mirror image—with different colored hair and younger but the same asymmetrical smile, droopy eye, and her version of a small left ear. We stared in amazement and then began to share our stories. Kristy's sister had dug out the name Microtia from the internet. No doctor or audiologist had named it for us. Once I had this name, I could find others who had it, but most importantly, instead of insulting myself: "Well, I have one bad ear." "This one doesn't work right" and worst, "That's my deformed ear," I could now talk respectfully about my ear.

Kristy confirmed the progression of brain tiredness that a one-eared person has: Entering a noisy room, everything is chaos, then that progresses to straining and not being able to talk much, then a spacey feeling sets in. Finally, tiredness takes over and you cannot stay awake. It was good to have that common event confirmed. She also was trained as a massage therapist. We clicked immediately and began to do exchanges, finding that we had better intuition and understanding of each other's scar tissue than any previous healer. And just the fact of knowing there was someone else in the world with similar trauma calmed me in a major way.

Transformation

It was time to begin. Because I only had normal hearing in one ear, I had to have special headphones so that the sound could reach me through bone conduction on the top of my head as well as through the headphones to my right ear. This arrangement would stimulate both sides of the brain. The way in which I was presented these phones and the general lack of shame in the atmosphere of the centre made me feel special, not different and not a 'problem.' This was a repair experience for my childhood shame around my disability.

The adult listening room had several people already hooked up to audio systems designed to filter and adjust the sound in three ways. One progressively emphasizes the high end of the sound spectrum, which helps with discriminating between tones and auditory processing. Two, the "gating," stimulates the middle and inner ear by alternately bringing the music from background to foreground and from low to high frequency, which makes the tiny muscles inside the ear contract and release, helping with their functions (regulating the loudness and adjusting the eardrum). Three, the balance function, modifies the volume in the left ear, shifting it more to the right ear to stimulate the language center on the left side of the brain.

I was told that this program of sound would feed my brain with "good sound" and help balance out my bad experience of the low-range sounds that I had been subjected to with the hearing-aid implant. After this "feeding" I would begin the active phase of the program in the second

fifteen days. So, I hooked up and began to listen. The soothing sounds of
Mozart filled my head and resonated in my body. Suddenly, I felt how
truly tired I was. Being in the world with one ear is an experience of
strain and struggle. My Listening Centre experience let me admit how
exhausted I had become.

With headphones, the sound was close. I didn't have to strain to hear
and the listening therapists were attentive to get the volume just right.
Just before I closed my eyes in a deep sleep, I looked around and saw the
art hanging on the walls. There was a whole range of images and many
pictures with Listening Centre themes—headphones, reading, and so on.
I thought to myself that I'd like to draw a picture too.

I don't remember much about the first fifteen days except sleeping,
sometimes having irrational bouts of irritation, and drawing pictures
filled with color. Halfway through the program, my Eustachian tubes had
a major clearing. After a session toward the end of the fifteen days, I had
a sensation in my chest of opening and warming. (This was the effect
of the improving function of ears/brain on my vagus and facial nerves,
which are closely connected to ear function.) I felt so nurtured that The
Listening Centre became like a "good parent." The music was like arms
holding me, and in my interviews, the precise questions they asked me
regarding my perceptions were those of a truly listening parent.

Learning to Like My Voice

The first active session was humming. I was taken upstairs and plugged in
with the addition of a microphone set in front of me. I was instructed to
take a well-balanced posture, similar to an Alexander posture, where each
body part is aligned and supporting the part above it. Then I listened to
a monk humming a few notes of a Gregorian chant, and in the space
following, I would repeat what he had sung. Both my own voice and that
of the monk were filtered, gated, and balanced to achieve the listening-
training effect. Shortly after I began, I realized that, other than when
I could hear my voice from outside my head, as in a recording studio,
I had always hated the sound of my voice, especially my singing voice.
When Paul told me that this was a normal experience for someone with
my ear/brain pattern, I had an insight: This hatred had been blocking

me. I hated to tape record and listen to myself, even though I had been instructed to do so by my teachers. This reluctance to listen and my fear that I sounded as awful to everyone else as I did to myself had stopped my development as a musician. The humming aspect of the program was filled with emotion—despair, anger, and on a good day, hope. Several times I left the center crying. Luckily, I knew my own emotional process and knew I was working out musical traumas from my past.

Further into the active sessions, I noticed that my voice lessons were getting easier. I could also hear more instruments when I listened to music. Before the program, I had mainly listened to the vocals or just the rhythm. Now I could hear the bass and keyboards as well. My experience of music became broader. Before I went to The Listening Centre, visual art did not interest me. Now I was drawing pictures and began to notice other people's drawings in a new way. The colors seemed more vivid. I began to enjoy art of all kinds. My senses were opening up. My speaking voice was softening, and friends noticed that it sounded friendlier and more resonant. "You seem more relaxed," they would say. I was sleeping better and experiencing fewer symptoms of inflammation.

The next big shift I experienced was that fall at a song-writing festival where I was performing (my song had been a semi-finalist in the song-writing contest). Though the conditions were bad—I was disappointed that I had not won the contest; I was alone, and I had spent more money than I should have—I felt a new level of confidence while performing one evening. Suddenly, it was fun. My fingers knew where to go, my voice stayed strong, and I could focus on the audience and my playing at the same time. My shoulder, which had been hurting on the drive there, was pain-free. I had succeeded in expressing what was inside me.

No Miracles, Just Solutions

I followed the centre's normal schedule for boosts: yearly five-day listening programs designed to remind my listening ability and my brain to stay on the new track. I soon discovered that listening curves and brain patterns have considerable inertia.

Before my next scheduled boost, I noticed that my symptoms got worse. I was nervous and mildly depressed. Musically, I was going downhill. Paul mentioned when he saw my face that it had "fallen." He surmised that this might be caused by the effort of straining to hear—an activity that affects the stirrup muscle, which is stimulated by a branch of the facial nerve (the one that was cut). He said there might be a negative feedback loop between my ear and face. I took this as a cue and began to let sound come to me. It created a whole new perspective on the world of sound and was much less effort.

After the boost, I improved on all fronts. This surprised me. I had done no biographical or emotional therapeutic work, yet I felt happy and connected. I realized how much my listening problem, an inner disconnection, had contributed to my isolation. As Paul put it, "The problem is the faulty wiring that goes to your right brain. It lacks development because of the lack of stimulation through your left ear. The emotional and musical functions of your brain are there, but you have had only intermittent access to them." This accurately described my experience of my voice, both spoken and sung, and the pattern of my relationships, which manifested as difficulty in bonding. I often felt on the outside or as if no one noticed me.

I could see how my perceptual disability had affected my consciousness, my emotional and social functions, and my personality. I knew it was a tough road, but I was determined to learn how to bond and to enjoy music.

After The Listening Centre, I began to protect and pay careful attention to my left ear. I was fitted for a musician's earplug, which I wore in noisy environments, and I made sure to rest after occasions where there was noise from more than one source or very loud sounds. I refrained from judging myself for being extra-tired after parties or performances.

I also noticed several things that proved to me that the program was bettering my ability to bond. I was able to ask family and friends for help and attention in a much more direct way. I also had more calmness and patience when I was working with clients, and my friends said I was more open. I felt love coming toward me and mine going out to them on a much more regular basis. I was able to bond with the children of several of my friends. It was a whole new world of relating.

The Power of Knowledge

I continued to make progress with my music, feeling competent as a guitarist and gradually improving with my voice. As my singing teacher said, "Now you can hear when it becomes uncoordinated and fix it. That was not the case before." Performing alone and with others became fun instead of a struggle. I could tell when I was becoming overloaded with low-frequency sounds and knew what to do about it. I could feel my voice in my body. I became comfortable in social situations and didn't try to force myself to hear if conditions were bad. Allowing the sound to come to me, I was much less anxious. I often felt that heart-warming sensation that told me I was emotionally unified.

There was still room for improvement. I was not always able to hear or compose melodies as readily as I would like to. I guessed that this was because melody is a function of the right brain and there was still that tenuousness of connection to a creative flow. I compared myself with my friend Suzie, a professional singer, whose melodies flowed out constantly, although she had a hard time finding the words. This difference made us good songwriting partners.

In my later boost sessions, I was struck with how quickly I could feel the positive results. I felt a deepening and calming of my interactions with others after the boost. As I was discussing my struggles with my voice with Paul, he said something that struck a chord. "It amazes me how persistent you are with something as difficult as your voice. Maybe you have an innate sense that working with your voice is what keeps the rest of you healthy. As if somewhere you know that if you did not pursue satisfaction with your voice that your listening capacity would deteriorate and narrow your experience down to a place where you would become trapped in yourself. I admire your persistence." I am so deeply grateful to The Listening Centre and all the people there who helped me learn that neither my brain, my ear, nor the world was my enemy.

I composed the following poem, "Attuned, resonant, balanced," about my time there:

As I leave The Listening Centre
The colours of the trees leap out
Sparkling my eyes with their brilliance

Under the clear blue
My breath is deep
I'm solid on both feet
Noticing the smiles of people walking by
Life is a flower
I have found a way to her sweet nectar
And it sustains me

Music Heals the Body

In the late nineties, I tried the Nashville adventure again. I packed my guitar and drove down to Nashville to learn songwriting in the centre of a country music scene that was rapidly changing to pop. I came from a jazz/folk background and didn't fit in very well with the high glamour and fast pace of Nashville in the nineties. However, I did have my new-found confidence in my voice and sang at open stages, co-wrote songs, survived the noisy song camps, and got lost (more calmly this time) on the twisty streets.

Many times, lost in the Nashville swirl, I would just get stuck listening to other's ideas, never having (or taking) the chance on my words or my voice. However, I learned many songwriting tricks and principles that served me well when I returned to Toronto and joined the Songwriting Association of Canada (SAC). One propitious night, I went to an event called "Date with a Tape." (Yes, people made tapes back then!) The encouraging feedback I received propelled my creativity forward, and I hooked up with three other songwriters, David Leask, Debra Alexander, and Suzie Vinnick, whose songs I admired. We started a support group to write together and cheer each other on. We called it "The First Ave Song Writers Group" because I lived on First Avenue and was the convener. Two of our members were active performing songwriters and two of us less so. We wrote in different combinations and my co-writes with David and Suzie were recorded on their CDs and began to earn money (I framed my first royalty check). It seemed amazing to me that I was succeeding in getting out into the world, and I learned so much from our collaboration.

I created community within the songwriting association by hosting a monthly open stage at a popular folk club. That was really fun and good for me. I made demos of my songs sung by professional singers. (I could sing but knew I did not have a "selling voice.") I entered them in contests and got many honorable mentions and a few wins. I was hooked on the process of songwriting because it felt like my "calling."

Losing My Voice ... Again

My persistence was about to put to the test. I began to lose my voice in 2003, and this was discouraging and shameful. I could barely admit it to myself: It was happening *again*.

My songwriters open stage that I had been running for several years wound down, and except for the First Ave group, I had no musical focus. At the time, my main healing work was through acupuncture and micro-current therapy on my face. Micro-current therapy is an electrical-current therapy developed for pain but often used for cosmetic purposes. Its signals are weak and have coherence with the body's own electrical current to make it more effective, which it was for me. I was still receiving therapy sessions and doing Tai Chi. But despite those efforts, I quit singing lessons after some disastrous performances. I felt envious of people who could sing. I sadly gave up.

Hope Springs Eternal

On the table receiving micro-currents in 2004, I commented to Elaine, the practitioner, that she seemed to have more energy than usual. She said, "I have been doing a new meditation." I asked, "What is it?" She said, "Well you drink a tea and then sing." I was very curious and immediately wanted to know more. Shortly after this conversation, I went to my first meditation. I had an intuition that the tea, which was made of the medicinal herb Ayahuasca, would help me to sing. I was so hopeful at the beginning and tried hard to have a miracle happen to my voice. There was no miracle.

The meditations eventually helped me to sing, but first I had to face myself on many levels and get additional help. When I first joined the group, I played guitar. This allowed me to hide the fact that I was going through a period of not being able to sing, thereby engaging in my old habit of secretiveness. But I knew that my "singing" heart was breaking to hear everyone else singing beautiful Brazilian hymns when I couldn't. I began to fall into a depression. Then, gradually, I began to receive intuitions in the meditations, but they weren't very clear. I got "speech therapist" and "brain."

I investigated speech therapists and the first one I found was very wrong for me and frustrating. Then I found a speech pathologist, Aaron, who worked with singers. He helped in several ways. He told me to stop trying to sing entirely. That was very hard, because I wanted to sing so much and now and then I could get a note or two. He massaged my throat and had me do unusual exercises. I was no stranger to trying new things, even when they seemed odd at first. After a year, I felt more comfortable with my voice in general but still couldn't sustain notes (though I did write a song with very short notes). I didn't know at that point that I would learn even more—read on.

I am grateful to Aaron for two things. He defined more clearly what my problem was: vocal tension dystonia (spasmodic vocal dysphonia), a condition where vocal folds (cords) do not meet properly, so any kind of vocal production is difficult, from talking to singing. Each person with dysphonia has slightly different manifestations and a variety of triggering incidents. My incident was probably intubation during my operation and the post surgery facial paralysis. It manifested as an inability to produce a clean, sustained singing tone. This diagnosis decreased the shame I felt about losing my singing voice. He also told me about his niece with one hearing ear and normalized many of my behaviors with stories about her. This decreased my isolation but did not solve the puzzle of my off-and-on-again voice. The only "brain thing" I could think of was The Listening Centre. I went back, and though it would help me relax, it didn't bring my singing voice back

The Saga of My Singing Voice

It took many years to figure out what was going on physically when I couldn't sing. Here is a brief review. The trauma of having my voice come and go with no named cause was heartbreaking. I was lacking the information about dystonia and the vagus nerve that would eventually bring understanding. Because of a very specific set of circumstances (weak muscles, sporadic brain and nerve connection), my vocal folds would not meet reliably in a way that would produce a sustained singing tone, especially in combination with consonants that were still hard for my weak lips on the left side of my face to pronounce. In my younger years, it made certain notes difficult, hence it was easier to sing melodies I wrote skipping these notes; later the problem was more widespread, and I couldn't sing anything. Glottal sounds, such as yodeling, jump started the fold closure and made me feel like I could sing. I discovered I could yodel even when I couldn't sing while riding my horse, Cinnamon, on the island when I was thirteen. I had no idea why I could yodel but not sing "Happy Birthday"—no one around me thought to ask, and I asked no one. It became part of the mystery. I had no idea why I could sing while under the influence of LSD and later Ayahuasca but learned in Dr. Farias' seminar that drinking alcohol is a common self-medication for dystonia. Somehow these substances interrupt the 'habit' of the dystonic brain. In later years, when I began to understand more about vocal-fold closure and singing production in general, I experimented with chanting, singing, talk-singing, that sounded like spoken word poetry, and wild experiments with vocal sounding when I was in safe settings. I still had no idea why I could do vocalizing in my many singing lessons but could not reliably sing songs.

Another problem was my ear-voice connection. When on stage, it was extra-difficult to hear myself without monitors, and my voice quality deteriorated quickly. Every singer struggles with this kind of audio environment, but a one-eared person struggles more because of audio-directional difficulties, and in my case, a bad internal sound in my left ear. This struggle set off a chain reaction in my vagus nerve, which very quickly spread to my vocal-production muscles.

For a long time, I had no way of articulating my weird disability symptoms. Now, having received enough help and information about synkinesis, dystonia, the brain, and the nerves and muscles involved in singing, I can reliably bring back the sustained tone of a singing note under special circumstances. A relaxed mind, body, and a good acoustic atmosphere are essential for developing my 'true' vocal folds. I had been lost for a long time in all the false compensatory muscular effort that eventually added up to dystonia and dysphonia.

But from 2004 to 2008, I struggled emotionally and musically. My main comfort was a new guitar. It had nylon strings and a pickup for amplification. It felt very comfortable to hold and had a lovely sound. My frustrated melodic brain, which had been on hold for four years because of not being able to sing, began to find its voice on the soft strings. I began guitar lessons with a guitarist who specialized in Latin rhythms. He encouraged my compositions enthusiastically. My melodies were influenced by a mixture of flamenco (the last time I had played a nylon-string guitar was when I was fourteen and studying flamenco), Brazilian music, and jazz. I was attracted to minor melodies, waltzes, and odd time signatures. Somehow, though still being technically challenged, I managed to home-record them. Still, I did not have a musical place.

Finding My Musical Place

In 2007, my guitar teacher said, "I want you to meet a friend of mine, Diego. He might be a possible producer for your compositions. We're playing a gig next Saturday. Why don't you come down and meet him." It was an early summer evening and the bar was small. My teacher played guitar and Diego played percussion. I listened for a set, and then, over a beer, began to talk to Diego about the project I had in mind (A CD to accompany a book I was co-writing). I must have sounded some-what together, because he said, "Come and meet my co-producer, Juan." As soon as I met Juan and played them my composition "Caminho de Irineu" (the path of Irineu), we all knew we had some kind of creative magic happening. I knew I had found high-level mentors and a good musical place.

I also found my musical place in a new meditation group, where I was the only guitar player and in charge of rehearsals. I was playing my new guitar, and it was satisfying to use all my knowledge to make the music better.

I began to write lyrics for my CD project. One of the songs, "If I Can Sing" was about my trauma. My fellow songwriter Debra Alexander helped with the re-writes ending up a co-writer, and because I still couldn't sing well enough for the song to sound the way I wanted, I hired my friend Suzie to sing it. In Juan and Diego's hands, it became a full production, and it is one of my favorite songs.

> I sang my song with a young girl's freedom
> "Til the accident crushed my soul
> It sent my voice and the sound of my music
> Down the jaws of a deep black hole
> But I had a dream that a horse came running
> On the waves of a bright blue bay
> He came to me with a song he was singing
> His words guide me to this day
>
> Chorus
> If I can sing you can do anything
> You'll go walking on the water like me
>
> He gave me hope my horse on the water
> I believed I would sing once more
> And note-by-note if I fell or I faltered
> I'd hear him from my place on the shore
> So I found myself in the seat of the saddle
> And I chose to ride through the heat of the battle
> And the song I sing to you is a miracle dream
> come true
>
> —Kristi's song lyrics

My Changing Brain

In early 2008, I was on Elaine's table, and she said, "I just heard about a method of neuro-feedback you might be interested in." My attention perked up, and I thought, *Maybe this is the 'brain' thing that my intuition is nudging me toward.* I researched Low Energy Neurofeedback System, then ordered the book *The Healing Power of Neurofeedback* by Stephen Larsen and knew it was the next help curve for me.

Low Energy Neurofeedback System

Low Energy Neurofeedback System (LENS), is a method of communicating with our brain. The feedback is an incredibly tiny radio wave that lasts a matter of seconds and is slightly offset from and travels in tandem with the electrical signal of the cortex at any particular spot that is being engaged in that moment. The feedback system is designed as a disruptor of fixed, non-beneficial patterns such as occurs after brain injury or other trauma. It can also interrupt anxiety loops and depression. The suppressed energy in these patterns becomes released in the feedback process, and this promotes better neuronal connectivity, better brain/body connection, a relaxation response in the nervous system, and the wonderful, open possibility of doing things in a new way. The amount of radio wave signal in the feedback is very tiny—less than a digital watch. It works because it is precise and attuned. This results in brain learning and brain healing because of the brief on/off nature of the wave signal is similar to how the brain talks to itself. For more, see ochslabs.com.

But there was a problem in accessing treatment: The nearest practitioner was in upstate New York, a nine-hour drive south. After recovering from a driving phobia, because of my father's dying in a car accident, I had become more comfortable driving over the years. However, if I was tense, I would have fears of the car suddenly falling apart. Every weird sound would activate my body's alarm system—heart beating, jaw-clenching tension. The drive down was an endurance test.

I arrived at the Stone Mountain Center for my first appointment, exhausted, nervous, hopeful, and depressed. After a long, detailed interview with Sam, the LENS practitioner, in a dark room cluttered with knick-knacks and paper, I had my first treatment. I remember he kept encouraging me to drink water, but I resisted, not wanting to be told what to do and not understanding why water might be important. (Later I found out that water facilitates changes in the brain.) He attached the small electrodes to my head and pressed some buttons. It was over in a few minutes. Had I felt anything? All I had felt was a few tingles, and I prepared myself to be disappointed. But when I did some Tai Chi outside a little later, I noticed that my left ankle, which had been giving me problems, was suddenly better. *Hmmm,* I thought. *Here is some hard evidence.* I received two more treatments before the drive back to Toronto and felt progressively happier and more stable. The difference between the drive home and the drive down was night and day. I felt confident and in tune with my car. The hours sped by.

Much as I was being helped by LENS, it soon became apparent that I could not keep going to New York state for treatments. I decided that I would buy the equipment and train to operate it on myself and others. This accomplished, I began giving myself treatments, as well as a few friends. Gradually, as I took more courses, read relevant literature and became a LENS practitioner, I began to treat some of my clients.

Through doing therapy and having Ayahuasca experiences, I knew the ins and outs of releasing suppressed energy and believed in the benefits of shaking up habitual patterns. What surprised me in LENS treatments was the sharp increase in well-being. I had experienced some of this at the Listening Centre, but LENS gave me more of these "comfortable in my skin" feelings. I also experienced the emotional storms that can accompany the release of suppressed energy: sharp spikes of emotions and accompanying memories like flashbacks. But these were shorter in duration and had better resolution—even without therapy. It was as if my inner therapist/healer had gotten a big boost. As I gradually learned, this was a signal of a better connection with my Pre-frontal Cortex—the place in our brain with executive functions and perspective—the place where our inner therapist resides.

It Takes a Team

When my Pre-frontal Cortex function improved from neurofeedback, I could make better choices about what was good for me. One of these was a chiropractor who knew how to get my fascia moving.

Her name was Katarina, and I called her a "fascia magician" because she was so good at deep muscle and fascia work. She began to untwist and loosen the considerable scar tissue I had, as well as work on the postural tensions I had been collecting from years of turning my head to be able to hear with my hearing ear, the right one. Her treatments were painful and challenging, but very effective. For most people who have a combination of scar tissue and dissociation, there are mysteries held in the mechanical structures of our fascia. Her intuitive fingers were like detectives, revealing the true culprits of tension problems, resolving them and leaving me with a more flexible and more known body. She also kept pointing me to the psoas muscle as the source of some of my pain.

The Psoas Muscles

The psoas muscles are attached to the inner surfaces of the lumbar vertebrae from L1 to L5. Some fibers from the superficial branch of the psoas attach on to T12, an insertion in common with the diaphragm. The psoas then passes though the abdomen to join with the illiacus muscle, which attaches on the inside of the hip bone, the muscles then go through the pelvis to attach on the inside of the femur (thigh bone). They look like fans and act like flexible pillars. They have many functions: stabilizing the lower spine, flexing the spine forward, lifting the legs, and helping to keep the hips and lower back flexible.

Understanding What "Core" Means

I was motivated to learn about my psoas muscle, because it was speaking to me loudly, contributing to a painful spasm in my lower mid-back. The psoas is an often-misunderstood core muscle. Exercise teachers encourage us to strengthen our core and "pull it in" and this is good advice, but most people don't know how to do this or what the implications of a "weak" core are. Because the psoas is part of our survival-system muscles—helping us go into fetal position when there is danger—they often go into in a state of hyper alertness. The psoas is susceptible to stress states. When it is not constricted or weak, it works in coordination with the gluteal muscles and the lower-back muscles, allowing a good posture and ease of movement.

If it is unhealthy—weak, tense, or twisty—it can cause back pain, hip pain, knee pain, postural problems, and because it strongly influences the diaphragm, breathing constriction. I use the word "twisty" as a way of describing the feeling of a muscle where some of the fibers are strong and some weak in a way that causes an imbalance or twist. Often the psoas is ignored because the muscles it affects (such as the lower-back muscles) speak more loudly, and because of its deep location in the abdomen, it is hard to feel and treat. Postural problems like hips forward, hips back, lordosis (swayback), one hip higher than the other, and many more, can have their source in trauma or in too much sitting. These problems are caused by and also cause psoas weakness.

In addition to posture, PTSD can affect the psoas through low-level fight-or-flight reactions that put the psoas in a chronic state of "survival" position—breath held, slight contraction in the lower back, and tension in the front of the neck. My psoas was weak from PTSD and twisty from a long-time habit of rotating my torso to the left to be able to hear.

As Katarina released the tissues, I slowly worked through the emotional issues that surfaced from the work on my psoas with EMDR (see chapter 7) and strengthened the released muscles with Pilates, yoga, and Tai Chi. Each of these exercises worked on different aspects: the yoga breathing and upward /downward dogs released the diaphragm and lower-back vertebrae; the Pilates strengthened my abdominal muscles and balanced my left and right sides; the Tai Chi, with its gentle twisting moves, coordinated (oiled) the whole core area. I also learned some "do it yourself" psoas releases that helped me to "be" with the muscle and release the fight-or-flight energy lurking in its fibers. (See the techniques at end of this chapter.) The final result was surprising: I became light on my feet and could kick higher in my martial-arts practice. I was calmer. This was because my psoas was finally strong and balanced.

Singing Lesson

I added another very important person to my "team" about three months after starting LENS. I found a new vocal coach, Lucas Marchand, who teaches a technique called Speech Level singing. In this technique, the vocal exercises are designed to capitalize on the ease of speech to help improve singing. When I started lessons, I could only sing very short notes in limited combinations. He coached me on the songs for my

CD and working with him gradually brought my voice back to a place where I could sing songs, though still in a limited way.

In a lesson that was a turning point, I worked on the jazz standard "All of Me." Scale practice had been fine that day, but as soon as I started singing the song, my voice got heavy and strained. Lucas and I worked hard, but it was just stuck. During the following week, I reviewed my lesson, and I could not bring myself to approach the song again. I felt discouraged and wondered if there were any songs easy enough for me to sing. At the next lesson, I told Lucas that I didn't think I could do the song. He looked at me and said, "I think you can. Let's pitch it in a lower key." It was much easier to sing in the new key, but there was still stiffness when I transitioned to singing lyrics from vocalizing sounds. Lucas said, "Okay, just speak the words." I did that no problem. Then he had the idea of me speaking the words while he played the accompaniment. The second time through, I spoke the words in the shape of the melody, and suddenly I could feel them! In this moment, I realized what I had half known: When I sang, I would lose expression. Doing this speak/sing, I could stay present and express with feeling. At the end, Lucas said, "That was really good, and it touched me." I wish that he had been there when my twenty-year-old self was so confused about my voice and singing.

The Almost-Miracle

In the fall of 2008, I was in my regular meditation group and we were doing an acapella set of hymns. Suddenly, I opened my mouth and I could sing—really sing—not just a few notes or phrases but several hymns in a row. This was the miracle I had been waiting for! But wait … why did my singing voice go away again? Why couldn't I sing without the help of the Ayahuasca? Why couldn't I sing in large group settings? I began doubting that it had happened and asked my fellow meditators, "Did you hear me sing?" Sometimes they said, "Yes," but more often, "I wasn't listening." I was left once again with mysteries to solve on my own.

I added a language coach to my team and would speak/sing the Portuguese hymns in rehearsal with him. I found a mentor for the LENS work and got coaching from him on different treatment protocols. I regularly half-sang one set of hymns in my group. I began to have intuitions about the way sound affected me. I tried several earplugs without much success, trying to block "bad" sounds from my left ear. I experimented with positioning as much as I could. I often felt discouraged, but the LENS work had lifted my depression, the work on the CD had given me a musical place to belong, and I felt I had a good team.

Another Piece of the Puzzle

I was very happy with my finished CD but didn't quite know how I was going to share or sell it. I knew there was something still missing in my life that was hard to put into words.

I did not know how to explain to myself or anyone else the flashbacks of embarrassment (of not being able to hear or keep up with jokes or conversations in groups); of lingering shame now combined with fears about having an aging body and voice, which made me afraid that no one would want me; and the fear of never being able to sing again and conversely to sing and then lose my voice again. Because of this confusion, my past disappointments repeated like a movie in my mind-body. This is common for people with PTSD. Any of these emotional situations could give me low-level flashbacks, which then were suppressed by my mind but continued in my body, which did not know how to feel reliably 'safe'.

The vagus nerve is an arbiter of the nervous system, both sending messages to the brain from the body and from the brain back down to the body. We can improve this two-way system from the body end by changing our "state" through physical means, or from the brain end by changing our minds with new concepts and mental practices. A strong (well-myelinated) vagus nerve can help a person regain stability after a frightening or shocking event. However, if those events are frequent, the more primitive part of the vagal system (the dorsal vagal branch) becomes dominant and we 'freeze and collapse' and eventually fall into a state of dysautonomia—a disorder of the autonomic nervous system. That was my situation.

When an old friend stopped by to tell me about an osteopath he had been working with to help his singing voice, I paid attention and began another Help Curve. Six months later, in a sparsely furnished, quiet room, I met an energetic Hideki Kumagai, the healer who would put it all together for me and provide the information I needed to take the next step forward. What I learned was well worth the wait.

He explained to me about the vagus nerve (one of ten cranial nerves) and its many functions, two of which are important to this story. The vagus is affected by shock, including low-level fight-or-flight states (trauma flashbacks) and some fibers innervate the singing muscles—bringing the vocal folds (cords) to meet and raising the soft palate. Because I could talk but not sustain a singing tone, he deduced that it was the nerve nucleus in the brainstem that was problematic, because it was not providing the energy necessary to keep the nerve firing.

This was an intense revelation to me because I could see the connection between my left-middle-ear problems, struggling to hear and voice production. I could also see how chronic flashbacks had affected the state of my vagus nerve. It was upsetting and hopeful.

I began a program of carefully calibrated exercises and learning about how the cranial nerves are related. Many things became clear: On behalf of my voice, I would need to take better care of my ears; I would need to speak up about background sounds and regulate the amount of time spent in noisy surrounding; I would need to learn how I felt in my body when my ventral vagus nerve nucleus was in a healthy state—yes there is a feeling that goes with that—and figure out what to do to keep it there.

Here are some of the things I changed: I limited myself to one and a half hours in noise, because I discovered that was the amount of time I could handle sound sorting (the most difficult task for a one-eared person) before going into a dissociative state. If I had scary or shocking experiences, I would shake them out of my body as soon as possible. I would vocalize early in the morning to make use of time when my vagus nerve was strongest, and then by singing vigorously, increase the strength of the nerve nucleus. I found out where background noises were coming from, and if I could do anything about them. I paid attention to optimal positioning in any group situation and stopped expecting the impossible of my ears and voice. I made sure to get cranial massage, neurofeedback, and acupuncture to keep my middle ear healthy and energized.

This new level of advocacy healed many of the "freeze and collapse" habits (dorsal vagal states) that I had collected from living with a disability and ongoing audio/vocal flashbacks. I also felt more noticed and taken care of, because the people around me knew my particular needs. As my vagus nerve became stronger, I felt more at ease and at home in my body and in my communities.

The meditation group I had been attending disbanded. I finally found another one to join, but they already had a guitar player. I would have to learn to sing for real! It was a journey and a half! One good thing I did when I joined was to come out of hiding to reveal my disability and how it affected my voice. The leader at one point said, echoing Paul Madaule's words, "It's interesting that you chose a spiritual path that is so difficult—that challenges your greatest weakness."[2] Gradually, I learned what I needed: to learn the hymns in my own peculiar way that did not involve singing them but rather playing the melodies on guitar and then speaking the words in meter (having checked my pronunciation with a new Portuguese coach). Under the influence of Ayahuasca, I encountered again my fear of not being able to sing that I felt each time my voice would not hold a sustained note. The sensation is like being stopped by a mysterious force when you really want to do something. Then, when I began to sing, I would often have panicky feelings that calmed after a bit. I realized that singing challenged the muscles and related brain areas that had shut down in the original trauma, thus triggering a small, physical-level flashback.

I kept up my LENS treatment, not caring that my brain was taking so long to heal; I was making progress. I could feel the good effect of regular singing on my vagus nerve: how being calm and well rested would help my singing. I understood why large group gatherings were not good for me: too much strain on my ears and brain.

Good social relationships also helped me strengthen my vagus nerve. I began to pay more attention to receiving love from communities and individuals I felt known by, as well as giving back to them. The "being known" aspect was important to me, because of all the time I had spent unconsciously pretending and dissociating.

I had learned good skills and perspectives from my personal experiences of changing my brain. I passed these on to clients by providing LENS treatments and teaching them the life skills of dealing with their trauma, fascia tissues, and their psoas muscle. I asked my clients how they felt emotionally, and how they perceived and comprehended the world. I asked how their thoughts and imagination worked. My experience at The Listening Centre underlined the importance of recognizing my clients and listening to the way they described their reality. Often, this was expressed in metaphors. Healing can be a long journey for all of us. It's important to involve specialists and interdisciplinary practitioners, combined in a customized, creative approach to your needs, to support you as you embark on multiple Help Curves. The concept and practice of teamwork in the healing journey is important, because not one person or method is going to have the "answer."

My favorite Pilates teachers always bring in new ways of doing exercises in order to keep the brain fresh and well stimulated with novelty. I do this with my clients by asking the "right question," like my uncle Dick did in his practice, and having many options for how to approach the mind-body system. Sometimes, this means my client will show up for a massage expecting sixty minutes of blissful silence and instead find that they end up telling me about their stressful year at work. Sometimes, a client who has been coming for coaching is just too tired and instead I give them a cranial sacral session. We construct the journey together, and at the end, they have perspective on their patterns and a bag of tricks to do "self-work."

Combinations of techniques, for example Pilates, yoga, and massage, or therapy, neurofeedback, and meditation have given me the best results. Sometimes doing many techniques is an avoidance of committing to one thing in order to go deeper, but in my experience, this was not the case, and everything worked together. Nowadays, my brain feels good, and I know what "feeling good" is: a cheerful calm feeling. I would not give up my "new brain" for anything!

Innate Intelligence Letter

Dear Kristi,

Wow, what journey! It is wonderful to see how much more observant you are now that you are not just rushing and tumbling through life. I am happy you are making better choices for yourself. I am happy that you have become more realistic about what you can and cannot do.

You are getting perspective on your "being in the world" because you have more information about how your disability works. This perspective is beneficially influencing many other things in your life: health, relationships, and your ability to take it easy while still giving.

The healers you have collected around you are perfect for you. You will continue to grow. Keep paying attention in your intuition—that is where I can speak to you.

Oh, and by the way, loneliness will soon be a thing of the past. Get ready!

With cheers,

Innate Intelligence

Techniques for Keeping the Body in Mind

How do we begin to map out our brain patterns and tendencies? There are many books on the subject, but the science of how the brain works is still in the beginning stages. There is so much we don't know. Reading books has helped me find a starting place for my observations, such as by learning to observe how things affect my nervous system and my body and doing experiments to see what works to improve my well-being. You can do the same. I developed the following technique when I was first learning about left and right brain function and how music could help.

Both Sides Now

This is a simple brain gym exercise for activating both sides of the brain, thus improving flexibility and energy levels. Music activates both sides of the brain, rhythm for the left side and melody for the right. If tapping on your body feels too stimulating, or if you feel dizzy, it is probably not the technique for you.

What to Do

Play a piece of music you like that is about waltz speed (not too fast). Then place your right palm on the front of your left shoulder and your left palm on your right shoulder, as if hugging yourself. As you hear the music's rhythm, allow your hands to alternately pat the shoulders in some kind of pattern, such as three pats on one side and three on the other (any pattern will work). If you wish, you can move your hands down your outer arms, down your torso, continuously patting, down to your legs, and if your back allows, all the way down to your feet. If it feels good, come all the way back up to your shoulders. Finish by tracing a small figure eight in front of you with your nose, allowing your head to move loosely and release your neck.

What to Expect

You may feel more coordinated and able to stand on both feet equally. Your eyes may feel better and your thinking clearer.

Psoas Self-Massage Release

Releasing the psoas muscle takes patience, awareness, and a slow approach. It is helpful to get a practitioner to treat it first, so you have more of a sense of how it feels. When you do it yourself, focus more on the feeling in the body of "rightness" instead of the feeling in your fingertips. There are layers of muscle in the abdomen, including the obliques, the transverse and the rectus abdominis. Looking at a picture of the anatomy is helpful. Once you find the tight part of the muscle, hold a steady, medium pressure, relax the rest of your body, and patiently wait for it to let go. If your hands feel too weak or it feels too scary to massage your stomach, try a psoas muscle stretch (see below).

What to Do

There are two positions in which to do the release. Try both and see which works best for you.

Position 1

1. Lie on your stomach and slide one knee into a bent position on the floor. It should be more than a ninety-degree angle to your hip. Turn your head in the same direction as the bent knee. This allows some weight to fall to the opposite side, which is where you will put your fingers.

2. Place both hands at waist level, toward the outside edge of your waist. Use one hand to support the other. Press your fingers into your muscle and wiggle the muscle tissue back and forth. Focus on the internal feeling. Gradually go deeper, paying attention to any stop signals from your body (such as agitation or too much discomfort). If you feel a tight strand of muscle, just hold steady until it releases a bit and then move up or down. Take several deep breaths to release the diaphragm.

3. Press and wiggle the muscles on the inside of the hip bone, pressing the bone down and out. This should release your sacrum. Spend up to fifteen minutes exploring and waiting for the release. Then stand up and see if your posture and walking feel different. It is good to finish with a brisk walk outside swinging your arms.

Position 2

1. Lie on your side with your head on a pillow.

2. Place the fingers of your up-side hand on the front of your waist and your thumb slightly around the back. Begin to press and wiggle the muscles gradually working up and down the psoas.

3. To release the muscle on the inside of your hip (the illiacus), place the thumbs of both hands on the inside of the hip and press toward the feet and away from the centre of the body. This is a good position to release hip pain caused by a tight psoas and related muscles. Be patient and slow and take deep breaths. Spend up to fifteen minutes on each side.

What to Expect

If your tight psoas is causing knee or lower-back pain, you should feel a loosening of those related muscles. You may need to do more than one session. You may feel some release of fear or another emotion. The release will help you to sleep better.

Basic Psoas Stretch

There are many ways to stretch and strengthen the psoas muscle. If you are just beginning to get to know your psoas, or if your pain level is high, this stretch may be useful to you.

What to Do

1. Starting with the less-affected side, lie on your back on the side of your bed and let the outside leg slowly drift off the edge until you feel a stretch in the front of your hip. (If it hurts your back to do this, seek professional help).

2. Take several deep breaths, and then, engaging your abdominal muscles and holding your lower back toward the bed, lift the leg back up. Bend the knee and gently pull it toward your chest with your hands on the hamstring.

3. After several breaths in this position, lower the leg to the bed and observe any changes. Repeat this exercise at least three times on each side.

4. Get up and walk around, observing how your body feels

What to Expect

If this is the right exercise for you, you will feel lighter in the lower half of your body, less pain in your back, and it will be easier to walk. If it doesn't work, seek guidance from a professional.

Chapter 10
Belonging:
The Essential Nectar of Life

At the top of a mountain is a starhouse
In it I feel the sky, I feel the earth
Singing in my soul
There's room in the star house for dreaming
Room for every kind of being

Invisibility and Loneliness

Being seen and being known are basic human needs. When they are not met, we feel lonely. In a recent article in the *Globe,* Sam Roberts writes about Dr. Cacioppo, a social neuroscientist:

> He likened loneliness to hunger, explaining that it helps naturally gregarious humans establish mutually beneficial relationships that meet social needs vital to survival. He estimated that 1 in 4 Americans are lonely, without any confidants, and social isolation results in negative emotional and physical consequences. ... He drew a distinction between loneliness and being alone. "In animals, it's not separating a monkey from any companion, it's separating them from a preferred companion," he said in an interview last year with *The Atlantic* magazine. "Being with others doesn't mean you're going to feel connected and being alone doesn't mean you're going to feel lonely.[1]

When social needs are met, we are comfortable in our own skins. Connected. When we are comfortable in our own skin, our needs are more likely to be met by others, because we reveal ourselves. My experience of having hidden disabilities (my ear and singing voice) and a "no talk" rule about my obvious one (my face) made me feel invisible. I was not comfortable in my own skin and much of my energy went into proving I was worthy. The feeling of invisibility made me almost give up many times. The shame of it made me smaller. In contrast, precise recognition and questions that helped me reveal my hidden brokenness and my hidden talents brought visibility and increasing ease in my whole self. I had many layers of telling the truth.

When memoirist Pauline Dakin was interviewed by radio host Shelagh Rogers, she answered a question about how she felt when she told the truth after years of hiding it and being told not to tell anyone with, "Transcendent. It's all out there. No more need to hide."[2] I recognize this feeling and probably everyone with a hidden disability or the burden of secrets does.

I have come to see as ideal for me a "Kintsugi" repair: visibility and healing without hiding what was broken.

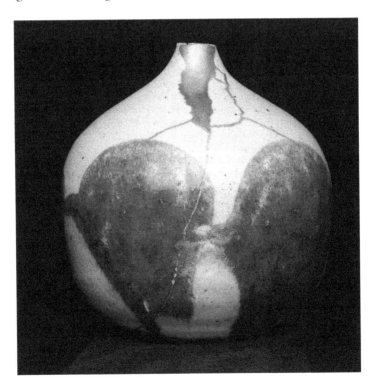

Translated to "golden joinery," *Kintsugi* (or *Kintsukuroi*, which means "golden repair") is the centuries-old Japanese art of fixing broken pottery with a special lacquer dusted with powdered gold, silver, or platinum. Beautiful seams of gold glint in the cracks of ceramic ware, giving a unique appearance to the piece.

This repair method celebrates each artifact's unique history by emphasizing its fractures and breaks instead of hiding or disguising them. Kintsugi often makes the repaired piece even more beautiful than the original, revitalizing it with new life.

What appeals to me most about this idea is that what is broken is not hidden, nor is it considered weak. Anyone working with trauma will recognize this logic. It's like taking pride in our scars. They tell the story of what we've been through, battles fought, and wounds repaired.

Community and a Mystery Solved

I had a way of finding community even as I was hampered in receiving from those communities because of my hearing difficulties, vocal difficulties, and PTSD. This talent was a positive result of growing up having a true "home" on the island and in the island community. It was also influenced by my parent's dedication to many kinds of communities—Friends Meeting, American Friends Service committee, dance groups, political action groups, and land-use (environmentalist) groups. The island was a physical surrounding that in itself produced a feeling of belonging. In a journal from my youth, I write:

> "This is the first time I've been back to Eagle Island after living somewhere else [Seattle]. I never realized how much I missed it until coming back: sitting in front of the fire and feeling the warmth flowing through me; going outside in the clear, peaceful fall mornings when the sun is just rising and the air is chilly; walking around eating a winter delicious (apple), rustling my feet in the golden poplar leaves, and listening to the quietness. I feel like I'm inside a diamond, everything is so sparkling."

However, as is the case with many people, I had significant blocks to a felt sense of belonging, even on the island. I had to learn through trial and error what kind of effort it took from me to construct places and ways of belonging. In the last layer of uncovering my family history, and finally understanding my dystonia in a complete way, some of the mystery was solved and solutions became apparent.

Just being a member in a group doesn't guarantee a sense of belonging. If someone conceals their shame (around a disability or anything else), they are spending their energy engaged in secrecy and trauma-driven "protection" behaviors. They will often make themselves small. Influenced by my Norwegian background and attitudes towards people with disabilities when I was a child, that is what I did. The opposite action is to draw myself up to my full height, so to speak, to take up space, and to ask for what I need. Showing up in community and not feeling like I have to pretend. This is belonging and this is what I am learning.

In the process of writing this book and digging deep into my past, I heard about a movement specialist and researcher, Dr. Farias, who had done research on dystonia and created an excellent online platform, the Dystonia Recovery Program. Though my intuition said I needed to get in touch with this man, I put it on the back burner, telling myself it was too much to handle both the archives of my life and learning new things about my voice. I completed my book, and in the process, made a coherent narrative of my trauma experiences, which was deeply healing. Then I applied for the dysphonia (dystonia) seminar, sending a video of me singing a very quavery sustained note (due to my dystonic vocal folds). Then I waited. During that wait, I realized how much I wanted to go to the seminar. I felt my fear of not being worthy of help—not being 'disabled' enough to qualify. What if the seminar was only for people who had difficulties speaking? What if I was told again that I couldn't be helped. This feeling was a trigger I was familiar with, having had my vocal disability misunderstood many times.

In the weeks before the seminar, I became very curious about who the participants would be and whether they would have singing or speaking dysphonia. Even though I had become much more familiar with revealing my compromised voice, there was some deep resistance going on in my unconscious, and my diaphragm and psoas muscle on my right side began to tighten up, eventually causing my knee to hurt. (This was supposed to be my strong side!!) However, thanks to my trauma work,

I knew what was happening and knew it was a mind-body symptom that would release once I saw the reality of the present-day situation.

As we went around the room introducing ourselves, I felt a resonating recognition and began to relax deep in my abdomen. When Dr. Farias explained his research and normalized the experience of dysphonia and the common adjunct of underlying trauma, I felt known. I felt validated by several pieces of information, such as dysphonia being an off and on condition, that diaphragm tension is common, and that compensation habits for weak muscles must be stopped so the true vocal folds can strengthen. Also, that being in a trauma state is not good for learning new muscular habits. He encouraged us to strengthen our vagus nerve system and get to 'know' our abdominal muscles. I felt good that all my work on trauma recovery was paying off, and shortly after I arrived in the group, the old fear of revealing myself dissipated and I was happily absorbing the new pieces of information, as well as feeling validated for what I had already accomplished. These were my people. I belonged. I could contribute. I was part of a dystonia community. The last bits of mystery and shame about my singing voice were melting away as information, clarifications, and techniques sank in.

For a person with a disability, a sense of belonging often depends on having the right tools to help their body adjust to the environment or the right environmental accommodations to make belonging possible. Sometimes these needs impose on others, but ultimately, we are all better off when someone who has a different body can be a part of the society we live in.

The movie *Breathe* is a portrait of how the accommodation of a wheelchair, specially designed by a friend, and the ability to live at home transformed the life of Robin Cavendish, who had been paralyzed from the neck down at age twenty-eight. It was beautiful to see how everyone came together as a team to help with the wheelchair project, and how in turn, people were changed by helping Robin belong in his community of family and friends. His story took place in the sixties and seventies when people with disabilities were often hidden away (as he says "imprisoned") in institutions. There were no adequate chairs then and his ventilator was an iron lung. In these days of advanced technology, it is hard to imagine not having wheelchairs of all shapes and varieties and fancy support machines. Disability is openly talked about now, but there are those of us that still struggle with difficulty in belonging because of lack of accommodation.

My disabilities are sensory and spasmodic in nature, and accommodation for these conditions is still at the beginning stage. Historically, dystonia was viewed as a 'possession' because of the on-off symptoms. Rejection and shunning were the norm. My residual shame and fear lead to compensation and tension, especially when I am having a PTSD flashback. My goal of belonging, as you can see from my story, was to be able to sing and be socially comfortable in groups of people instead of 'lost in sound'" and 'weird'.

The first step in accommodation is being able to name and talk about your own disability. Once the shame lifted from me, I could begin to ask for and find accommodations. For my ear, I realized that I needed to be in the right location in a room to be able to hear without strain. I needed to have a person I could get close to in noisy situations to tell me where sounds were coming from, so I wouldn't be on hyper-alert all the time. And to translate if I had missed a word, so I could keep up with jokes and so on.

Accommodating My Hearing

The reasons why noise environment and positioning have been important to me was not apparent until this later stage of my healing. I now had enough stability to stay present in noisy places and do experiments. Here is what I discovered: When I enter a room, the sounds are very chaotic, because I can't locate what sound is coming from where. If I don't dissociate but instead start looking around at the different noise sources (fans, furnaces, dishes clanking, conversations, recorded music, dogs barking), I can relax and figure out what or who I want to hear.

Next comes the screening efforts. I discern where the best place for me to sit or stand is so that background noise (what I don't want to hear) stays in the background and I can sort out what I do want to hear, such as a person speaking. This is both a brain focus and a hearing effort. I do some lip reading, if I am facing the person I want to hear. A corner position is good for a one-eared person but not always possible. Likewise for having my right hearing ear close to what I want to hear. Often the background noise creeps into the foreground (even if it is quiet) and I am sonically lost. I usually leave the noisy environment to take a sound break when that happens to recover my audio perspective. So positioning is key for me.

For my dystonic voice, which is related to my hearing disability, I needed a monitoring system so I could hear my voice in my right ear and be able to sing. This was very hard to find. I am still looking for the perfect solution. I tried headphones and a mike with an amplifier, which worked but was not terribly portable. Then I found "hearfones," which work fairly well. Often used in choirs, these are non-electrical devices that feed back the sound of your voice. Somewhere in all my experimentation, I also found that, if I held the left side of my face, I could hear my voice better. I still don't know why that works!

When I became sound sensitive in my left ear, I needed earplugs on certain noisy occasions. I tried five different musicians' earplugs and a complete sound blocking earplug but eventually came back to drugstore foamies because the others all were physically uncomfortable (getting a mold of the inside of my left ear was very tricky).

Singing in a group is difficult, because I can't always have the perfect "place" from which to hear myself as well as others. I like familiar rooms, because I can get used to where all the sounds are coming from and therefore relax. When I relax, my diaphragm lets go, my vagus nerve kicks in, and my vocal folds can come together producing the steady sustained sound of singing. I also need a music stand and a particular chair that is suited to my short legs, so I can sit upright and get maximum resonation from my bones. I have become used to my equipment, but sometimes I envy people who can just come with a book and open their mouths and sing. However, the rewards of singing in a group are worth every bit of effort. These are the moments when I have a deep sense of belonging. I will give the last word on this to a dream:

> I am attending a musical/spiritual event. I am carrying a chair and hoping I have arrived early enough to find my right place. When I enter the room, I see most of the chairs are filled. There is only one at the front and one at the back. I wander back and forth.

A woman asks me to give up the chair I am carrying, but I say loudly, "I need this chair." Eventually, I decide to sit at the front, even though I am afraid it will be too loud. There is a large man sitting there, and I say, "I hope you don't mind that I am sitting close to you—it may seem overly affectionate but with my one-eared status I need to be close to one person." He says he doesn't mind. Then the speaker, a previous group leader of mine, comes to the microphone. His voice is too loud. I plug my ear and think, "Maybe I will approach him afterward and see if he is doing any small workshops like he used to." I have a memory of how he supported me in those workshops to find my voice.

In this dream, I identify and speak up about the accommodations I need, as well as know what is wrong in the moment.

By looking at myself clearly, naming things and asking for what I need, I am transforming a history of staying quiet, concealing my truth, and feeling wrong and isolated. It required considerable growth and work to get to this point. Not getting stuck in shame or fear states in the body is a huge part, as is telling other people what is going on. The risk of being honest with other people is that sometimes they let you down. Sometimes you ask for help and the help isn't there. No one is perfect. We all are being influenced by our traumas and family inheritance and as a result will let others down. One way of healing (and it's not necessarily the best or the only) is to allow forgiveness into the equation—forgiveness for ourselves and others.

Forgiveness

This is my story of how forgiveness worked to bring me out of isolation and into a feeling of belonging. There are many kinds and levels of forgiveness. What they have in common is releasing us to move on in our lives. The grief released by forgiveness washed away the bitterness. Imagining being in the other's "shoes" expanded my universe. When I no longer had to chew on the bones of hurt feelings, I could use the released energy to move my life forward and connect to those around me. It wasn't about forgetting the pain; it was about changing the foreground by making the background more understandable—everybody's part in it. Then I felt a part of things again instead of the isolated, neglected victim. Forgiveness was like a medicine bringing calmness to my body and peace to my mind.

Sometimes understanding the deeper story of the person who has hurt you helps the process of forgiveness. In the course of writing this book, I had the opportunity to talk with Raoul, my teenage boyfriend to whom I had sacrificed my guitar. The first thing he said was that he was sorry for how he had treated me, and while sharing memories, he admitted that he had been an angry young man, and I remembered that his parents had abandoned him. It must have seemed to him that I had everything he didn't: a big loving family. In that moment, the last remnant of bitterness faded, and I forgave him.

The hardest "forgive" for me was of my parents. It took a long time for true letting go, because I had pretended on their behalf that I was okay when I wasn't. First, I had to be honest with myself and then events like the following story, recorded in my journal, happened:

> *I feel unsettled from a dream—I do some Tai Chi and it helps a bit. I do EFT, Emotional Freedom Technique—a method of tapping the body—which calms me, but I know I need human contact. I go next door to see my friends Dorn and Norma. I show them my baby pictures, feeling better as they say, "Yes, we can see what you mean." And, "Yes, there is the original small ear." Dorn says in his lovely slow voice, "I remember your dad talking to me before the operation, wondering whether it was a good thing. I think he knew then that it was a risk."*

> *Norma says, "Maybe afterward they felt so bad they just couldn't talk about it."*

> *Later my friend Meredith says, "I know my mother was very opposed to it and talked to your parents." I feel recognized and forgiving of my parents and the community. These reality checks help me to feel that I have a place, a group of people who know me and my reality.*

Another forgiveness story: Steve, another one of my childhood friends, came across the field to visit one summer, during the writing of this book (he had not read any of it yet). Settling himself at the kitchen table with a cup of peppermint tea, he said, "I have come to apologize."

I was startled, because I did not have a memory of him doing anything to hurt me. We reviewed our friendship, both remembering the innocent crush we had had on each other when he was in eighth grade and I was in the third grade, just before my operation. We remembered walking along the road holding hands and the secret notes I had sent (which were very fun to write and hide). At that time, I had talked and he had listened.

Now he told me what I didn't remember, which was that when I had been off island for my operation, he had decided that he was too old to be close with a younger girl and that he would break off our friendship when I returned. He remembered seeing my bandaged head and my crooked smile then, caught up in the momentum of his decision, had "Wordlessly and awkwardly" pushed my hand and my affection away. He said he realized now that it must have felt to me like a rejection for the way I looked. I told him that I didn't remember that part—probably it had been lumped in with my general feelings of isolation. I felt warm and forgiving and said that it was okay. There was a familiar easiness that came back between us. It is never too late to give and receive apologies, and this one helped me in my forgiveness process.

To thoroughly forgive my parents, I felt compelled to do more digging. This was literal digging though the dusty boxes in the archive of our family home on Eagle Island. I found photos of myself when I was a child, letters from my mother who saved many random papers and useful family history. After spending time with old letters, I talked to my friends and family, each of whom had a unique perspective that I could learn from, once I was ready to really take it in.

Forgiveness of self can be as important as forgiving others. In one instance, I was talking with three of my childhood friends, including Meredith. We sat in the Ludwigs' lovely cabin and reminisced. I felt safe enough to tell my friends the story of how I lay in the hospital bed in Bellingham, imagining I was missing the boat trip of a lifetime and it was my fault for being 'different'! My friend Belle said, "Well, really you didn't miss much. It was a rainy day, and we stood for hours waiting until they fixed the motor, and then there wasn't time to go to Victoria, so we went to Sydney and only had time to walk up the street and back. We were cold and hungry and had uncomfortable orange kapok life jackets on." We laughed at the funny way she told it and the old " my fault for being left out" feeling melted away.

From this place of belonging with my long-time friends, and the safety to confess an old hurt, I was able to forgive myself for feeling left out for so long and embrace a deeper feeling of belonging.

Another night, after reading several heart-breaking letters of my mother's, I dreamed that I was at a spiritual gathering with music—a waltz—and I saw two women dancing. I saw my mother and felt warmth. I put my arm around her in companionship. I saw what we had in common: a spiritual struggle to know and understand ourselves, to reach beyond the confines of what was given or not given to us by our parents.

In a spontaneous role reversal (after decades of psychodrama, these happened easily and were a great tool for accessing empathy and gaining insight), I realized the unbearableness of the operation trauma was too much for my mother to handle with the ghost of her mother whispering in her ear, "I knew you couldn't handle being a mother." My mother proved to be much stronger than her mother predicted, having five kids, living on an island, teaching for many of those years, and having an active hand in local politics. Still, I believe she had a fear of not being good enough that made her unable to admit her mistakes, and therefore, unable to grow in certain areas, even though she believed in personal growth. I was the main fatality of these fears, but oddly, she also gave me some tools to overcome them, such as writing and self-reflection.

Then I had another dream: I am watching my mother walking and dealing with a disability. She is doing it with grace and dignity. She indicates that she does not need my help but wants me to go do what I want. I feel admiring and relieved of duty.

Alchemy

I was scrolling through an online list of musical events in Toronto, and I impulsively signed up for a workshop called "The Alchemy of the Voice." I didn't think much about my motivation until the day of the workshop, and then I began to call myself crazy for exposing my fragile, unpredictable voice in an environment where I knew no one and had no idea of the format. Would they make me sing long-sustained notes? Would I be exposed as someone who can't sing? How would I handle my disability? What was I hoping to get? Alchemy implies some kind of transformative process. I am always longing for more transformation of my voice.

I arrived in a renovated semi-basement space. Soul7 was quiet and beautiful, with large singing bowls prominently placed, sacred artwork on the walls, and a series of rooms with odd-looking equipment. In one, the leader of the workshop, Laur Fugere, greeted me. Having previously rehearsed it in my mind, I said, "I am not sure I am in the right place. I have a vocal/singing disability and can't sustain long notes." She reassured me that I would be fine (I felt cynical). Slowly, the other three participants arrived—two about my age and one younger person.

As soon as she began to talk, I realized that I was in the right place, and it was not scary. I was familiar with the concepts and practices she referred to, and I began to observe my experience in a slightly objective way.

As illustration of how important one's "own" voice is, she told a story about herself. She was a professional singer, for many years singing in musicals, but one time she was out with family and they asked her to sing a song. She realized that she didn't have "songs," she just had her professional repertoire that did not fit the occasion. So, she decided to open her mouth and just sing an improvised piece. This experience let her come out of the "box" of musical theatre. Her "own" voice was improvisation.

Daniel Levitan writes:

> Safety plays a role for a lot of us in choosing music. To a certain extent, we surrender to music when we listen to it—we allow ourselves to trust the composers and musicians with a part of our hearts and spirits; we let the music take us somewhere outside of ourselves. Many of us feel that great music connects us to something larger than our own existence, to ourselves or to God. Even when music does not transport us to an emotional place that is transcendent, it can change our mood. We might be understandably reluctant to let down our guard, to drop our emotional defenses

for just anyone. We will do so if the musicians and composers make us feel safe.[3]

I believe that when we feel "safe" in the above way, we naturally become attached to that music and those performers or composers. This attachment process deserves respect. It's why we feel love for our favourite performers although we've never met them.

In the workshop, Laur talked about this vulnerability (we reveal ourselves with our voice) and demonstrated her improvising with a large singing bowl. The sound of the bowl was entrancing, and she used a little monitor system that she said enhanced certain harmonics in her voice. Next, she explained that we need to hear our voices through our bones, and that "we can only sing as well as we can hear." I certainly resonated with that, having learned it at The Listening Centre! We aligned our posture to allow the voice box to vibrate against the neck vertebrae and from there up and down the spine. Our speaking became more resonant. We practiced breathing and releasing our bodies by shaking and moving.

I was feeling safer and safer in the workshop, and though beforehand I was sure I would say no to any exposure of my voice, I was now ready to reveal it. The next exercise was to lie on the floor in a circle with our heads to the center and improvise a sound (I had done this type of exercise many times in the past). As we lay there, everyone else began making long sounds, and I tried a few without success. I could feel my body tensing and discouragement building. I remembered those past times when my voice was an instrument of spirit and I could trance out with it or join others in a web of sound. I remembered how it was when I lost that ability. I felt sad.

Then I thought, I can use my "friend" rhythm, so I began making short sounds. This was better, but I was still very sad. When we sat up to share, I let myself feel and show my sadness. I said that I missed my "long voice" meaning my sustained tone. I revealed my uncertainty about finding the right place for my voice. I revealed my sadness at being "different" in many musical situations. It felt good to be known and not hidden.

Then she said, "We each have our own soul melodies." And we sat in front of her, one by one, to improvise vocally with the singing bowl.

The singing bowl is a Tibetan instrument that first you hit with a mallet and then slowly circle the mallet around the bowl to produce a sustained sound. This particular bowl had a deep sound, and when I sat in front of it, my whole body felt encompassed by it. My throat opened up. I chose a waltz rhythm (my soul melody is a waltz) and the word "one" to improvise with. I was feeling more confident. I found my melody and my voice within it. Afterward, I realized that I had a "belonging" experience through music.

More Music and the Brain

I have explained the many ways that music has affected my brain and my "being" in my life. It has enhanced my social relationships in many ways. My friendship with Diane is one of those musical friendships. We began playing together in the 2000s—she on flute and me on guitar. We both loved jazz, Celtic, and klezmer music. During one spell of our playing together, we performed, mainly in retirement homes. It was rewarding to perfect our pieces, and often playing and talking together would change my mood for the better. It kept my hands strong and my musical brain active, and the music made a bond between us. It provided a regular steady "music as healer" experience for us both.

Robert Jourdain writes:

> "Music overcomes Parkinson's symptoms by lifting the brain to a higher than normal level of integration. Music establishes flow in the brain, at once enlivening and coordinating the brain's activities, bringing its anticipations into step. By so doing, the music provides a stream of intention to which the Parkinson's patient can entrain his or her motions."

I found this to be true when helping my mother with her Parkinson's. He further states:

> "The magic that music works on Parkinson's patient is no different from the magic it works on us all. [Music] lifts us from our frozen mental habits and makes our minds move in ways they ordinarily cannot. When we are embraced by well-written music, we experience understandings that outstrip those of our mundane existence

and that are usually beyond recollection once the music stops and we fall back into our mental wheelchairs."[4]

When my musical brain is awakened by playing or singing with others, or with my guitar composing, or at a concert, or dancing tango, I feel the magic. A scene from a "happening" at my uncle Dick's memorial reveals this magic. The evening after the official ceremony, my family gathered at a restaurant. An idea was proposed—let's have a sing-along! A quiet private room was found. Those not too tired drifted in. I was not sure that I would be able to sing but decided to sit in and enjoy the others' singing. We all had been raised on folksongs, so that is where we began. Various people led a Pete Seeger or Woodie Guthrie or Peter, Paul and Mary song and then moved on to jazz and musical theatre. The younger generation found lyrics on their phones and sang along. I tried a few words here and there and found I was singing the easy downward flowing melodies—my body was remembering how good it felt to sing these songs as a child. Then my sister Melanie noticed I was starting to sing. She came over and engaged me, eye to eye, and sang toward me but not too loud so I could join (entrain) with her voice. It worked! I sang complete songs. I went to bed satisfied with a quiet ecstasy.

Jourdain says,

> "It's for this reason that music can be transcendent. For a few moments, it makes us larger than we really are, the world more orderly than it really is. We respond not just to the beauty of the sustained deep relations that are revealed but also to the fact of our perceiving them. As our brains are thrown into overdrive, we feel our very existence expand and realize that we can be more than we normally are, and the world is more than it seems. This is cause enough for ecstasy."[5]

In the past I had practiced some of this "ecstasy" in holotrophic-breathing therapy groups, which use breath and music to produce an altered state in which to explore the psyche and release emotional blocks. The music helped me to understand myself on a deeper level.

Dancing Tango is a unique way of experiencing the power of music, and I believe it was the cherry on the cake of my social healing. I went to classes for three years before venturing into the less safe world of milongas (a public dance) and large groups. I would arrive worn from my work week to my Friday-night class. Tango music would accompany warm-ups, and then after learning a few steps, we would begin to dance—switching partners often. Though I often felt resistant to contact at the beginning, by the end of the class, my mood was shifted—always. I noticed this and began to count on my Tango classes.

And then I met my boyfriend to be. With him, I began to dance in the close embrace. With him, I was brave enough to go to Milongas. With him, I loved to waltz and was inspired to write my first Tango waltz, "Invitation." It was a way to enter a relationship softly. Now Tango is crucial to my health. Moving to music and in coordination with another person does healing in my brain and body.

The Kids Next Door

To be able to pass on this musical path to ecstasy has much meaning for me. In 2011, I began doing music with the children who lived two doors down from me, Anna and Joseph. They were eight and five and their mother, Kathryn, also joined in. We sang folksongs and protest songs. One day Anna said, "I wrote a song. Do you want to hear it?" She opened her mouth and sang, "Squeakity eakity eak, I am a hamster." What followed was a perfect little gem of a children's song. I realized that she had song-writing talent, especially in melody writing. She could take a poem with a strong regular meter (rhythm) and improvise a beautiful melody. She would often forget the melody as soon as she sang it, but luckily, I had a smartphone by then and could capture them. Our sessions became half folksongs and half writing sessions. By summer the next year, we had accumulated several very good children's songs. It was time to record. In the fall of 2012, I taught them microphone and "counting in" skills and other things necessary for the recording studio. My producer, Juan, was able to do it in his home studio. We recorded a seven song EP under the name Ankajoma. We gave it to friends and family for Christmas presents that year. It was a proud moment for all of us.

The next step was to challenge Anna to write ten completed songs with me, and at the end, I would give her a recording device. We managed to do this over the next year and presented it to her family on her birthday. She had some unique titles and subject matter: "The Markets Call"—a song about a girl in the Middle Ages; "The Overflowing Bead Tray"—a song about cleaning her room; and "Little Gecko"—a song from a gecko's point of view. We also began singing Beatles and other pop songs in our weekly sessions, intended to develop Anna's and Joseph's ears and skills by singing well-constructed songs.

In the next couple of years, we performed as a group and continued to write songs together. I gave Joseph a Cahon, which is a box drum used in Latin American music and jazz. After I gave them ukuleles the next year, Joseph began to write melodies and interesting rhythmical progressions. I introduced them to the fun experience of harmony singing with some vocal lessons from a previous vocal coach of mine.

In 2017, Anna had her first role in a musical—*Beauty and the Beast*—and was accepted into an arts and music program in a well-known arts high school. I was happy to be able to write her letter of recommendation and see her spread her wings into the big world of music study. I realized that I had given her what I had wanted when I was her age. In 2018, Anna had the starring role in the musical *Annie,* and Joseph began composing melodies on the ukulele. At a kitchen party, he sang his first vocal solo performance and harmony with his mother. Their accomplishments gave me a warm feeling because I could see that I had helped to nurture their musical abilities to a point where they could take it out into the world.

Facing the Music

I have made four professional recordings to date. I have made many more demos with other people singing my songs. I have early live recordings of small gigs I did in Toronto. I did not listen to my early recordings much after doing them, because when I had thought about it, I just couldn't raise the courage to listen. I felt afraid that they would be so bad that I would feel terrible shame or they would be good and I would feel sadness for what I had lost (my voice).

Finally, after a therapy session working on letting go of my trauma around my first loss of voice, I found the tapes and began to listen. I had the loan of an old cassette tape player with a nice speaker. The first thing that struck me was how long I could hold the notes—this had been an 'on' time for my vocal folds. Then I heard the song-writing talent and the vulnerability in the lyrics. I noticed I was writing my life and healing myself with the songs. Next, I noticed that the songs were pitched too high and did not make use of my lovely low-range notes. Then I heard how much work the musicians who supported me put into it. They cared about my music!

I wish I had had a song-writing coach to trim the rough edges. I felt sad that I had abandoned my musical self several times and that the 'mystery' of vocal dysphonia had frequently stolen it. I felt a deep sorrow and respect for my younger self in those difficult and confusing dissociative years. Facing this music I had made "then" meant facing "now"... the other painful things that had happened to me, such as being a workaholic, co-dependent, and oversensitive songwriter. I am sure I was way too prickly around my music to receive constructive criticism.

Having a Secure Work Identity

Our work identity is important in establishing a feeling of belonging. Mine has matured over the years—I can see what I am and what I am not. This book is a further defining of my role as pioneer, teacher and healer.

During a closure session with two of my supervision students, I can see how they have grown with the information I have given them. One of them says, "One of the most special things about you as a teacher is that you have humanized the process of being a teacher. You don't hold yourself above us. You share who you are." The other one says, "You made it comfortable for me to share myself in a group when it had always been scary before. I feel known and connected. This has carried over to other group situations." Coincidentally, later that day, I had a conversation with one of my very first students. She said, "You were the first person to see me and what was difficult for me. You pulled me out of my stuck place but very gently and gradually. And you didn't have 'rules.' It wasn't a rigid system so I felt free to learn what you taught at my own speed. I still have my vision board drawing, and I take it out every so often and say to myself, 'Yes I am doing it.'"

These statements bring me a deep feeling of satisfaction, a knowledge that I have given them a new way to think and be as healers themselves. I realize that even though I was a "wounded healer," I was capable of taking every bit of new learning I received and passing it on to others in a good and kind way. My work on myself has been a gift I give. A one-eared client of mine recently confirmed that I made him feel safe in the world saying, "I don't say this enough, but I'm very lucky to have found you. Having a role model and mentor who also went through Microtia has been so helpful for me. Don't ever move!"

A Right to Feel Comfortable in My Body

During a visit to my ENT in 2016, he said something simple that made a huge impact on me. "Kristi, you struggled with your ears most of your life, and then it was stable for many years, so now that there is a new landscape of problems—it's no wonder it feels hard." I felt enormous relief, both physically and emotionally. It felt so healing to have a doctor listen to me and appreciate my challenges and my feelings. The little girl inside was happy.

A few days later, I heard a program on CBC, "White Coat Black Art," that was about a woman who woke up during her operation. She described similar feelings to mine (I especially identified with her description of the PTSD she felt going into the environment of hospitals) and described the difference between a professional who listened to her and one who didn't. She now gives talks to doctors about her experience to educate them on what works for surgery patients: validation of their reality in a non-defensive manner.[6]

We all need this careful 'listening to' for whatever disease we are dealing with. We need advocates and survivors of trauma who will talk openly about their experiences. We need to be seen for who we are. We need science and art and community. We need partners in the task of deducing what to do when feeling uncomfortable in our body. We all have a right to feel comfortable in our bodies and to belong, whatever the colors, shapes, and conditions are.

A Song for the People

There are many manifestations of PTSD. Mine is what I would call a survival pattern. I become extraordinarily functional in some capacities, in order to hide and compensate for my disabilities, inadvertently keeping my system locked in the past and unbalanced. This has meant making my life smaller than it should be. I remember a psychic reading I had once. The psychic said, "I see you inhabiting only a small corner of a large room. You need to allow yourself to be in the whole room." At the time, I resisted this image because I thought, *How can I be in a corner when I am so busy running from activity to activity?* What I couldn't see then was that all this activity happened in a very narrow sphere. Some other manifestations of PTSD are addiction and dysfunctional relationships. They also make for a smaller life that is "hooked" to the wrong things.

The following dream illustrates the idea of an antidote to smallness:

> *I am working with a team of people to clean out a basement. We complete the job and are admiring the clean space feeling satisfied. Then I am with a meditation group in a sharing circle. We are doing back extension (strengthening) exercises. I notice there is a theme emerging from what everyone is saying. I think to myself, I could make a song and sing it to everyone. So, I quickly summarize the group themes in a song and sing it. It has the words "let go" in it and a nice melody. Everyone enjoys it. I feel competent and satisfied.*

This dream signifies the unity of my different parts and our working together to clean up my unconscious (the basement). We complete the job with satisfaction. Then I am able to write songs "for the people"—a spontaneous coming together of my musical and healing skills.

Innate Intelligence Letter

Dear Kristi,

You have been doing well in your openness to my guidance and in breaking the "habits" of your old self. I know you feel discouraged and triggered by the strange noises and sensations in your ears. I know you have felt waves of shame for your behaviors of the nineties as you go through your archives. That was a dark time. And you were struggling. You had courage but not always openness. You had undiagnosed PTSD, and there is a tendency for "survivors" to unconsciously relive their trauma. You were reliving both your attachment trauma and your ear and voice trauma. No wonder you were depressed and isolated!

Now you are just remembering it—the trauma is no longer happening.

The process of writing for a PTSD survivor is tricky. You have seen some of your writer clients go through this—odd physical symptoms and waves of emotional stuff from the past. You know how to combat this: Don't invest in the idea of "everything's going to turn out a disappointment." That is one of your habitual core sentences to let go of. Then receive the help you have constructed: your treatments, short-term therapy, and exercise (especially dance). Thirdly, continue to grow bigger than your past.

I have sent you six message dreams. I will remind you of their messages here:

Message 1: After the anxiety that steals your energy is released, you can see the resources that are available to bring consciousness to all parts of you and freedom from the past.

Message 2: Even if there are technical difficulties (like hearing) that make you feel far away from people, the strong ones will forge a connection anyway and you will receive their love.

Message 3: Let go of the "smallness" feeling from the past—understand that you are bigger now. De-clutter your unconscious and believe that things can be "repaired."

Message 4: Trust the mother in you, your actual mother "in spirit," and the "mothers" around you to have your best interests at heart and the competence to help you finish your trauma story with repair and dramatic power so it will touch others.

Message 5: It is time to allow the love of your parents to register and know that their apologies and acknowledgements count.

Message 6: Believe in the forward movement of your career; it is now time to go out in the bigger world with your truth. You can pick the fruits of your labour and receive complete acceptance.

You will notice that there is a happy feeling at the end of each dream. That is indicative of the healing of depressed and disappointed times. You are not back there now. Keep registering the happiness of the present. Write about the past, but don't take up residence there!

With love,

Your Innate Intelligence

Techniques for Keeping the Body in Mind

The Emotional Freedom Technique

When I first heard of Emotional Freedom Technique (EFT) in the early 2000s, I knew it was good for two reasons: one, it involves tapping on acupuncture points for calming; and two, it uses contrast between the acknowledgement of uncomfortable feelings and self-love. Contrast and paradox work to unlock our brains and the patterns that have been trapped there. Paradox can make us laugh, can make us see from a new perspective. An example of an emotional paradox is to laugh and cry at the same time—a very magical feeling.

I have used EFT for close to eighteen years for myself and others. I use it when I can't sleep, when I am nervous, for stage fright, for depression, and for figuring out what is bothering me. It is much easier to think productively about oneself when in a calmer body.

What to Do

There are many versions of EFT on the Internet. Find the one that suits you. I prefer versions that incorporate eye movement and humming and counting, as those are additional ways to unlock stuck brain/body patterns. You will know when you have the right version for you because it will make you yawn (a signal that the ventral vagal system is activated).

What to Expect

The tapping and eye movements interrupt many kinds of locked mind-body states and their accompanying symptoms (except of course an actual disease process such as fever or infection), and through this interruption, allow the mind-body to reset. Therefore, many small problems can shift, and the intensity of bigger ones can be lessened. Expect to feel some differences in your body and mood. How much will depend on the severity of the problem and your ability to notice body-state changes. The technique itself is a training for body awareness.

Forgiveness of the Body

Sometimes when we sustain an injury or have a disability, we feel angry. We take that anger out on our body by hating the part that prevents us from doing what we want, or having the appearance we want, or getting what we want. To be present in our body, to heal as much as possible, and to find creative solutions to working with our limitations, we need to acknowledge and then let go of our bitterness. This technique of acceptance is designed for that. You may need the help of a professional to carry it through.

What to Do

Identify the body part, injury site, or surgical scar that you have not come to terms with. Then identify the bitterness, anger, sadness, or fear associated with it, toward your body, toward others, and toward God. Release this emotion vocally, if you want, as fully as you can. Then take on the energy of forgiveness, like that embodied by your Higher Self, the good father or mother, an angel, your dog, God, or whoever or whatever can have that role in your mind. From this role, express your acceptance and love to that vulnerable part of your body, preferably out loud. Imagine yourself in the injured part receiving that acceptance and forgiveness. Notice your body response. If this technique has a feeling of "fakeness," pause, back up, and ask yourself, "Am I ready to do this now? What might need to come first?"

What to Expect

Each person's road to self-forgiveness is different and will bring different results. With this technique, you may just feel resistance and more anger or struggle with yourself to do it "perfectly." If this is the case, find an interim step, such as contemplating that though not possible now there could be a time in the future when it will be, and then practice acceptance of the "now" feelings with the EFT technique above. This process promotes relaxation and motivation for self-care. Our words to ourselves and others can become more kindly ones.

Forgiveness with Others

No parent is perfect. No spouse, lover, friend, or self is faultless. Mistakes are made; deeds based in fear are committed. We must grieve what did or did not happen and gain the courage and energy to move forward. Forgiving others enables us to free ourselves. Forgiving ourselves brings healing in the body. It is not to say something did not happen or did not hurt. It is not a bandage hiding an infected wound. We must tell the truth of how we have been hurt or how we have hurt others. Forgiveness helps us to gain humility and lose arrogance, because it requires that we spend time in the other person's shoes, and this takes us out of our locked positions of rightness and allows humility (I am not the only hurt person here) to grow. In a state of forgiveness, we do not put ourselves above others. It makes us free of what hooks us to the past, free to change and heal. There are many ways to enter into forgiveness. This is just one. Choose a method that speaks to you.

What to Do

In a therapeutic setting or in a journal, tell the story of the hurt again. Express your feelings fully to whoever you are intending to forgive. Allow the language of your feelings to evolve from blame and finger pointing to direct expressions such as "I feel really, really angry." Next, role reverse (see "In Their Shoes" in chapter 7's "Techniques for Keeping the Body in Mind") and feel and express the other person's history and emotions.

Come back into your own role and think of a location—real or imaginary—that could hold both of you. This imaginary place acts as a container for intense feelings, and as such, brings safety and a more complete expression of emotion as a consequence of that safety. Absorb the energy of this place into your body and imagination, and then say, "I fully acknowledge my own pain and yours, but I am letting go of the entanglements of knots between us. I forgive you and myself for holding this pain. I let go of my anger and blame. I forgive you." Sit with the feelings that emerge (especially the feelings of resistance or protest from other parts). After everything in you has been acknowledged, if you are ready, role reverse with the other person.

This technique can and may need to be repeated. This does not mean there is something wrong with you. True forgiveness takes time.

What to Expect

After this process, you can expect to be less obsessed and more able to relax around the person or topic.

Backward Mapping

Sometimes we need to surprise ourselves out of faulty self-concepts, procrastination, and habits of low self-esteem. Backward Mapping, which I learned at a songwriting workshop, is a technique for this. By starting at the furthest endpoint and then working backward by increments of five years, one year, six months, and one month, we can often find a missing action, an emotion that is blocking us, or a negative belief that we did not know we had. Simply thinking in a different way can mobilize us.

What to Do

Choose an end point for your project. Let's say it's building a house. Imagine yourself five years in the future—what your house would look like, how you would feel? Be detailed in your answers. Notice any inner resistance or negative beliefs. Take notes. Then imagine yourself four years in the future. What have you done to get to this point? Look with your mind's eye and take notes. Imagine yourself three years in the future and repeat the process. Then go to six months into the future and repeat. Finally, go just one month into the future. What have you done to get to where you are on your house project? You are now constructing a "to do" list with your future firmly in your mind.

What to Expect

Whenever we succeed in getting to a different viewpoint, new insights occur.

Done List

We need techniques to combat perfectionism and the inner critic. Most people focus too much on the "to do" list and beat themselves up in the process. This is a technique to help shift that focus.

What to Do

In the evening or at the end of a week, compile a list of things you have done. Include small things as well as big. Go to a mirror and read it aloud to yourself. Then choose some of the following statements, or any others that come to mind, to say directly to your image in the mirror:

> » I love you.

» I'm grateful to you.

» I believe in you.

» I trust you.

If you are using the technique to chill out the critic, practice it every day until the critic is quieter. You could make a chant or song with the positive words you have found. Do not make your "to do" list right after using this technique, because generally, we need space without self-expectation to integrate self-love. Make your to-do list in the morning.

What to Expect

Language is an important method of change. In the same way that if we change our posture our emotional state can change, if we change our language our feelings will change.

Conclusion:
Finding Peace along the Pathways of the Vagus Nerve

But if something you learn or observe or imagine can be set down and saved, and if you can see your life reflected in previous lives, and can imagine it reflected in subsequent ones, you can begin to discover order and harmony. You know that you are part of a larger story that has shape and purpose—a tangible familiar past and a constantly refreshed future. We are all whispering in a tin can on a string, but we are heard, so we whisper the message into the next tin can and the next string. Writing a book, just like building a library, is an act of sheer defiance. It is a declaration that you believe in the persistence of memory.

—Susan Orlean, *The Library Book*

Writing things down, mostly in the form of letters, dream journals, and songs has brought definition to a thread (string) that has led me through growth, awakening, engagement, peace, and finally to a healing of my vagus system, an understanding of how it affects my dystonia symptoms and musical satisfaction.

A few facts about the vagus nerve to remember: It is long and extensive; it has fibers that send messages out from the brain to the body, and from the organs and tissues back to the brain. It has two branches: One branch connects to organs below the diaphragm that reflect and affect the working of organs, defense mechanisms, and body states of fight, flight or freeze; the other branch connects to organs and muscles above the diaphragm that reflect and affect our social engagement and balancing mechanisms. The vagus nerve affects many aspects of our basic functioning (the heart, lungs, viscera, and more) and our sense of well-being. Here are my reflections on following its winding pathways:

The phrase "self-shaking" was one I used at the beginning of my journey, when I was new to body awareness. I sensed that, in order to "be" in my body, some old order needed to be shaken up. I know now that this was the constrictions of trauma and dissociation that produced a low level of depression—a survival mode.

The next phrase I used was "living from the gut," by which I meant finding the intuitive part of myself (I felt it was in my gut) and using it as a guide instead of my habitual worries. I was learning to have "time out of mind" away from looping thoughts and obsessive feelings and into my body's sensations and intuitive knowing. The methods I used at this time to break up the default mode of worry were Tai Chi, bodywork, and music.

When I was in my psychodrama years, "breaking the pattern" was my favorite saying. I was using emotional release and role play to experience "getting out" of my habitual self and thus gaining energy, insight, and new ways of doing things.

"Practicing my way out of a pattern" was an idea I developed after reading John Ratey's book *Shadow Syndromes*. In the book, he describes mental disorders (depression, ADD, obsessive-compulsive disorder, and others) as being on a continuum. I self-diagnosed that I had "shadow" OCD and realized that I needed to break up my thought loops by developing a practice of doing activities such as laughing, smelling good aromas, receiving touch and massage, noticing colours. Little did I know at this time that I also had a dystonic pattern that is closely linked to obsessive pushing/rushing habits that don't allow time for "smelling the roses'. My experience at The Listening Centre helped with these efforts, and I felt much less obsessive after I had a listening session.

My experience with Ayahuasca helped me to learn the feeling of "being able to think about everything," being outside myself enough to temporarily stop the constant self-referencing and then being able to flow in my thoughts and feelings in many directions without the constrictions of a rigid self-definition. After these experiences, I would be more flexible in my approach to life and to other people. However, I am not generally recommending the Ayahuasca path even though it has become legal as a religious sacrament in a few places. It is difficult, unpredictable and contra-indicated for some. It requires the right context, a high degree of stability, self-knowledge and self-responsibility to produce change. It is not about getting "high". There are many ways to achieve this same step of growth.

"Disrupting the pattern" and "releasing suppression" are two concepts I learned doing LENS. It seemed to me that there was a strong similarity between what I felt after (not during) an Ayahuasca experience and what I felt after a good LENS treatment. LENS was much milder in effect, but there was a steadying of my nervous system state and an increase in social engagement that I felt reliably from both. And they both helped me to sing. My analysis was that they strengthened the ventral vagus nerve system, in part because they "shook" me out of my mental/physical patterns of isolation and tension.

Working on my dystonias, I learned that letting go of 'compensations'—those muscular and mental habits we construct to make up for or to hide weak or disconnected muscles (and disconnected parts f self) —is the first thing to do. Then the brain can reconnect to the muscles and the body-mind resumes more effortless movement.

The idea of "seeing beyond default modes" is new wording for a familiar idea. It emerged as a synthesis of my experiences with the reading I have been doing about the new research being done on the Poly Vagal theory and the Default Mode Network discussed in chapter 6 of Michael Pollan's book *How to Change Your Mind*. The Default Mode Network (DMN) consists of three parts of the brain working together to provide us with a sense of self, shortcuts in thinking (metacognition), and what he calls, "time travel": "Mental time travel is constantly taking us off the frontier of the present moment. This can be highly adaptive; it allows us to learn from the past and plan for the future. But when time travel turns obsessive, it fosters the backward-looking gaze of depression and the forward pitch of anxiety."[1] We need, and will have, a certain amount of DMN activity to maintain a working self (psychosis is an example of severe loss of self) and an efficient life, but I know that I have often been caught in the net of habit and worry (obsessive DMN). I have needed to see beyond my default modes.

In my efforts to promote as frequent ventral vagal states in my nervous system as possible, I have found that I can't be in my overactive DMN (what I have traditionally called my "pattern") and my ventral vagal state at the same time. I now frequently use "switching tricks" to jolt me out of ruminative patterns and reboot my system to a better (less depressed) state. Once in this better state, I can act or rest more effectively. I can engage with people more fully. I can "feel my heart" and "smell the roses." These questions are now in my mind: How is an overactive DMN related to trauma and PTSD? Could "keeping the body in mind" be a reliable way to reboot? (I think so.) And could vagus nerve techniques (among which is meditation) help to break up the patterns caused by an overactive DMN? The answers are still to come, but here are some stories about more comfortable vagus states:

I am on Eagle Island. The saltwater in the bay is cold! I do my water therapy for my vagus nerve every day—slowly working up to a five-minute dip. I feel my muscles strengthening from the twice-weekly yoga. I go barefoot as much as possible to feel the soft spring grass. I breathe in the incredible smell of sea air and Scotch broom flowers. The birds tweet in the quiet, and I am connected. I receive hugs from my boyfriend and can feel my trust building as I manage to fall asleep in his arms.

On another island, I visit a childhood friend who has ALS and is mostly paralyzed and can hardly speak—his spirit and his love are still strong. I make eye contact, and layering our hands together, we make a "hand sand-wich." I read the lyrics from my CD to him. He tells me that he is proud of me. We have a brief conversation about our childhoods, and I am able to put his mind at rest about a few facts, because I have my "coherent narra-tive" close at hand—I have done the investigative work. I improvise on the guitar while he rests, and then I gently massage him. We are present with each other. I am aware of all the learning that contributes to my ability to be comfortable in his presence. It is meaningful on many levels.

Nature nurtures the vagus and so does music. Community stimulates the social engagement aspect of the vagus system, and in turn, the vagus is strengthened by community. We connect to our body's pleasures (sex, bonding, and relaxation) through the vagus system. Being touched or touch-ing others (in a safe way) also brings contentment to the system. Our voice is influenced by our vagus nerve and using our singing voice strengthens it. Thus, singing or playing music with others or walking/playing in nature with friends brings energy and health to our whole system. Throughout my life, I had instincts to engage in these activities, which I am sure, offset the terrible shock and damage done not only to my face and ear but also to my vagus system by my operation. The wellbeing that I had been robbed of was gradually healed by music, singing, and touch.

Though the knowledge about the vagus nerve has only recently been widely available, I experienced it and tried to describe it at the age of twenty in a letter to Melanie: "Even when my life events follow a roller-coaster course, I can blip into a state of calm consciousness that allows me to see a broader scope and have the sensibility to take the next small step in front of me." Instinctively, I knew how important that "calm" state was. When I was finally educated by Dr. Farias, my osteopath, Hideki and various books in the past five years, many pieces of my trauma puzzle and healing journey fell into place. This included the mystery of my dystonia being solved. Because dystonias are often triggered by shock/trauma or high stress, I can't help but think the vagus nerve (as well as the brain) plays a big part in its resolution. As the information about the vagus nerve and its signs of health or imbalance comes into the public eye, I believe many people will find resolutions to their conditions.

A friend who is a trauma survivor and struggles with her vagus system says, "I know, when I talk to you about this stuff (trauma symptoms), I can feel restful because I don't have to try to explain all of my strange symptoms and behaviors." I would hope that, eventually, there will be enough general knowledge in society so that a survivor's struggle to be understood takes less effort and there is not stigma associated with it.

I would hope that the power of connection wins over the power of suffering for everyone. That we continue to learn how to keep the body in mind, that we find the teams of healthcare providers we need, and release the expectations that there are "magic" fixes out there. I would hope that activities and techniques to heal our "out of balance" brain, body, and mind systems become commonplace, and that we as a society learn to value the activities of connection and well-being that are so closely tied to a healthy, balanced system.

I hope that the scientists continue their researches into the brain and what activities can promote well-being, and that the activists keep pushing for the security and recognition that all people need in order to pursue well-being. My part will be strengthening minds and bodies and teaching people how to listen.

I am grateful for the peace I have found in pursuing my study of the vagus nerve, this giant nervous system that can bring us home to our body, make us comfortable in our skin, engage our senses, help us to build relationships, provide energy to take on the stresses of life, and help us to sing beautifully. Keeping the body in mind rests on the foundation of the vagus system.

At the completion of this manuscript, a significant thing happened: On Eagle Island for holidays, riding my bike on the dirt roads, a melody came to me as many other melodies had come in the past. Returning to Toronto, I listened to the melody I had luckily recorded and quickly lyrics arrived. This was one of my strongest experiences of "channeling a song." The song, titled "Seeking," feels like an important message from my Innate Intelligence for myself and my readers:

> Deep in the dark night we see the star shine
> Illuminating every mind
> It will lead us through the old pain
> And beyond the chains of shame
>
> In stormy waters we find the lifeboat
> That will lift us to the shore
> Where our guides will come to greet us
> And reveal eternal love
>
> When we are walking the barren desert
> The moon's light will take us further
> 'Til we find the green oasis
> That allows our souls to rest
>
> We know that seeking is our journey
> To find a true path, a destiny
> We can ask and we'll be given
> All the lives that we must tend

Notes

Introduction

1. Daniel Siegel, *Mindsight: The New Science of Personal Transformation* (New York: Bantam Books, 2010).

2. Tara Westover, *Educated: A Memoir* (New York: Penguin Random House, 2018), 304.

3. Pauline Dakin, *Run, Hide, Repeat: A Memoir of a Fugitive Childhood* (New York: Penguin Random House, 2017).

4. Antonio Damasio, *Descartes' Error: Emotion, Reason and the Human Brain* (New York: Penguin/Putnam, 1994).

5. Richard M. Magraw, *Ferment in Medicine: A Study of the Essence of Medical Practice and of Its New Dilemmas* (Philadelphia: W.B. Saunders Company, 1966), 25.

Chapter 2

1. J. Bowlby, *Attachment and Loss,* Vol. 1: *Attachment* (New York: Basic Books, 1973).

Chapter 4

1. Johann Hari, *Lost Connections: Uncovering the Real Causes of Depression and the Unexpected Solutions* (London: Bloomsbury Publishing PLC, 2015), 245–6.

Chapter 5

1. Bessel van der Kolk, *The Body Keeps the* Score*: Mind, Brain and Body in the Transformation of Trauma* (New York: Viking/ Penguin, 2014), 42.

2. Van der Kolk, 91–2.

3. Stephen Porges, *The Polyvagal Theory: Neurophysiological Foundations of Emotions, Attachment, Communication, and Self-Regulation* (New York: Norton, 2011).

4. Georg Groddeck, *The Book of the It* (Vienna: Psychoanalytischer Verlag, 1923).

5. Peter A. Levine, *In an Unspoken Voice: How the Body Releases Trauma and Restores Goodness* (Berkley: North Atlantic Books, 2010).

6. David Berceli, *Trauma Release Exercises: (TRE) A Revolutionary New Method for Stress and Trauma Recovery* (Scotts Valley, CA: Create Space, 2005).

Chapter 6

1. David Berceli, *Trauma Release Exercise*s: *(TRE) A Revolutionary New Method for Stress/Trauma Recovery* (Scotts Valley, CA: Create Space, 2005), 97.

2. Bessel van der Kolk, *The Body Keeps the* Score: *Mind, Brain and Body in the Transformation of Trauma* (New York: Viking/Penguin, 2014), 70.

3. Adriaan Louw, Sandra Hilton and Carolyn Vandyken, *Why Pelvic Pain Hurts: Neuroscience Education for Patients with Pelvic Pain* (United States: International Spine and Pain Institute, 2014), 112.

4. John Sarno, *Healing Back Pain: The Mind-Body Connection* (New York: Warner Books Inc., 1991).

5. Steven Ozanich and Taylor Krzsowski, *Dr. John Sarno's Top 10 Healing Discoveries* (Warren, OH: Silver Cord Records, Inc., 2016).

6. Candace Pert, *Molecules of Emotion: Why You Feel the Way You Feel* (New York: Scribner, 1997).

7. John Schwartz, "Candace Pert, 67 Explorer of the Brain, Dies," *New York Times*, September 19, 2013, https://www.nytimes.com/2013/09/20/science/candace-pert-67-explorer-of-the-brain-dies.html.

Chapter 7

1. J. Bowlby, *Attachment and Loss,* Vol. 1, *Attachment* (New York: Basic Books, 1973).

2. John Ratey, *A User's Guide to the Brain: Perception, Attention, and the Four Theaters of the Brain* (New York: First Vintage Books, 2001), 263.

Chapter 8

1. Mark Wolynn, *It Didn't Start with You: How Inherited Family Trauma Shapes Who We Are and How to End the Cycle* (New York: Viking, 2016), 23.

2. Helen Epstein, *Children of the Holocaust: Conversations with Sons and Daughters of Survivors* (New York: Putnam, 1979).

3. Wolynn, *It Didn't Start with You*, 6.

Chapter 9

1. Shania Twain interview with Tom Power, *Q*, CBC Radio, November 30, 2017.

2. Paul Madaule in conversation with the author, May 2002. See Madaule's book *When Listening Comes Alive: A Guide to Effective Learning and Communication* (Norval, ON: Moulin Publishing, 1993).

Chapter 10

1. Sam Roberts, "John Cacioppo, Who Studied Effects of Loneliness, Is Dead at 66," Obituary Section, *New York Times*, March 26, 2018, https://www.nytimes.com/2018/03/26/obituaries/john-cacioppo-who-studied-effects-of-loneliness-is-dead-at-66.html.

2. Pauline Dakin interview with Shelagh Rogers, *The Next Chapter*, CBC Radio, March 15, 2018.

3. Daniel Levitan, *This Your Brain on Music: The Science of a Human Obsession* (New York: Penguin Group, 2006), 242–3.

4. Robert Jourdain, *Music, the Brain and Ecstasy: How Music Captures Our Imagination* (New York: Avon Books, 1997), 305–6.

5. Jourdain, 331.

6. Donna Penner interview with Dr. Brian Goldman, *White Coat, Black Art*, CBC Radio, September 16, 2016.

Conclusion

1. Michael Pollan, *How to Change Your Mind: What the New Science of Psychedelics Teaches Us about Consciousness, Dying, Addiction, Depression and Transcendence* (New York: Random House, 2018), 386.

Further Readings

Books have always been important to me. Here are some that have illu-minated and encouraged me on my path as I hope they might on yours:

Blakeslee, Sandra, and Mathew Blakeslee. *The Body Has a Mind of Its Own: How Body Maps in Your Brain Help You Do (Almost) Everything Better*. New York: Random House, 2007.

Blatner, Adam, and Allee Blatner. *Foundations of Psychodrama: History, Theory and Practice*. New York: Springer Publishing Inc., 1988.

Bradshaw, John. *Healing the Shame That Binds You*. Deerfield Beach: Health Communications Inc. 1988.

Dakin, Pauline *Run, Hide, Repeat: A Memoir of a Fugitive Childhood* (New York: Penguin Random House, 2017).

Damasio, Antonio. *Looking for Spinoza: Joy, Sorrow, and the Feeling Brain*. Orlando: Harcourt Inc., 2003.

Dashtgard, Annahid. *Breaking the Ocean: A Memoir of Race, Rebellion, and Reconciliation*. Toronto: House of Anansi, 2019.

Dispenza, Joe. *Breaking the Habit of Being Yourself: How to Lose Your Mind and Create a New One*. New York: Hay House Inc., 2012.

Doidge, Norman. *The Brain That Changes Itself: Stories of Personal Triumph from the Frontiers of Brain Science*. New York: Penguin Books, 2007.

Elliot, Clark. *The Ghost in My Brain: How Concussion Stole My Brain and How the New Science of Neuro Plasticity Helped Me Get It Back*. New York: Penguin Books, 2015.

Fields, R. Douglas. *The Other Brain: The Scientific and Medical Breakthroughs That Will Heal Our Brains an Revolutionize Our Health.* New York: Simon & Schuster, 2009.

Fosha, Diana. *The Transforming Power of Affect: A Model for Accelerated Change.* New York: Basic Books, 2000.

Gelb, Michael J. *How to Think Like Leonardo da Vinci: Seven Steps to Genius Every Day.* New York: Random House, 1998.

Goldberg, Elkhonon. *The Wisdom Paradox: How Your Mind Can Grow Stronger as Your Brain Grows Older.* New York: Penguin Books, 2005.

Grossinger, Richard. *Planet Medicine: From Stone Age Shamanism to Post-Industrial Healing.* Berkeley: North Atlantic Books, 1980.

Grosz, Stephen. *The Examined Life: How We Lose and Find Ourselves.* New York: Random House, 2013.

Hammer, Leon. *Dragon Rises, Red Bird Flies: Psychology & Chinese Medicine.* Barrytown: Station Hill Press Inc., 1990.

Hari, Johann. *Chasing the Scream: The First and Last Days of the War on Drugs.* London: Bloomsbury, 2015.

Harrington, Anne. *The Cure Within: A History of Mind-Body Medicine.* New York: W.W. Norton & Company Inc., 2008.

Iacoboni, Marco. *Mirroring People: The New Science of How We Connect With Others.* New York: Farrar, Straus and Giroux, 2008.

Jackson, Marni. *Pain: The Science and Culture of Why We Hurt.* New York: Random House, 2002.

Kurtz, Ron. *Body-Centered Psychotherapy: The Hakomi Method.* Mendocino: Life Rhythm, 1990.

Li, Cynthia. *Brave New Medicine: A Doctor's Unconventional Path to Healing Her Autoimmune Illness.* Oakland: Reveal Press, 2019

Lipska, Barbara K., and Elaine McArdle. *The Neuroscientist Who Lost Her Mind: My Tale of Madness and Recovery.* New York: Houghton, Mifflin, Harcourt Publishing Company, 2018.

Masumoto, Kiiko, and Stephen Birch. *Five Elements ad Ten Stems: Nan Ching Theory, Diagnosis and Practice*. Brookline: Paradigm Publications, 1983.

Mellick, Jill. *The Natural Artistry of Dreams: Creative Ways to Bring the Wisdom of Dreams to Waking Life*. Berkeley: Conari Press, 1996.

Menakem, Resmaa. *My Grandmother's Hands: Racialized Trauma and the Pathway to Mending Our Hearts and Bodies*. Las Vegas: Central Recovery Press, 2017.

Miller, Alice. *Thou Shalt Not Be Aware: Society's Betrayal of the Child*. New York: Farrar, Strauss and Giroux, 1981.

Mindell, Arnold. *Dreambody: The Body's Role in Revealing the Self*. Boston: Sigo Press, 1982.

Moreno, J. L. *The Essential Moreno: Writings on Psychodrama, Group Method and Spontaneity by J. L. Moreno*. Edited by Jonathan Fox. New York: Springer Publishing Company, 1987.

Orlean, Susan. *The Library Book*. New York: Simon & Schuster, 2018.

Pollan, Michael. *How to Change Your Mind: What the New Science of Psychedelics Teaches Us about Consciousness, Dying, Addiction, Depression and Transcendence* (New York: Random House, 2018).

Porges, Stephen. *The Pocket Guide to the Polyvagal Theory: The Transformative Power of Feeling Safe*. New York: W. W. Norton and Company, 2017.

Ratey, John, and Catherine Johnson. *Shadow Syndromes: The Mild Forms of Major Mental Disorders That Sabotage Us*. New York: Bantam Books, 1997.

Rebick, Judy. *Heros in My Head: A Memoir*. Toronto: House of Anansi Press Inc., 2018.

Rosenburg, Stanley. *Accessing the Healing Power of the Vagus Nerve: Self Help Exercises for Anxiety, Depression, Trauma and Autism*. Berkeley: North Atlantic Books, 2017.

Seem, Mark D. *Acupuncture Imaging: Perceiving the Energy Pathways of the Body*. Rochester: Healing Arts Press, 1990.

Teege, Jennifer, and Nikola Sellair. *My Grandfather Would Have Shot Me: A Black Woman's Discovery of Her Nazi Past.* New York: The Experiment LLC, 2015.

Thien, Madeleine. *Do Not Say We Have Nothing.* New York: W. W. Norton & Company Inc., 2016.

Trungpa, Chogyam. *Meditation in Action.* Berkeley: Shambala Publications, 1970.

Van der Kolk, Bessel. *The Body Keeps the* Score: *Mind, Brain and Body in the Transformation of Trauma* (New York: Viking/Penguin, 2014).

Wolynn, Mark. *It Didn't Start with You: How Inherited Family Trauma Shapes Who We Are and How to End the Cycle* (New York: Viking, 2016).

Acknowledgements

A special thanks to my sisters, who remained open to my writing about our childhood, bravely read the chapters about my medical and other traumas, and gave me invaluable feedback.

I am grateful to my parents for pointing me to the path of seeking, and to my uncle Dick for his support of my project during the last years of his life.

Many thanks to my childhood friends, whose enthusiasm and contributions spurred me on: Meredith Ludwig, Steve Ludwig, Chris Weaver, Josie Weaver, Kurt Thorson, Susan Bucknell, Dorn Campbell, and Shawn Huntley.

Many thanks to my friends and colleagues who read chapters, expressed their enthusiasm, and made corrections: Madeleine Byrnes, Diane Granfield, Libbie Mills, Lisa Merrifield, Mary Reins, Susan Arndt, Emily, Leon Levin, Randall Kempf, Norma Fried, Dorn Campbell, Fred and Donna Adams, Petra Bergant and Robin Freeman. A deep appreciation goes to Jeana Bird who helped edit the technique section, making the techniques clear and comfortable for trauma survivors. A special thanks to my friend Kristy Micklewright for being my sounding board for what it's like to live with one ear and medical trauma. Credit also goes to the many friends, students, colleagues, clients, and extended family members, who said, "Yes, you should write a book" whenever I wavered in my perseverance.

Thanks to my healers, Hideki Kumagai, Jeanette Han, Mary Hao, Dr. Chung, Dr. Halik, and Katarina Bulat, for keeping my body strong and healthy. Thanks to my exercise teachers, Rebecca Bell and Paula Ryff, and my long-time martial-arts work-out buddy, Shirley Russ.

I am grateful to my therapists, who helped me to follow my body-mind and my dreams: David O'Connor, Alf Walker, and Ronn Young. To my psychodrama directors and group leaders, among them Madeleine Byrnes and Liz White, you gave me the belief and experience of changing my inner reality; thank you. Thank you to my peer support group, Don Warrington and Deborah Stewart-Finestone. I am grateful to my early teacher in body knowledge, Donna Adams—you inspired me. I am grateful to all the people (you know who you are), who connected me to important resources that changed my life.

Thanks to my spiritual leaders and buddies who cared for me in difficult circumstances.

Thanks to my musical mentors, past and present, who all believed I could be a musician and a singer: Gloria, Eileen Smith, Lucas Marchand, Juan Valencia, Diego Las Heras, Kim Ratcliffe, Michael Bard, Donna O'Connor, Dunstan Morey, Frank Falco, Fred Adams, and Jeff Edge.

I owe much to my book coach and first editor Michelle MacAleese, without whose caring and expert help I would not have had the courage to face my trauma stories with the confidence that I could write them well. I am grateful to Kendra Ward, my second editor, for all the smoothing and streamlining, and for helping me birth my book properly. Thanks to Marni Jackson for the endorsement that makes the front cover draw people in.

I am grateful to Sandy Peic for executing my ideas in the visual realm in a way that expands my message.

Deep thanks to Tijmen Tieleman, my partner in dance and life, for his chapter reading, constant support, and faith in me as a writer. His encouragement, being a writer I respect, held the weight of approval I needed to keep going in the difficult bits.

I am grateful to the peace and beauty of my island, where much of the book was written.

About the Author

Kristi Magraw is known for having developed a unique synthesis of Eastern healing (Five Element theory) and Western ways of working with the mind, called the Magraw Method, which she established in 1979. This method uses metaphoric language and release techniques to help people heal physical and emotional pain.

She is a certified Director of Psychodrama and a Registered Massage Therapist with additional certificates in Reflexology, Shiatsu, Polarity, Cranial Sacral therapy and LENS (Low Energy Neurofeedback System). She also integrates Tai Chi, Kung Fu, Qi Quong and Yoga in her practice. A gifted teacher, she has conducted training and supervision groups for over twenty years. Her communications courses for the Kikkawa massage school became the curriculum template for massage schools in Ontario. She is a member of Ontario Massage therapists Association and a clinical provider of LENS. She is a retired member of the American Society for Group Psychotherapy and Psychodrama, the Ontario Society of Psychotherapists and the College of Psychotherapists of Ontario.

Kristi is also a musician and composer. She has received several song-writing awards, and has had her songs covered by other artists. Her CD "Everybody has the Gift to Heal Themselves" inspires people to trust themselves and their self-healing processes. She is a member of Nashville Songwriters Association International, Songwriters Association of Canada and SOCAN, Canada's performing rights organization.

CPSIA information can be obtained
at www.ICGtesting.com
Printed in the USA
BVHW021533220920
589367BV00023B/780